Ex-Kaiser William II

THE KAISER
AND ENGLISH RELATIONS

BY

E. F. BENSON

AUTHOR OF 'QUEEN VICTORIA,' 'KING EDWARD VII,'
'AS WE WERE,' ETC.

WITH ILLUSTRATIONS

LONGMANS, GREEN AND CO.

LONDON · NEW YORK · TORONTO

1936

LONGMANS, GREEN AND CO.
114 FIFTH AVENUE, NEW YORK
221 EAST 20TH STREET, CHICAGO
88 TREMONT STREET, BOSTON

LONGMANS, GREEN AND CO. LTD.
39 PATERNOSTER ROW, LONDON, E C 4
6 OLD COURT HOUSE STREET, CALCUTTA
53 NICOL ROAD, BOMBAY
36A MOUNT ROAD, MADRAS

LONGMANS, GREEN AND CO.
215 VICTORIA STREET, TORONTO

BENSON
THE KAISER AND ENGLISH RELATIONS

FIRST EDITION

PRINTED IN THE UNITED STATES OF AMERICA

NOTE

I gratefully acknowledge the permission of Mr. John Murray to quote from *The Letters of Queen Victoria,* and the permission of Messrs. Macmillan and Co. Ltd. to quote from *Letters of the Empress Frederick,* by the late Lord Sysonby (Sir Frederick Ponsonby).

CONTENTS

LIST OF ILLUSTRATIONS

THE KAISER

AND ENGLISH RELATIONS

THE KAISER
AND ENGLISH RELATIONS

CHAPTER I

VICTORIA, Princess Royal of England, was not yet fifteen years old, and her parents were in two minds whether she was not rather young to be engaged to be married, when, one September morning at Balmoral in the year 1855, Prince Frederick William of Prussia asked their permission to propose to her. He had seen her for the first time when he came to England four years ago to attend the opening of the Prince Albert's Great Exhibition in Hyde Park, and since then the project of this marriage had received the private approval of his father and mother and of his uncle the King of Prussia. The girl's parents also approved, and they had asked Prince Frederick to spend a fortnight at Balmoral in order to give him ample opportunity to see what he thought of her now. From their point of view it was an absolutely ideal match ; indeed, if Queen Victoria and Prince Albert had been bidden to select any young prince from all the Royal Houses of Europe to be Vicky's husband, they would have chosen Fritz.

Physically he was a splendid young fellow, tall and stalwart and handsome, and in character most estimable. He had no dazzling intellectual qualities, but he was sensible and kindly, upright and conscientious, and, for all her immaturity, he was really in love with her. These points weighed very strongly in his favour, for neither the Queen nor Prince Albert would have dreamed of allowing their beloved daughter to marry a man who was not likely to make her happy in her home life. Apart from all such primary considerations, he would succeed his uncle and his father on the throne of Prussia, and of all the clauses in Prince Albert's political and international creed the one that was dearest to his heart concerned his beloved native land of Germany and her relations with England. He was also convinced that friendship between two nations was greatly strengthened by marriages between their Royal Families. What then could be more perfect ? Vicky, wedded to an admirable husband, would one day be Queen of Prussia.

So at once Fritz had the support of both the father and mother of his desired bride, for the Queen was not only as pro-German in her sympathies as her husband but looked upon him as the supreme incarnation of wisdom and right judgment in all things, and for herself she found Fritz 'a dear, excellent, charming young man.' As far then as the parents were concerned the prospective suitor was warmly accepted, but what about allowing a girl of fourteen to answer the supremely important question just yet ? Her father thought she was hardly of ripe age, and he wrote to Lord Clarendon, the Foreign Minister, to say that though he and the Queen as well as Fritz's parents were all in favour of the match, they thought it wiser that 'the child' (as indeed she was) should not be told of the destiny that awaited her decision until after she had been confirmed in the following spring. Confirmation — so, we gather, his thought ran — would enable her to make her choice with a more enlightened sense of its gravity. The young man would then be allowed to propose to her, and would 'receive from her own lips the answer which is only valuable when flowing from those of the person chiefly concerned.' Lord Clarendon was told that he might pass on this news to the Prime Minister, Lord Palmerston, but at present it must otherwise be kept a strict secret. Next day the Queen wrote, again in confidence, to her Uncle Leopold, King of the Belgians, who was very much interested in Vicky's future, just as he had been in her mother's, saying what joy this proposal had given to Albert and herself, and that she felt no doubt that Vicky would accept it.*

But reflection brought a change of mind to the parents. They were extremely anxious that the engagement should be stamped and sealed, since, both domestically and dynastically, it seemed so ideal, and it could not be definite unless the answer 'flowed from the lips of the person chiefly concerned.' Six months was a long time to wait : Fritz doubtless urged on them a more immediate permission, for not only was he in love with her and wanted to have it settled, but it would be a fiasco to return to Berlin with his avowed purpose postponed and unaccomplished, and a week later he was allowed to speak. On Michaelmas Day, 1855, the Queen and Prince Albert and the two young people went for a ride up the hill Craig-na-Ban, and Fritz picked a piece of white heather, which brought good luck, and gave it to Vicky. As they returned down Glen Girnoch, the parents went on ahead or loitered behind, and the young man, as the Queen wrote in her Diary, 'was enabled to make an allusion to his hopes and wishes,' and Vicky accepted him as her mother had foreseen. The girl did not know that her parents had allowed her lover to make this 'allusion,' and, terrified at having done anything so unmaidenly bold, went to them with tears when she got home and confessed her fault, only to find that she was already forgiven.† Though the engagement was not yet made public, it somehow leaked out, perhaps through the indiscretion of those who had been let into the secret, and very soon everybody knew. Public

---

* *Letters of Queen Victoria*, 1st Series, iii. pp. 146, 147. These are subsequently referred to as *Letters*.

† *Leaves from the Journal of our Life in the Highlands*, p. 107; *Greville Memoirs*, Dec. 12, 1859.

opinion in England was far from enthusiastic, for the German sympathies of the Queen and Prince Albert were very unpopular, and *The Times* defined the Hohenzollerns as 'a paltry German dynasty,' a stigma from which they presently freed themselves.   In any case, as Prince Albert very sensibly remarked, 'What the world may say we cannot help.' *

It was indeed no wonder that Prince Frederick William fell for this precocious and fascinating girl.   From her babyhood she must have had that indefinable quality called charm, and with it the engaging spice of original sin which is so appropriate to a very attractive and lively child, and which made her mother record with fully as much pride as dismay : 'Pussy is amazingly advanced in intellect, and, alas, also in naughtiness. . . You have no idea what a *knowing,* and I am sorry to say, *sly* little rogue she is, and so *obstinate.'* At the age of three she could express herself with fluency not only in German, which was often in her ears at home, but in French and English as well.   In her linguistic ease there lurked a defect which was subsequently characteristic of her in more significant matters, for she spoke English with a German accent and German with an English accent.   Unlike her eldest brother she was remarkably quick at her lessons, and could apply them practically, for one day, after learning a verse of Lamartine by heart, she turned to her French governess as they rode in Windsor Park, and exclaimed 'Violà le tableau qui se déroule à mes pieds.'   That was more like what a person of twenty would say, thought her proud mother, than a child of three.†   She was ardently affectionate, she had tearing spirits, and as she grew she developed keen intellectual curiosity, and shared her father's

---

* The Queen had some correspondence with Mr. Disraeli about the marriage, but her letters were destroyed by King Edward VII. *Journals and Letters of Lord Esher,* ii. p. 256.

† *Letters I,* ii. p. 3.

artistic tastes. Now at the age of fourteen, without being a beautiful or even a pretty girl — her mother sometimes lamented her plainness — she must have been bewitching, as indeed Fritz found her. The blue of her eyes was shot with the green of the sea, her nose was short and tip-tilted, her mobile mouth was expressive equally of obstinacy and of disarming tenderness. Her face was the swift vehicle for shades of infinite variety ; at one moment it was pensive and serious, then a smile was kindled in those sparkling eyes, the radiance spread and an irresistible merriment of laughter bubbled up. Prince Frederick was surely in luck when he came a-wooing to Balmoral, even as was his future brother-in-law when, not many years later, he sought, on Princess Frederick's recommendation, his Danish bride.

Next spring the Crimean War came to an end, the Princess was confirmed, and the news of her engagement officially announced. It was arranged that her marriage should not take place till she was seventeen, and it was fortunate that more than a year and a half must elapse before that, for the sympathies both of the German Court and of the nation were strongly pro-Russian, and it was as well that those hot feelings should have time to cool down. A couple of months before the wedding there occurred a slight hitch, for representations were made from Berlin to the British Government that it was the custom for Prussian princes to be married at home. The Queen dealt with such monstrous impertinence in her most summary style. She wrote to Lord Clarendon : 'The assumption of its being *too much* for a Prince Royal of Prussia to *come* over to marry the *Princess Royal of Great Britain* IN England is too *absurd* to say the least. Whatever may be the usual practice of Prussian Princes, it is not *every* day that one marries the eldest daughter of the Queen of England. The question therefore must be considered settled and closed.' Settled and closed it was ;

instead the Princess's future Court came to England a fortnight before the wedding. 'Which,' said her mother, 'is a
very good thing, so that she will get acquainted with them.'
Agonising were the farewells : 'The poor child was quite
broken-hearted, particularly at parting with her dearest beloved papa, whom she idolises.' *

Yet in that parting there were many high reflections to
uplift and sustain them both. Princess Frederick was following in her father's footsteps, for had he not, just eighteen
years ago, in answer to the call of duty and self-sacrifice, left
his beloved Coburg to be Consort to the sovereign of a foreign land ? That had been a terrible wrench, and he had
written to his adored stepmother when he accepted Queen
Victoria's devotion : 'Life has its thorns in every position, and
the consciousness of having used one's powers and endeav-
ours for an object as great as that of promoting the good of
so many will surely be sufficient to support me.' † Nobly had
he performed his duties, and now his daughter was similarly
called by marriage to make her home in a foreign land and
in Germany to fulfil just such a splendid mission as had been
his in England. In many talks with her before that parting
he had imbued and inspired her with the vision of what
it should be hers to do for the nations of her birth and
her adoption. Germany and England were natural allies,
and Germany (such was his constant aspiration), united under the hegemony of Prussia, must get to work on such
programmes of progressive liberalism as had been inau-
gurated in England by the Reform Bill of 1832. Vicky, as
both her father and mother knew, was a girl of far greater
ability and of far stronger will than her husband — she 'had
a man's head,' the Prince Consort told him ‡ — and it would
be her task, in the years that elapsed (thirty of them, as it

* *Letters I,* iii. pp. 253, 254.
† Grey, *Early Years of the Prince Consort,* p. 238.
‡ Martin, *Life of the Prince Consort,* iv. p. 174.

proved to be) before he came to the throne, to establish her influence with him on these lines of wisdom and foresight. The invincible combination of Germany by land and England by sea, inspired by the most exalted ideals, would bring peace and prosperity to distracted Europe. She must be in Germany what her father had made himself in England ; he as Prince Consort, now near the untimely end of his laborious days, had long, by his paramount influence over the Queen, been virtually King, and she in the next generation, as Queen Consort of the King of Prussia (enlarged, it was to be hoped, beyond all telling), must wield just such an enlightened supremacy over husband and children. She, with her quick, imaginative intelligence, was eagerly receptive of her father's conception, and, Brünnhilde to his Wotan, she was the maiden of his will. Once more, with a vaster prospect in view than Windsor Park, she might have exclaimed : 'Violà le tableau qui se déroule à mes pieds.' Moreover she loved power and influence, and here there were illimitable opportunities — opportunities as large as she could make them — of acquiring both. The memory of these talks, the thought of the magnificent and congenial work that opened before her and her intense affection for her husband, mitigated the pangs of parting. She was royal missioner to Prussia for the propagation of her adored papa's faith, and her emotions and her intelligence alike were enlisted in this service. The enchanting smile beamed like a rainbow against her tears as the *Victoria and Albert* put out into the wintry mists of the North Sea.

The Princess was only a few months over seventeen when, laden with this tremendous task, she was shipped to a foreign land, where she would be surrounded by watchful eyes and censorious ears, to take up her delicate and difficult position. Her father's ideals, passionately shared by her, were a stimulus to that active, eager mind, which was really much more in need of a sedative. A transcendent tact was required, for Prussia just now, tingling with the sense of growth and military expansion, would be quick to notice any hint of a patronising or Anglicising tendency in its new Princess and eager to resent it: evidently it would be easier for her to make critics than friends. If she was to be an effective missioner she must shed, or at any rate effectively conceal, her Englishness. In that respect she would have to do better than her father. Eighteen years ago, on his marriage, he had promised his stepmother that he would never cease 'ein treuer Deutscher und Coburger zu sein,' and his adherence to that ill-advised resolve had been the main reason why, in spite of his wise and unwearied labours for England, he had never been trusted there, except by his wife and those few Ministers who rated him at his true worth, and had remained a foreigner. If now his daughter was to succeed she must pass the scrutiny of the most penetrating and Prussian eyes in all Europe. Bismarck was not yet in power, nor for several years yet would he be established at Berlin, but within a few months of her marriage he had seen her and given his verdict : she must become a Prussian through and through, she must 'leave the Englishwoman at home' and let her remain a sleeping Princess in suspended animation save when she revisited her native land. He thought her clever 'in a womanly way,' but not able to disguise her feelings, a grave defect in Bismarck's eyes.*

Successfully to manipulate these trances and resuscitations would have taxed the wisdom of Solomon, and with all her dazzling cleverness Princess Frederick was not wise. She could not adjust herself to these difficult quick changes, and even as when, a bilingual child, she spoke each of two languages with the accent appropriate to the other, she now

* Busch, *Bismarck*, i. p. 139.

made a like confusion in her conduct, and her eldest brother
was not far wrong when he said 'Vicky is always pure Prussian when she is at home, and pure English when she is in
Prussia.' Moreover she cultivated her artistic pursuits with
a publicity which the Germans, with their strict limitations
of the proper spheres for a woman's activities, considered
strangely emancipated. She kept up her painting, and indeed she was a very good artist ; she modelled in clay, and
sent photographs of her bas-relief of the Princes in the Tower
and of her statuette of Lady Jane Grey to her father, who
thought very highly of them and urged her to take up the
study of architecture. She asked artists and musicians to dine,
introducing the leaven of the arts into the heavy dough of her
Court, and that was a staggering innovation in royal circles
in Prussia. There again she was following her father's example, who in the early days of his married life had tried to
mix the same leaven into evenings at Windsor. The Queen
had not approved of that, nor now did the Princess Frederick's entourage. The Prince Consort again, though a very
devout Christian, permitted a certain rationalism in Biblical
criticism, but that Princess Frederick should hold such loose
notions was an abomination to the pietism of Prussia : 'She
is quite Renan in her ideas' was the horrified comment of
the Queen.* In more material ways she protested against
the sanitary inconveniences of the Old Schloss in Berlin
where she and her husband were at first lodged, and her expressed yearning for the superior plumbing of Osborne and
Balmoral was not tactful. She found it odd, too, that when
she asked for an egg-cup at breakfast she was told that the
Prussian mode was to use a liqueur glass. Or, commenting
on the decoration of dinner-tables, she observed that two or
three merchant families in Liverpool had more silver plate

* Princess Catherine Radziwill, *Empress Frederick,* p. 59.

than the entire Prussian nobility. But on the whole she was
received with great friendliness in Berlin : there was evidently a desire to give 'die Engländerin' a fair trial, though
in the very word 'Engländerin' there was an implied reserva-
tion ready to express itself.

It would have been wiser if her parents had let her alone
rather more in these early days in order that she should
realise and adapt herself to her position. But every Wednes-
day her father wrote to her with careful and detailed advice :
he reminded her that 'her place is that of her husband's wife
and her mother's daughter' : he offered to look through her
private budget of allowance and expenditure, recommending
her to put aside a handsome margin for unforeseen contingencies : she promised to impart to him the progress of
of her inner life and he 'to take a constantly active part in
fostering it.' To her mother she wrote almost daily and
sometimes twice a day. The Prince Consort came to stay
with her and her husband in June, five months after her marriage, and expressed himself pleased. 'I have had long
talks,' he wrote to his wife, 'with both of them, singly and
together, which gave me the greatest satisfaction,' and only
two months afterwards he came again and stayed for a fortnight, accompanied by the Queen, who brought with her
two of her Ministers and Lord Clarendon, her late Foreign
Minister : this gave a slightly official air to the visit, which
was perhaps a mistake. The Queen also hardly appreciated
the fact that if her daughter was to make herself acceptable
to a foreign and jealous Court, she must identify herself with
Germany, as Bismarck said, and cease to be English. Instead she wanted to continue to exercise parental control, and
constantly wrote her very severe letters, telling her that she
ought to be more mindful of her own country and her own
family. She encouraged the Princess's tendency to be too

English to suit German sensibilities, when she should have done her best to discourage it.*

Both England and Prussia were soon rejoicing in the prospect of an heir of the third generation to the Prussian Crown. This happy event, which for a while looked as if it might end in just such a double tragedy as that which had befallen Princess Charlotte of Wales, daughter of the Prince Regent, took place on January 27, 1859. The delivery was very difficult, and while the cannons of Berlin and its pealing bells saluted the infant Prince, it seemed doubtful whether medical skill could induce him to take up the burden of life at all and his mother not to lay it down. So desperate indeed seemed her condition that messages were sent to the chief newspaper offices to set up obituary notices. During those hours the primary needs of mother and son so occupied nurses and doctors alike that none observed how grievously the boy's left arm had been injured : the shoulder-blade had been nearly wrenched from its socket and the surrounding muscles badly torn. Incredible as it seems, this was not discovered till the third day after the baby's birth, when it was noticed that there was no power of movement in this limb. With the boy's slender hold on life the German doctors did not attempt to adjust it, and it was lucky that Sir James Clark, the English doctor whom the Queen had sent over for her daughter's confinement, made no attempt, for when the irreparable nature of the damage was known, there would surely have been just such an outcry over the meddling mismanagement of English medical men as occurred twenty-eight years later.

* Bülow, *Memoirs*, 1897–1903, p. 529 ; *Greville Memoirs*, Dec. 12, 1859 ; Ponsonby, *Letters of Empress Frederick*, p. 17 ; Martin, *Life of the Prince Consort*, iv. pp. 176, 177, 207, 216, 217, 241 ; Busch, *Bismarck*, i. p. 500.

Prince Frederick William Victor Albert thus started life with a grave physical disability, and far graver perhaps were the psychical consequences of his tortured entry. Knowing as we do now that the earliest, even the prenatal, impressions which a child's mind subconsciously receives are often, though lost to memory, indelibly stamped there and, with maturing years, are among the most powerful of formative influences, it may well be that those first days of William's life and even the physical maiming at his actual birth bit deep into the soft wax that hardens into character and temperament. Torturing and empirical applications of electricity were subsequently tried, but found to be in vain, and Nature was left to perform such spontaneous healing as she could. In other respects the child throve well, and six weeks later the Prince Consort recommended his daughter to try the bracing effects of sea-air and washing in cold water. She wrote to her mother that the baby was exceedingly lively and required to be constantly danced about.

A political crisis prevented the Queen from going to Berlin for William's christening : 'Never,' she wrote to her Uncle Leopold, 'have I felt *so* bitterly disappointed *about anything* as about this. . . It is a *stupid law* in Prussia, I must say, to be so particular about having the child christened so soon.' * But Prussia would not revise the rubrics of her Church at a moment's notice, and the Queen did not see her grandson till she and the Prince Consort went on a visit to Coburg in September 1860, when William was twenty months old and already had a sister.† She detected Fritz's eyes and Vicky's mouth in his baby face, and he behaved beautifully, and her heart went out to him in an affection and tenderness which outlasted many trying occasions. As

---

* *Letters I*, iii. p. 324.

† By some curious mistake, the Emperor William II informed Mr. Frederick Whitridge that the Queen had held him in her arms when he was only a few hours old. (Private information.)

might have been surmised, he had an English nurse, and, rather unexpectedly, the Queen mentioned his 'very fine shoulders.'

The King of Prussia, Frederick William IV, had been insane for several years, his brother, Prince William, the father-in-law of Princess Frederick, acting as Regent. In January 1861 the King died, and Prince Frederick on his father's accession became Crown Prince. The new Crown Princess was becoming very unpopular : she certainly was not 'leaving the Englishwoman at home,' and the campaign of violent attacks in *The Times* against everything Prussian was certainly damaging to her.* She ordered her nurseries in the English mode, and her Treasurer was Baron Ernest Stockmar, the son of him who had lived so long in England on the most confidential terms with her father and mother : now with her added dignities she would be more closely and jealously watched than before. Lord Clarendon, who officially attended the coronation of William I, wrote most glowingly of her to her mother, but the very warmth and quality of his praise should have conveyed a warning. Speaking of the new King, he said : 'If His Majesty had the mind, the judgment of the Princess Royal, there would be nothing to fear, and the example and the influence of Prussia would soon be marvellously developed. . . Lord Clarendon has had the honour to hold a very long conversation with Her Royal Highness, and has been more than ever astonished at the statesmanlike and comprehensive views which she takes of the policy of Prussia, both internal and foreign, and of the *duties* of a Constitutional King.' † That was high praise, and the Prince Consort was rightly proud of the daughter who had proved so apt a pupil and was carrying on her mission so keenly. 'I spare no pains,' wrote her father about the new Crown Prince and Princess, 'to

* Martin, *Life of the Prince Consort*, v. p. 399.   † *Letters I*, iii. p. 459.

encourage and stimulate them in the path they have chosen.' * She sent him a long and able memorandum suggesting that ministerial responsibility should be defined by law, but was there not a dangerous quality in her very brilliance and her grasp of Prussian politics ? As long as she kept her views completely to herself there was no harm in her holding them, but Prussia did not desire the Crown Princess to be statesmanlike and foreseeing and authoritative on the duties of a constitutional king, and her father should have mingled his appreciation of her gifts with emphatic cautions. Already she had established a very strong influence over her husband and had imbued him with the liberal principles of government which she derived from 'home,' as she still called England. These liberal views and her husband's adoption of them were known and resented, and the risk of trouble to come was the more serious because the new King was strongly reactionary : even the Prince Consort felt discouraged about his mission of bringing Prussia and England together when he read his speeches about the divine right of kings.† He did not intend to govern on liberal principles, and nothing was further from his thoughts than to consult either his son or his daughter-in-law on affairs of State. In this Queen Victoria was really of a like mind with him, for her eldest son was fifty years old before she allowed him any voice in matters of internal or international policy. Why then should not King William of Prussia resent the young Crown Prince, now just thirty years old, airing liberal views so directly opposed to his own, especially when he knew that these poisonous doctrines were inspired by the even younger 'Engländerin' ? Already she had been too emphatic on the superior excellence of all things English, and now, as Crown Princess, she became more emphatic yet. Within a year of King William's

---

* Martin, *Life of the Prince Consort*, v. p. 292.   † *Ibid.* p. 407.

accession occurred the lamentable death of the Prince Consort, and more than ever his daughter felt the sacredness of the mission with which on her marriage he had entrusted her. More than ever it was her duty, now that he was gone, to inspire her husband with his noble ideals and aspirations. Her father's death had but strengthened the spiritual tie between them, and with the added prestige of her new position she pursued his will.

Next year, 1862, came the determinative moment for the future history of Prussia. The Reichstag refused to vote the enormous sum which the new King demanded for the reconstitution of the Prussian army, and he recalled Bismarck from the German Embassy at Paris. From then till his dismissal from the post of Chancellor by the Crown Princess's eldest baby, then aged three, he dictated the policy of Prussia. Autocracy took the place of constitutional government, and 'blood and iron' were its methods. His principles, in fact, were the precise opposite of those of the mission of the Crown Princess, and while completely conscious of her influence over her husband, he as completely disregarded them both. They were entirely negligible : they were the Anglo-Coburgs.

The first collision occurred before Bismarck had been a year in office. He restricted, or rather abolished, the liberty of the Press. The Crown Prince twice wrote in protest to his father, and also to Bismarck : he got an angry reply from the King and none from the Minister President. In order to dissociate himself publicly from so unconstitutional a measure he arranged that, while he was paying a military visit to Danzig, the Ober-Bürgermeister, Von Winter, should allude to it in a speech at the Rathaus : the Crown Prince would thus have an opportunity of declaring his disapproval. The device was strongly backed up by the Crown Princess, who wrote to her mother : 'I did *all* I *could* to induce Fritz to do so, knowing how necessary it was that he should *once* express his sentiments openly and disclaim having any part in the last measures of the Government. I hope you will make his conduct known to your Ministers and to all our friends in England.' *

Anything more injudicious could scarcely be imagined. The Crown Princess was, of course, at liberty to tell her mother about the trouble, but Prussia's internal policy was no concern of the Queen's Ministers. One can imagine what the Queen's feelings would have been if the Princess of Wales had begged her husband to make a public speech at Manchester attacking some measure that had received the Sovereign's approval, and had written to the King of Denmark asking that his Ministers should be told all about it. Or does not imagination boggle at so prodigious an idea ? . . . In Prussia the natural and proper consequence of the Crown Prince following his wife's advice was that the King was furious with his son and told him publicly to retract what he had publicly said. This he refused to do, and offered to resign all his civil and military offices and live in retirement. The Princess, in her passion for what she felt was right, was delighted with her own impetuous folly, and her gaily pugnacious comment was 'I enjoy a pitched battle (when it comes to it) exceedingly.' Indeed her enjoyment was scarcely tempered by the knowledge that her counsel to her husband had led to a very bitter quarrel between him and his father, for she was quite convinced that she had only urged him to do his duty, and would do the same again 'in the face of all the Kings and Emperors of the whole world.' † A further result was that she earned for them both a more abundant measure of Bismarck's hostility.

---

* *Letters II*, i. pp. 87, 88 ; Busch, *Bismarck*, iii. p. 238.
† Ponsonby, *Letters of Empress Frederick*, pp. 41, 42.

This episode is illustrative of the conscientious but tactless blunders that the Princess was making in the propagation of her mission. Her changes of front also were highly bewildering, as was shown over the question of the Duchies of Schleswig and Holstein. It was exceedingly complicated : Palmerston said that only three people had ever understood it — the Prince Consort, who was dead, himself who had forgotten about it, and a German professor who was now insane.* The claimants were the King of Denmark, Duke Frederick of Schleswig-Holstein-Sonderburg-Augustenburg, and Prussia in combination with Austria. Just before the war broke out, the Crown Prince and Princess were staying with the Queen at Windsor, and this family gathering was far from harmonious. The Prince and Princess of Wales were naturally pro-Danish, as was also the general sympathy of the nation ; the Queen, mindful of the Prince Consort's conviction that neither Denmark nor Duke Frederick had any valid claim, was pro-Prussian ; while the Crown Prince and Princess, out of detestation for Bismarck's policy of brigandage, were upholders of Duke Frederick. War broke out, and instantly the Princess became as Prussian as Bismarck himself. She could not blame an English person, she wrote to her mother, for not understanding the question, but to 'us Germans' it was as clear as daylight. The English sympathy with Denmark was monstrous ; the attacks on Prussia in the Press were absurd, unjust, rude and violent : 'The continual meddling and interfering of England in other people's affairs has become so ridiculous abroad that it almost ceases to annoy.' †

Only a few weeks ago she had been convinced that Duke Frederick was the rightful claimant in the sight of God and man, but now her husband was on active service in the vic-

* Strachey, *Queen Victoria*, p. 226.
† Ponsonby, *Letters of Empress Frederick*, p. 53.

torious Prussian armies, and that made the whole difference : Bismarck was right, she was sorry for the poor Danes, she hoped her sister-in-law was not too much distressed, and the claims of Duke Frederick vanished into thin air. Precisely the same thing happened in the ensuing quarrel between Prussia and Austria. 'Not a day passes,' she wrote to her mother, 'when the wicked man does not with the *greatest* ability counteract and thwart what is good, and drive on towards war.' The Queen agreed with her, and went so far as to write to the King of Prussia, telling him that 'he was being deceived by one man,' and begging him to use all his influence to prevent war. But her intervention was fruitless, and when the Seven Weeks' War came to a swift conclusion with the battle of Sadowa in July 1866, it was perhaps too much to expect of human nature that the Crown Princess should not have looked on 'the wicked man' with different eyes, for Prussia, of which her husband would one day be King, was marvellously expanding under his unscrupulous dictatorship. Certain German states, of which her near relations were the rulers, such as the Kingdom of Hanover and part of the Grand Duchy of Hesse-Darmstadt, were absorbed into Prussia, but it was their fault. They had been told beforehand what they might expect, and they had chosen to stand in with Austria, poor things. The abhorred policy of blood and iron, so utterly opposed to the spirit of the mission with which her father had entrusted her, had won vast aggrandisements for Prussia, and she positively lectured her mother on the importance of keeping her natural sympathy with relations quite separate from a cool judgment of political necessities. 'Nothing,' she wrote, 'will or ever can shake Fritz's principle of sound Liberalism and justice, but you know by experience that one must proceed in the direction given by the political events which have come to pass. . . I cannot and will not forget that I am a Prussian, but as such I know that it is very difficult to make you or any other non-German see how our case lies.' *

It was not really very difficult ; anyone could see (and her mother certainly did) that Vicky wanted to have it both ways. She and Fritz did not give up their sound liberal principles, but they thankfully accepted the immense territorial acquisitions which the abandonment of those principles had won. Indeed, nobody but a Prussian could fully sympathise with such unscrupulous appropriations. As such, she had certainly left the Englishwoman at home, and disowned her prejudices. But the cherished liberal principles, it must be understood, were not really abandoned : they were just put away in a safe place for the time, and when Fritz came to the throne — for some reason no one suspected that his father would live much longer — they would be brought out again.

In 1870 Bismarck was ready to prove more convincingly than ever before that the Hohenzollerns were not the 'paltry German dynasty' which *The Times* had once called them. His design, as usual, was of that subtle simplicity which makes lobster-pots so effective : the prey finds it perfectly easy to get into the trap, but impossible to get out. He induced Marshal Prim, who had become head of the Spanish republic after the deposition of Queen Isabella, to ask Prussia to nominate Prince Leopold of Hohenzollern-Sigmaringen for the throne of Spain. King William duly nominated him, and this had the desired result of causing France to veto the appointment. Prince Leopold, only a pawn in the game, withdrew, and France, thinking she had scored a tremendous diplomatic triumph, instructed her ambassador at Berlin to demand the King's promise that this attempt should never be repeated. That was just what

* *Letters II,* i. pp. 366, 367.

Bismarck wanted. No reigning monarch could submit to
such dictation, and the Chancellor by violent and insolent
attacks on France in the Press and in the Reichstag so inflamed public opinion in both countries that France declared war. Here the Crown Princess and her mother were
passionately at one. All the Queen's pro-German sympathies were stirred, and they both trembled for Germany's
very existence before the might of France. Oddly enough
the Prince Consort's mission, which Bismarck had been so
brutally misinterpreting, became a living force again. The
Queen remembered how on that state visit to France, just
before her daughter was betrothed, Prince Albert had by
no means shared her enthusiasm for the French. Albert
had never trusted Napoleon III, and as for France, he considered her a 'vainglorious and immoral nation.' What
would Albert have thought of her declaring war on his
pacific native land ? The Queen said to Sir Theodore
Martin : 'It was merciful that the beloved Prince was taken,
for had he lived I could never have prevented him from
joining the German Armies.' * Anxiety, however, as to the
fate of Germany was short-lived, for her hosts swept forward on a flood-tide of victory. On September 1, 1870, the
battle of Sedan broke the French, and the Crown Princess's
letters to her mother became as lyrical as the chant of Deb-
orah. Once again she was Prussian to the core, and she
lectured her mother on the bitter feelings which had pre-
vailed in Germany against England at the opening of the
war. The feeling had been (she wrote), 'If we are annihilated, England will be the cause : she knows and ac-
knowledges that we have been unfairly and unjustly attacked, and yet she will quietly see us go to the bottom
without stirring a little finger to help us ! . . . England is
suffering from obesity and too indolent to stir, it rather lets

* Esher, *Journals and Letters,* ii. p. 292.

us perish than speak a serious word to France. I think in the *main* Germany is right and her feeling legitimate.' *

In these first thirteen years of the Crown Princess's life in Germany, two events stand out infinitely more significant than all the rest. Between them they formed, so to speak, the theme on which her tragic life was based. The first was the maimed birth of her eldest son, the second the return of Bismarck from the German Embassy at Paris to Berlin.

* *Letters II,* ii. pp. 79, 80.

CHAPTER II

FROM the day when Princess Frederick had been recalled from the shadow of death after the birth of her first son, she had felt a special instinctive tenderness for the arm-crippled boy. She had wondered whether his condition was in any way her fault, whether it was a slur on her motherhood. But she, only just eighteen years old, had been lying unconscious between life and death for hours after the child had begun to live, and, very rightly, she had put from her the thought that she was responsible for his deformity. At the back of this peculiar tenderness, however, there was always the sense of pity, and it is easy to realise how this highly sensitive boy, as soon as he became conscious of his infirmity, shrank from it. It requires the most delicate tact to show pity without rousing resentment, and there could be nothing which such a child would more dislike than any display of it, for he would find in it a reminder of his maimed condition. But to affirm, as a very brilliant biographer of William II has done, that his mother 'instead of compassion cherished in her heart a secret grudge against her misshapen son, precisely because he *was* her first-born, and openly displayed a preference for her other children,' is an assertion which cannot be maintained.*
Such evidence as there is concerning the early relations of mother and son proves precisely the opposite, and we can only conclude that Dr. Ludwig has mistakenly attached to

* Emil Ludwig, *Kaiser Wilhelm II*, p. 6.

22

these earlier years the enmity between the two which sprang up later. It is, however, more than possible that the Princess's impulsive tenderness and pity often flicked the boy on the raw.

As soon as William emerged from the nursery and the guardianship of women, a strict and eminently joyless education was devised for him by his tutor Hinzpeter. Lessons started at six in the morning in the summer and seven in the winter, and continued, with intervals for meals and exercise, for the next twelve hours. We must assume that the Crown Prince and Princess approved this regime : indeed it conformed with German ideas of the education of children, and as it followed the lines which the Princess's father had laid down for the education of his eldest son, it had for her a pious significance. William was also subjected to very strict invigilation over his general conduct, and there, perhaps mindful of the effect of a similar bondage on her eldest son, Queen Victoria recommended a looser rein. 'I am sure,' she wrote, 'that you watch over your dear boy with the greatest care, but I often think too great care, too much constant watching, leads to the very dangers hereafter which one wishes to avoid.' * To William's educational course was added a system of physical exercises which should enable him, in spite of his paralysed arm, to fit himself for his future. It might have been permitted to a boy born in a less exalted sphere, who was not destined to be the head of the House of Hohenzollern, to devote himself to artistic and literary pursuits, in which this handicap would not have been so heavy, but for the eldest son of the Crown Prince of Prussia no such career was possible. Learning to ride was the most necessary and most difficult of these accomplishments, for owing to his infirmity he had no natural sense of balance. In order to

* Ponsonby, *Letters of Empress Frederick*, pp. 123, 124.

give it him he was made, at the age of eight, to ride without
stirrups, so that a loss of balance was instantly followed by
a fall, and tears and tumbles innumerable were his lot.
Such treatment was brutal, and it confirmed in him that
suppressed and humiliating sense that boys much smaller
than himself could do with ease what he, for no fault of
his, found so cruelly hard. In spite of all treatment no
power could be restored to his paralysed limb, and, in mod-
ern psychological terms, there developed in him a deep-
rooted inferiority complex. With a grit and a perseverance
wholly admirable he set his teeth and determined to overcome his physical disabilities and reduce to the smallest
possible the handicap under which he laboured. But what
he could not overcome was the inner sense of his inferiority.
From boyhood onwards he envied those who were stronger
than himself, and feared them.

From his earliest days he was steeped in militarism. He
remembered how at the age of five the allied Prussian and
Austrian forces, with his father in high command, returned
triumphant from the Danish campaign : two years later
these allies were at war, and once more his father came back
to Berlin at the head of his victorious troops after the battle
of Sadowa. On his tenth birthday he was given a commission in the 1st Infantry Regiment of the Guards, and
marched with them on parade before his admiring grandfather. When he was twelve came the most splendid pag-
eant of all, the last and the greatest triumph of German
arms that he was ever to see, when the troops returned from
the Franco-German War and made their entry into Berlin.
At the head of them rode the new Emperor, and Prince
William, now with an assured seat, followed his father on
a dappled horse.* The next time that German armies returned in force to Berlin it was not in the roar of triumph,

* William II, *My Early Life*, pp. 22, 23, 32, 47.

and he was not there to see that entry. But three times before he was thirteen years old he had seen victories by blood and iron snatch fresh territories for the Empire over which he would one day rule, and on each occasion it had been Bismarck who had been the architect of these enlargements.

That gigantic figure was now well known to him and heroic, but again and again he must have heard him spoken of at his father's table with dropped words of disparagement and dislike, or perhaps, when he was mentioned, a silence fell, not hard to interpret. William was a very sharp boy, and he noticed also how the nationality of the domestic atmosphere varied. Sometimes his mother was truculently English, sometimes she was as Prussian as anybody, but whichever was the favoured nation, Bismarck was to both his parents a sinister and untrusted figure. He was always very polite to William's mother, but surely irony underlay his formal courtesy, and the notion gradually formed itself in the boy's head that he did not pay serious attention to her. Sometimes she would argue with him, or she would treat him with a sort of chaffing humour, or with aloof dignity, but his demeanour was always the same : she didn't matter. These impressions, a touch here, a touch there, began to define themselves into permanent pictures, and the most vivid was that both his father and mother abhorred the great Chancellor.

It was odd : William's lessons in history with Hinzpeter had taught him that it was through Bismarck's astuteness and his creation of the great armies of Prussia that his country had acquired two duchies, two French provinces with a colossal indemnity, and, with an Emperor on the throne, was the head of Confederated and United Germany. Some day after the death of his grandfather and his father he would inherit these benefits. Count von Bismarck, whether William's parents appreciated him or not, was certainly a man to look up to. At present they were watching their son's development with great satisfaction. On his twelfth birthday his father recorded in his Diary the 'simple natural cordial relations that existed between them,' and simultaneously the Princess wrote to her mother : 'I am happy to say that between him and me there is a bond of love and confidence which I feel that nothing can destroy,' but she thought little of his abilities or of his strength of character. His crippled arm, alas, was no better, and it made him feel shy and helpless.*

The country outside Germany which William knew best was the little island with the big fleet where Grandmamma Victoria lived. It was linked up with the dawn of memory, and the scene of his earliest recollections was laid not at Berlin, but at her house at Osborne — 'a very original country-seat' — where, aged two and a half, he could remember being swung in a table-napkin by Grandpapa Albert, whose personality, he claimed, made a very vivid impression on him. But six months after that his grandfather died, and when next he visited England with his father and mother to be present at the marriage of his Uncle Bertie, he was four years old, and was fitted out with a Highland costume. The Queen was devoted to him : 'a clever, dear, good little child, the great favourite of my beloved Angel,' so she wrote to Uncle Leopold, and till her death, in spite of occasional ebullitions of fury with his intolerable antics, she retained her affection for him. He, too, had a real and deep regard for her, and with it was mingled a very salutary respect and awe such as he assuredly felt for no other man or woman in the world. Seldom during his boyhood did a year pass in which he did not spend a few weeks with her, and in this *annus mirabilis* for Germany, when he had ridden with his father and grandfather at the head of the

* Ponsonby, *Letters of Empress Frederick,* pp. 118–120.

triumphant armies returning from Paris, he and his mother and his brother Henry remained in England for a couple of months after his father had gone home again.

English national feeling just then was strongly sympathetic with France owing to the iron terms of peace which had been imposed and which, so it was believed, the Queen might have caused to be mitigated if she had used her influence with her German relations. Throughout the war she had made no secret of her Germanophil sentiments, and she was well aware that this visit from the ruling family would be very unpopular. But there were domestic reasons for it : the Prince of Wales's sympathies were ardently with France and he and the Crown Princess were at loggerheads. Throughout the war she had sent him most irritating messages : did not he envy Fritz who was doing such wonders for his country ? what did he and Alix (who still remembered with bitterness Germany's annexation of her father's duchies) make of these great German victories ? The Queen was determined that these family quarrels should be reconciled, and though the Press made 'vulgar and impertinent' attacks, and protests were raised in the House of Commons about the visit, nothing shook her. She was a widowed mother, and her children were quarrelling, and so Vicky and Fritz and William and Henry paid this long visit to make friends again. All happened as she had planned, for she and her son and her daughter and her son-in-law clasped hands over their common detestation of Bismarck. Fritz, the prospective beneficiary, so the Queen recorded, 'is so fair, kind and good, and has the intensest horror of Bismarck, says he is no doubt energetic and clever, but bad, unprincipled and *all-powerful* : he is in fact the Emperor, which Fritz's father does not like, but still cannot help.' *
This bond of a common hatred drew the family together,

* *Letters II*, ii. pp. 154, 155.

and so anti-Bismarckian was the Crown Prince over the appropriation of Alsace and Lorraine that the Prince of Wales believed that, when he came to the throne, he would restore part, at any rate, of the provinces to France. So sharp a boy as William could not fail to see how all his relations loathed the tremendous personage for whom he was beginning to feel a boyish hero-worship.

William was confirmed when he was fifteen. He tells us that Dr. Persius, who prepared him, did not give him much spiritual enlightenment, but that his own meditations resulted in 'a really elevating initiation' ; his tutor Hinzpeter quaintly observed that 'the Prince was to be free so to adapt the Christian faith himself to his own individuality that it might become the standard on which he could model his life.' * The Prince of Wales attended the ceremony in the Friedenskirche ; he himself had been through a similar ordeal in St. George's Chapel, and the Prince Consort in the Giants Hall at Coburg, and the Coburg use for the confirmation of royal princes was a formidable rite. The candidate was stationed by himself on a dais, in front of two rows of chairs where sat the Emperor and Empress and the Royal Family of Prussia, and for half an hour, as if on a theological rack, he answered without faltering, in a loud, steady voice, the forty conundrums put to him by the Court chaplain, who gave three long addresses. His younger brothers and sisters, whether from sympathy with William or from sheer fatigue at the appalling length of the ceremony, cried the whole time.†

The Crown Princess much distrusted the Emperor's notions as to William's education : she told her mother that his influence was very hurtful. But evidently on one point he had not been able to enforce it, for two days after this

---

* William II, *My Early Life*, p. 76.
† Ponsonby, *Letters of Empress Frederick*, p. 135.

ceremony William and Henry were sent off to the Grammar School at Cassel, where they remained for two years and a half. So democratic a course was quite unprecedented in the education of Prussian princes ; that the heir to the throne, as William put it, 'should be placed on the school-bench, thereby rendering him defenceless to the world's criticism,' had produced violent opposition in the family and Court circles. Hinzpeter, the Prince's tutor, had hatched this revolutionary idea, the Crown Princess had backed him up and they carried it through. William himself, when he was told what was to be done with him, disliked the idea as much as anybody, and in his memoirs of his early life he stated the quality of his objections with the most engaging candour : 'He was to learn with strange boys in a public school, was to compete with them, and — to come out lower in the list !' That rings true : he could not have made a juster piece of self-analysis. Competition, throughout his life, was intolerable to him, because it might demonstrate that sense of inferiority which always haunted him. An unchallenged supremacy on the most exalted pinnacle was the only setting in which he felt at ease.

But his mother got her way, and for these years William, in the obscurity and competitive atmosphere of school, living with his brother and his tutor in the Fürstenhaus at Cassel, was kept very hard at work, studying upwards of ten hours a day, on terms of equality though not familiarity with the other pupils. He kept a Diary, a *Curriculum Vitae,* and it reveals the boy as the legitimate father of the man. He made himself arbiter of the rival merits of the authors with whom he was now becoming acquainted : he settled that Cicero was a much overrated orator and his speech *Pro Sestio* a mere self-glorification ; he soon found that Horace was no gentleman, but of the lowest rank of hedonist ; no respectable person nowadays would dream of asking him to dinner. He founded a society for the study of mediaeval history, and a Sunday afternoon club to which he read a paper on Alexander the Great. He began writing a tragedy on the story of Harmodius and Aristogiton, but abandoned it when he found that young Prince Bernhard of Saxe-Meiningen had written a drama on this theme. He observed that his fellow-pupils had no feeling of *Civis Germanus sum,* 'such as,' he commented, 'I awoke later in the German people.' He was already intensely interested, thanks to his visits to his grandmother, in naval matters, and read William James's *Naval History,* and subsequently, so he tells us, often astounded British naval officers with the knowledge he had gained from it. His powers of observation were extraordinarily quick, he had an insatiable curiosity, and above all he fought his own timidity, encouraging himself to believe that his judgment on any point presented to his notice was infallible. Just before his eighteenth birthday he passed his final examination (which was not competitive) and returned home for his coming of age. Sweet, indeed, was his relief at his importance being recognised once more : his English grandmother sent him the Order of the Garter, which, he proudly records, was generally only given to the reigning sovereigns of Europe, and the Emperor invested him with the Order of the Black Eagle. The *Curriculum Vitae* testified that, as he had dedicated himself to God at his confirmation, he now dedicated himself to his military career.

Like his father he spent a few terms at Bonn as a student in the Corps 'Borussia,' reading jurisprudence, and there was a long visit to his grandmother at Balmoral. She gave him a Highland costume of Royal Stuart tartan, which he considered a mark of her special favour, since she was very proud of the tincture of Stuart blood that ran in her veins, and therefore even more attenuatedly in his, and sent him

The Crown Prince and Princess Frederick

out stalking for the first time. Of this experience he gave an account which baffles all efforts at interpretation. William sighted deer three miles off, and he and his gillie thereupon took 'full cover.' It was a long business before they could 'pick up the scent,' but after a three hours' crawl he got his first stag. This curious account is only mentioned because it so admirably foreshadows his constant conviction that he understood all the intricacies of international situations when he had not grasped the elements of them. At parting his grandmother urged him to do his best to become like the Prince Consort, but the resemblance was never very remarkable.*

For the next two years William lived with his regiment in an atmosphere saturated with Prussian militarism, and all the determinative influences of his early boyhood, the splendour of conquest, the expansion of the vastly extended Empire, now forming into character, began to range themselves against the liberal views of his parents. The general feeling in Germany just now, especially in military circles, was savagely anti-British, and the constant harpings of his mother on the superiority of all things English would have driven a young man of far less conscious self-importance than him into contradictiousness ; and when he returned to live at home again, this developed into a personal antagonism to her. When she heard disparaging remarks about England she acknowledged that she was wont to answer back pretty sharply, and occasions for friction multiplied.

No one could question her quickness and her cleverness, but she had none of the ballast of wisdom to give them weight. In both these characteristics, extreme cleverness and lack of wisdom, she and her son were extraordinarily alike, but their very similarity, instead of being a bond between them, only emphasised their antipathy. Both had

* William II, *My Early Life*, pp. 96–145.

the conviction that their view of any question, however hastily arrived at, was final and infallible, and both abounded in dogmatism.

But this similarity sprang from very different soils. William's assertiveness was partly due to conceit, but partly also was an antidote, self-administered, for his deep-rooted timidity and sense of inferiority, while his mother's was the expression of her dominating self-confidence. Each of them resented in the other what was common to them both ; what exasperated the mother with her son was the precise counterpart of that which exasperated the son with his mother. She considered it impertinent in him to set up his opinion against hers ; he took the Prussian view that, where political or national questions were concerned, it was impertinent of a woman to have any opinion at all. But instead of having none, she pronounced authoritatively and sometimes astonishingly on subjects of every kind : von Angeli, for instance, was the finest portrait-painter since Rembrandt, and Ebers had found an Egyptian mummy of a period long anterior to Moses, on the wrappings of which were inscribed the Ten Commandments word for word as they appeared in the book of Exodus.* Always brilliant, always voluble, she both counselled her husband on internal politics, and advised her mother about the affairs of Ireland or a change of Ministry. Indeed many of her letters to the Queen about this time, dealing with matters entirely concerned with the internal affairs of England, are conveyed in so responsible a tone that she seems to be carrying on her father's mission there as well as in Germany. She sympathises with the Queen in having to bear all these anxieties without his help and counsel, and at once overflows with urgent and minute advice. Just so, in later years, did William give his grandmother his views about the British Navy.

* Bell, *Randall Davidson*, i. p. 151.

With William then back again under his parents' roof, hot with militarism and exalted by the flattery of the young officers, it was inevitable that most topics in domestic intercourse should produce argument and collision. We may imagine the Crown Prince taking little part in these nimble skirmishes. His mind moved slowly but on an even keel, he considered a question before and not after he gave his opinion on it, and he still trusted his wife's swift dogmatic pronouncements as instinctively as he mistrusted his son's : she dominated his mind. He looked on William now as a young man inflated with monstrous conceit, but, after all, if he himself lived to anything like the span of life which a very healthy and abstemious man not yet fifty might reasonably expect, William, now worshipping Bismarck and all that he stood for, would have many maturing years in front of him yet, in which he would gain experience and possibly wisdom before he could be dangerous, and by that time Bismarck would have long vanished and the leaven of his own and his wife's liberal and pacific policies would be permeating Germany. For the present Bismarck had it all his own way, for his control of the Emperor was as thorough as his disregard of the Crown Prince, and there was something solider than sarcasm in his wife's bitter comment to her mother on Bismarck's position : 'I wonder why he does not say straight out "As long as *I* live both the Constitution and the Crown are suspended," because that is the real state of the matter.' * But the termination of that tyranny could not be very far off, for the Emperor was now in his eighty-third year, and though he was a hale old gentleman who could still enjoy a day's shooting and a visit to the play in the evening, he was mortal. He seldom saw his son or his daughter-in-law except on official occasions, and the Crown Prince could scarcely help looking forward

* *Letters II*, iii. p. 248.

to his father's death as the end of the regime which he and his wife, though large prospective beneficiaries, regarded with moral abhorrence. For twenty-two years they had been preparing themselves for power and for the realisation of the Prince Consort's dreams of his beloved Germany as an enlightened pacific state immensely powerful, which, in close alliance with England, would ensure the peace and prosperity of the world.

It was not, however, this domestic antagonism to his parents which attracted Prince William to Bismarck. It was his hero-worship of Bismarck and the militarism which had so enlarged Germany which caused him to regard his parents with contempt for their old-fashioned notions and with dislike for the snubs he continued to receive from them both. There was no longer real affection between the parents and the son, which would render domestic disputes matters of superficial friction, and these snubs reinforced rather than repressed his growing arrogance. Another relation whom William was beginning to regard with disfavour was his Uncle Bertie. Two years before, in 1878, the Prince of Wales had been in Berlin for the marriage of his niece, Princess Charlotte, to Prince Bernhard of Meiningen, and he had reported to the Queen that it was impossible to find a nicer boy than William. But those two years with his regiment had wrought a considerable change in his nephew, who now saw in the Prince a member of the English clique of Anglo-Coburgs of which his mother was the chief. A *flâneur* who called himself a soldier, but who had never seen active service, a friend of France, a meddlesome fellow, said Bismarck, one not to be trusted. And to the Prince's eyes, his nephew was growing up a swollen-headed young cub, who was rude to his father and mother and had shocking manners.

CHAPTER III

PRINCE WILLIAM was twenty-one in January 1880, and it was time that he looked about for a wife. He found one for himself in the person of Princess Augusta Victoria of Schleswig-Holstein-Sonderburg-Augustenburg. Her father, Duke Frederick, had been a claimant to the duchies which Bismarck had appropriated for Prussia, and Bismarck approved of the choice : his sardonic humour found a fitness in Duke Frederick's daughter marrying the young man who would inherit all that Prussia had grabbed from her father ; moreover, her uncle, Prince Christian, had married Princess Helena of England. Bismarck did not consider that the intermarriage of royal families was of much value in promoting cordiality between their nations or their governments — indeed for the last twenty years he had been demonstrating the opposite ; but he was beginning to consider whether a better understanding with England might not be valuable, and that the future Empress's uncle was the son-in-law of the formidable Victoria was possibly a small trump card. But most to his liking was the fact that the Princess would be an ideal wife to the future Emperor. Neither ability nor impetuosity marred her fitness for the post, and never would she seek to influence her husband in matters of State or concern herself in them, or preach the excellences of an alien home. She was quiet and mild, she had a certain physical distinction which would give her a creditable dignity when public

functions demanded her presence, and at home she ought to prove the perfect and submissive *hausfrau,* breeding children and going to church, and leading in her palaces the respectable life of a *bourgeoise :* that was what an Empress ought to be. It was of high importance, however, that William's grandmother should approve of his choice, and, before his mother set eyes on the young lady after her engagement, she was sent for to Windsor to be inspected. Luckily the Queen was satisfied : she found her 'gentle and amiable and sweet.' Such qualities, she too may have reflected, were more suitable for the future Empress of Germany than brilliant gifts and strength of will, and something of the same sort ran in the Crown Princess's mind when she remembered the early years of her own married life : 'It is a great blessing,' she wrote to the Queen, 'that Victoria is 22 and not 17, for in a place so difficult to get on in that is a great advantage.' As for William, she wished he could have seen more of the world before he married. Yet what was the use of travel to a young man who took no interest in Art, and did not admire the beauties of nature, and would not read a guide-book to give him information ? *
These were not just reproaches. William took a great deal of interest in Art, he had a prodigious memory for places he visited and he was passionately fond of travel. But the temptation to make these little digs at him was irresistible.

The young man came to England for a month in this autumn of 1880 to stay with his future uncle, Prince Christian, at Cumberland Lodge, and gave a taste of adolescent arrogance to the Prince of Wales. He had been bidden to Sandringham for the Prince's birthday, but broke off his visit the day before the anniversary and went back to Cumberland Lodge. It says much for the Prince's forbearance that he consented to go to William's wedding, and it is not

* *Letters of Empress Frederick,* p. 149.

surprising that the Princess of Wales did not accompany him. She took a great dislike to her nephew, which deepened as his qualities developed, and whenever possible she avoided meeting him. His wedding took place in February 1881, and his mother felt that pang of belated regret for those last inharmonious years which springs from sentimentality rather than sentiment. Frankly they disliked each other, and it was a relief to both that these daily contacts were at an end. That 'perfect confidence and love' which once existed between them was in tatters from incessant friction. They got on each other's nerves, and for such irritations there is no cure. Absence is the only possible treatment, and even that is only palliative.

The twenty-fifth anniversary of the marriage of the Crown Prince and Princess came round in 1883, and the Prince of Wales went to Berlin for the celebration of it. He still wanted, if possible, to be a friendly uncle to William, and, since Queen Victoria's gift of a Highland costume of Stuart tartan had been so much appreciated, he took him a new one. Stuart tartan, in fact, was becoming symbolic : it reminded William once more that he belonged to the Clan. He was delighted with it, and had himself photographed at full length, so that bonnet and sporran and kilt and the dirk in his stocking could all be manifest. But even while he looked at the handsome prints dark and subtle thoughts wove themselves in his brain, and when he distributed signed copies of these photographs to his friends he wrote in English under his name the Delphic sentence : 'I bide my time.' *
What that signified it is impossible precisely to conjecture, but its general import was certainly minatory. William, in Royal Stuart tartan, would some day have to be reckoned with. His uncle treated him like a boy of no account, and he must be taught better.

* Lee, *King Edward VII,* i. pp. 477–478.

As William's egotism expanded, it formed a sort of psychic alliance with his besetting sense of inferiority. The egotist is always profoundly aware that he is not sufficiently appreciated and admired, and that recognition was precisely what his inferiority complex demanded for his own comfort and encouragement. Both were now on a generous diet. He was married, his wife found him a perfect husband, and marked the flight of the years with punctual additions to the family, while, outside the domestic circle, Bismarck began to reward his hero-worship with serious attention. He did not think anything of William's abilities : it was more as if a master-carpenter had picked up from his bench some curious tool that might be fashioned into use for his lathe. He was a man who never neglected to provide for remote contingencies, and though the Emperor's immediate successor was a very healthy man still in the middle fifties, life was an uncertain business, and who could tell what might happen ? Then again it was pleasant to vex William's parents by a contemptuous unconsciousness of their existence, and by an advancement of their son. He saw much of William, he treated him with a benignant and respectful paternity : he brought him to the Emperor's notice, and the Emperor made much of his grandson. In 1884 he sent William to St. Petersburg, under Bismarck's advice, as his emissary to the Tsar Alexander III, for the celebration of the Tsarevitch Nicholas's sixteenth birthday, when officially he came of age. The Crown Prince therefore, who would properly have been his father's representative, was thus deliberately passed over, and his place taken by his son. There was certainly some reason for this, for the Royal message with which William was charged referred to the importance of the three Emperors of Russia, Germany and Austria standing firm to resist the encroachment of the liberal democracy of which the Crown Prince and his wife were avowed champions. This was the first occasion when William was enabled to be the mouthpiece of his grandfather, and he made the most of it, very characteristically, by warning the Tsar that the Prince of Wales was doing all he could to stir up the enmity of England against Russia. The Tsar, he said, was deeply impressed by this information.* Shortly afterwards his uncle was due to pay another visit to Berlin, and William pursued the theme by correspondence. He was sure that this design which he had spoken of was developing : there was conspiracy on foot, and his mother, his uncle and the Queen of England were all in it. Their object was to get Germany to join England against Russia. William thought the situation very dangerous, but his Royal cousin, the Tsar, must be reassured. He wrote :

'But these English have accidentally forgotten that *I* exist. And I swear to You, my dear cousin, that anything I can do for You and Your country I will do, and I swear I will keep my word. But only it will take a long time, and will have to be done very slowly.' †

Further opportunities occurred for putting William in the place that was rightly his father's, and Bismarck made the most of them. In 1885 a meeting was arranged between the Emperors of Germany and Austria at Gastein in order to cement the friendship of their countries. Bismarck contrived that William should attend these conversations instead of the Crown Prince. The very day that they were finished the Emperor despatched him on a further mission to Tsar Alexander III at Brest-Litovsk, where he was holding a military review. William, in his memoirs, professed himself unwilling again to supplant his father, but his grandfather told him that Bismarck would not consent to send the Crown Prince, as he was far too Anglophil to be an

* William II, *My Early Life*, p. 247.
† Lee, *King Edward VII*, i. pp. 485, 486.

acceptable ambassador ; Bismarck, when similarly applied to, shrugged his shoulders and told him that such were the Emperor's orders. So William, having made this effort of filial piety, went off to Brest-Litovsk to meet that colossal cousin whom he had sworn to befriend. Perhaps he was a little disappointed that his intercession on behalf of the Crown Prince had not found favour. It would have fed his soul to have been able to tell his mother that, owing to his entreaties, this mission to the Tsar was entrusted to his father instead of himself.

The mission was a complete failure. Bismarck seldom made a mistake, and even seldomer repeated one, but now he was guilty on both counts. Some years before (1877), in order to sow discord between England and France, he had declared that Germany would favour the permanent occupation of Egypt by England, but Lord Beaconsfield had intimated that if the Queen of England decided to do so, she would not require 'P. Bismarck's' permission. On the present occasion William was charged to tell the Tsar that if Russia decided to occupy Constantinople, Germany would raise no objection. The Tsar saw eye to eye with Lord Beaconsfield and Queen Victoria, and told William that if he wished to take Constantinople, he would do so without asking Bismarck's leave. In fact William was not very warmly received in his public capacity, and personally the Tsar did not take to him. 'Un garçon mal élevé et de mauvaise foi' was his brief comment.

William was conscious of having been snubbed, and it made him uneasy. He had already warned the Tsar that his Uncle Bertie was busy with treacherous designs against Russia, but the Tsar seemed to take no notice. Every summer the King of Denmark had a large family party at Copenhagen of sons and daughters and their wives and husbands. One son was the King of Greece, and one daughter was the Tsar's wife and another was the Princess of Wales. When, two years later, the informal party assembled, William somehow heard that the Tsar and his uncle seemed to be on very good terms, they had long talks together, and got on capitally. He did not like it : he suspected that they had been talking together about him. These suspicions were well founded, and their views about him were very similar. What was to be done ? He made a subtle plan. He went to Wittenberg where, on the conclusion of the Tsar's visit, the imperial train that took him back to Russia would stop. It was not yet dawn, but he boarded it, and the Tsar was awakened with the news that Prince William of Germany was here and would like to have a talk with him. No good : the Tsar sent a message that he was too sleepy, and William returned to Berlin.*

At home, as well as on foreign missions, Bismarck found opportunity for promoting William over his father's head. He obtained the Emperor's leave that he should enter the Foreign Office and gain experience in the handling of international relations. Under his rule the Foreign Office was nothing more than a department in the Chancellor's Office, and never had the Crown Prince been admitted into its outermost antechamber. Now his son was to be taught, under Bismarck's tuition, all that he himself had never been permitted to learn. To him that must perhaps have been the most stinging of all these casual but deliberate slights : it was as if his name was being erased from the succession, for indeed William was being treated as if he were heir apparent. For the first time under these ignorings of himself, the Crown Prince made a protest, but it was perhaps his wife's bitterness rather than his own which prompted it, for

* Lee, *King Edward VII*, ii. p. 682.

the sentiments and their expression are precisely those which occur so continually in her letters to the Queen about William's delinquencies.   The protest ran :

'In view of the immaturity as well as the inexperience of my eldest son together with his tendency to overbearingness and self-conceit, I cannot but frankly regard it as dangerous to allow him at present to take any part in foreign affairs.' *

It was very unwise. The Chancellor's chief object in putting William into the Foreign Office was to make his parents feel their insignificance, and he was pleased to know that the thrust had gone home.   How illogical, too, was the 'Engländerin' !   She gave William's inexperience as a reason why he should not be put in the way of getting experience ! He replied that such were the Kaiser's commands, and that he merely obeyed them.   She knew as well as he that the Kaiser's commands were Bismarck's wishes.

His parents were powerless, and Bismarck intended that they should feel it.   Three times within the last few months the Crown Prince had been pointedly passed over as if he did not exist.   He accepted his position in silence, his wife in bitter volubility to her mother, and it was directed not so much against the Emperor and his Chancellor as against William himself.   She had been horrified when he had been chosen to be present at the conference at Gastein, and she could scarcely believe that he was to be sent to Brest-Litovsk.   'It would make endless mischief,' she wrote, 'and do endless harm.   William is as blind and green, wrong-headed and violent on politics as can be.'   He was vain and selfish : he held superficial, rubbishy views, he talked rank retrograde chauvinist nonsense.†

Truly it was the most humiliating position, and one which

---

* Ludwig, *Kaiser Wilhelm II*, p. 21.
† Ponsonby, *Letters of Empress Frederick*, pp. 207, 214.

for a woman of her pride and love of power was intolerable. For years she had established this paramount influence over her husband, he was at one with her in all her liberal views, he shared her English sympathies and trusted completely in her judgment and ability, and now he was become an unheeded nonentity ; he did not exist for his father or for Bismarck, unless the Chancellor cared to amuse himself by yet another casual backhander at him. It was heartbreaking to think of the high hopes that had once been hers, and of that mission with which her father twenty-nine years ago had entrusted her. Today there was nothing of it left. Bismarck had established an iron militarism, an absolutism of the monarchy which he controlled, and which had trampled on all that had been so sacred to her. And how she had longed for a son who, brought up under the loving care of his father and herself, would carry on her pacific and noble policy ! Instead her first-born was Bismarck's creature heart and soul, and looked on his father and mother as an old-fashioned couple with ideas for Germany of the quaintest sort, put away, like demoded figures in pottery, on a dusty shelf in a cupboard.

Such were the relations political and domestic between these members of the House of Hohenzollern when on January 27, 1887, the Prince entered his twenty-ninth year.

CHAPTER IV

THE Crown Prince had been suffering this winter from a succession of colds, and they left him with a troublesome and persistent hoarseness. Professor Gerhardt examined his throat, and found a small growth on one of the vocal cords. He tried to burn it away by a course of electric cauterisation, but the Prince's throat was much inflamed, and for the present he abandoned this treatment and in April 1887 he sent him to Ems for the sake of his general health. This is important, for it shows that Gerhardt had as yet no serious apprehensions as to the nature of the growth, since, if he had, he would not have irritated it by cautery, nor would he have recommended a month's course of the waters of Ems. When the Crown Prince returned to Berlin, it was clear that Ems had not done any good to the local trouble, and Gerhardt called in the surgeon Dr. Bergmann. They both now suspected malignant disease, and, after other throat specialists had been consulted, they advised an operation for the removal of the growth by opening the larynx. The Crown Princess was informed of this, but it was settled that the patient was not to be told till immediately before the operation.* But the doctors decided first to call in for consultation some foreign specialist, and after considering three names they unanimously selected Dr. Morell Mackenzie, as being the

* Ponsonby, *Letters of Empress Frederick,* p. 231 ; Sir J. Rennell Rodd (Lord Rennell), *Social and Diplomatic Memoirs,* i. p. 113.

most eminent.* The Crown Princess had thus nothing to do with this choice, but, as it was made by the German doctors, she consented to it. This entirely disposes of the idea that it was she who was responsible for it, and of Bismarck's article in the *Norddeutsche Allgemeine Zeitung,* in which he stated : 'It is now established beyond question that an unimportant English physician of Radical political opinions took upon himself to play the Privy Councillor, and interfere directly in the history of the German nation.' The 'unimportant English physician' was chosen by the German medical staff in attendance upon the Crown Prince as being the first European authority on diseases of the throat. The relevance of Mackenzie's political opinions to his skill as a throat specialist was best known to Bismarck.

Morell Mackenzie arrived. It was understood that if he agreed with the verdict of the German doctors, the operation should take place. But, after looking at the Crown Prince's throat, he was not satisfied that the growth was malignant, and with the consent of his colleagues he removed two fragments of it and sent them to Professor Virchow for microscopical examination. Virchow's report was negative : in his view the structure of the cells did not indicate that the growth was malignant. A further specimen was submitted to him, and his verdict was the same. With the repeated opinion of the first pathologist in Europe to back him, Mackenzie advised against the operation, which, though in no way a serious one, would mean that the Crown Prince would never recover a normal speaking voice. He proposed to give him a course of treatment in England, and anticipated that he would be able to cure him in a few months. In spite of Professor Virchow's diagnosis, Gerhardt and Bergmann stuck to their opinion that the growth was cancerous, and that it was active. But both the Crown

* William II, *My Early Life,* p. 276.

Prince and his wife determined to try Mackenzie's treatment. There was a further reason why they were very anxious to go to England, for, in June this year, Queen Victoria was celebrating her Jubilee of fifty years' reign, and they arrived with Dr. Wegner, the Prince's personal physician, a week before Jubilee Day. Their luggage included three boxes packed with private papers of the Crown Prince. His wife was resolved that some day the tactics of the Bismarckian campaign against herself and her husband should be exposed, and justice be done to them. She had obtained her mother's leave to deposit these papers in a safe at Buckingham Palace, for she believed that Bismarck was quite capable of having them stolen and destroyed if they remained in Germany. The suspicion, wild as it sounds, proved to be well founded.

The Crown Prince could now only speak in a whisper. He took part in the cavalcade of princes, the Queen's sons, and sons-in-law and grandsons, who rode before her to the service in the Abbey, but in order to husband his strength he appeared at no other celebrations, and, at the desire of the German Emperor, was represented by William. He spent over two months in England under Mackenzie's care, but there was no sign of any improvement. Meantime in Berlin there was a strong and not unnatural feeling that he ought to return, for the Emperor, now ninety years old, was failing. Against this the Crown Princess fought, as she herself expressed it, 'tooth and nail' : indeed, it was impossible for a devoted wife to do otherwise. Life in Berlin with its inevitable duties and fatigues would be the worst possible thing for one whose health and resistance must be most carefully guarded. At the same time she was extremely anxious that William should not remain in Berlin, for she feared his influence with the Emperor, his growing importance in affairs of State and his continual intercourse with Bismarck at the

Foreign Office. Considering the past that was intelligible enough, but it was scarcely reasonable. In the Emperor's condition it was only right that, since she succeeded in preventing her husband from living in Berlin, he should be represented by his eldest son.

So, after leaving England, she and the Crown Prince went for a month to the Tyrol, and from there to Venice and Baveno. The growth, which Mackenzie still did not admit was malignant, seemed inactive, though assuredly it was not cured. But Mackenzie in October told the Crown Princess that he thought he might be quite well in a few months, for his general health seemed to improve. Early in November they went to San Remo, and immediately very disquieting symptoms appeared. Mackenzie was sent for, and, in answer to a direct question from the Crown Prince, said that the new growth looked malignant. The news was telegraphed to Berlin.

William had long ago made up his mind about his father's complaint ; his infallibility did not fail him. He was sure that so distinguished a specialist as Mackenzie must have known, as soon as he was called in, that this growth for which the German doctors had advised an operation was cancerous. Two motives, said William, had caused Mackenzie to declare that it was not : the first, that it would give him a valuable *cachet* professionally to have the Crown Prince under his care in England ; the second, that Mackenzie believed (and had stated) that if the Prince was pronounced to be suffering from malignant disease, he could not succeed to the throne.* Both these suggestions were untenable, for if Mackenzie had known that this was a case of cancer, he must also have known that his treatment could not possibly cure it, and that the resultant *cachet* would not be one which any specialist would covet. In the second

* William II, *My Early Life,* p. 278.

place, neither the family laws of the House of Hohenzollern nor the constitution of Germany contained any provision that could prevent the Crown Prince succeeding to the throne, even if he was on his death-bed. The decision therefore to adopt Mackenzie's treatment which the Crown Princess had successfully advocated gave rise to the most violent hostility between mother and son. William believed that a timely operation, not of a serious kind, which the German faculty had proposed would have saved his father's life perhaps for many years, whereas the adoption of the other course, known by Mackenzie to be fruitless, merely allowed the disease to progress unchecked.

The serious news from San Remo gave William an opportunity to assert himself. His father was under the care of the English doctor, whose treatment had so tragically failed, and of his assistant Dr. Hovell. He went to the Emperor and asked his permission to go to San Remo with three German specialists, whose presence Mackenzie himself now requested, in order that a joint report should be drawn up. The Emperor consented, and William was to see that this report was forwarded to him.

A ghastly scene took place between him and his mother on his arrival. The poor woman was worn out with anxiety and with constant attendance on her husband ; she had just heard that Mackenzie, on whom she had pinned her faith, now feared that the disease was malignant, even as the German doctors had said from the first. To her in this turmoil of shock and heart-breaking disappointment appeared William, arrogant and self-important, charged with this command from the Emperor that the doctors were to draw up their report, and that he was to see that it was done. William also represented himself as entrusted by Bismarck to tell his father that he must waive his rights of succession as being physically unfit to reign.* His mother lost her head : all the bitterness of the past years, William's hostility to her, his contempt for his father came in flood over her, and, according to his account, she at first refused to let him see his father at all. William's reminiscences are often in need of corroboration, but probably this was true, for she wrote to the Queen afterwards, saying : 'He [William] was as rude, as disagreeable and as impertinent to me as possible when he arrived, but I pitched into him, I am afraid with considerable violence. . . I said I would go and tell his father how he behaved and ask that he should be forbidden the house.' † In this crisis of tortured nerves she did not think how empty was such a threat, or how it would be remembered against her.

Then came the business with which William had been charged, namely, that the doctors should confer and that he should communicate their findings to his grandfather. Again his mother objected : the doctors must report to *her*, and not to William : *she* would forward their verdict. Again how unwise and how impotent a claim ! The Emperor had ordered this consultation of doctors, and it was only reasonable that he should have done so, for the English doctor's treatment had now confessedly failed, and he demanded that a fresh opinion based on the latest developments of his son's illness should be taken and brought to him direct. Prince William presided at this medical conference, and the first of the doctors to give his views was Mackenzie himself. He admitted that this new growth was malignant, and the rest unanimously agreed. The Crown Prince heard the sentence with the unaffected composure of

* Bülow, *Memoirs, 1849–1897,* p. 615.
† William II, *My Early Life,* pp. 278–281 ; Ponsonby, *Letters of Empress Frederick,* pp. 256, 257.

a man who was as courteous as he was brave. He thanked the doctors for the careful attention they had given to his case. The news was telegraphed to Berlin, and next day the *Reichsanzeiger* issued a bulletin definitely stating that he had cancer.

William returned to Berlin. With a frail grandfather of over ninety and a father whose death might come even more speedily, it was certain that he would not have long to wait for the day he so ardently desired, and he drew up an Imperial Edict addressed to the Princes of Confederated Germany, and to be despatched to them on the day of his accession. He sent this to Bismarck, who made a private copy of it for safe custody and returned the original to William, advising him to burn it at once. The Emperor of Germany was still alive, so also was the Heir Apparent. It would produce a monstrous impression if it leaked out that the Heir Presumptive had already drawn up an Imperial Edict. The fire was the best place for a document so indecently premature.*

But with the aged Emperor now losing his grip on life and often unable to write his name, however shakily, to any State papers that required his signature, and with the Crown Prince so far off, it was only proper that William should be appointed to act for his grandfather. But even this caused further trouble. Bismarck duly sent the notification of this to the Crown Prince, but his wife, thinking that it would worry him, kept it from him. A few days later Prince Henry came to San Remo, and gave his father a letter from William which alluded to his appointment. The Crown Prince was furious at not having received official notice from the Chancellor, and threatened to go back to Berlin at once to look after his rights. But it was the Empress and not Bismarck who had withheld from him this information;

* Ludwig, *Kaiser Wilhelm II*, pp. 43–45.

indeed throughout these terrible weeks the Chancellor was very careful of the Crown Prince's position and interests and jealously guarded them.*

In spite of the verdict of the doctors, now including Mackenzie himself, the Crown Princess would not admit the worst : perhaps it would be truer to say that she could not. Sometimes her unfounded faith broke down, and in despair she would tell her mother that she could not bear to think of the fate that awaited her husband. Then she would revoke her surrender and, relying on the negative and now obsolete pronouncements made months before by Professor Virchow, she ran up her gallant and pathetic colours again. She kept the German journals from her husband, but she read them herself, and the anguish of her love was aggravated by the cruel and continual attacks made on her. They blamed her for having influenced her husband to refuse to be operated on last May and for having adopted Mackenzie's treatment, whereas she had only done what every other woman would have done in the circumstances. She was blamed for inducing him not to give up hope and for keeping him from subsiding into the deadly depression into which sometimes he sank, and there indeed was a persecution for righteousness' sake. Her courage in this martyrdom was of the noblest and most splendid quality, but she had made many enemies, and now they pursued her with ruthless savagery. If ever a woman deserved sympathy it was she, but they hounded her with abuse. December passed, and in January Mackenzie came to England. What his real view of the case was it is difficult to say, for, though he had concurred in the verdict of the other doctors, he told the Queen that he 'fully believed' that there was nothing malignant in the Crown Prince's illness,† and that there might be no need to perform the operation of tracheotomy which had been suggested.

* *Letters III*, i. p. 376.   † *Ibid*. p. 377.

But in February his difficulty in breathing rendered it necessary, and once more, relying on the relief he experienced, the
Crown Princess wrote to her mother that he was beginning
to mend. The Queen, owing to these reports, maintained
her confidence in Mackenzie, and he promised her that he
would go back to San Remo and remain in constant attendance.

Early in March came news from Berlin that the Emperor's
condition was giving rise to great anxiety, and it might be
necessary at any moment to return. It was grievous to think
of leaving the sun and the warmth of the south. 'Six weeks
more,' the Crown Princess wrote to her mother, 'would have
set Fritz up, and he would soon have begun his walks and
drives again.' * On March 9, 1888, came news of his father's
death. The first act of the new Emperor was to telegraph to
Queen Victoria 'his sincere and constant desire for a close
and lasting friendship between our two nations.' †

The day on which the Prince Consort's visions were based
and for which his daughter and son-in-law had so earnestly
prepared themselves had come at last, but in circumstances
that rendered it but a travesty of fulfilment. She who had
made herself the inspiration of her husband in his high mission was now only the devoted wife of an Emperor con-
demned to death. For his part he realised the utter annihilation of all his political aims, and, instead of dismissing
from his post the Chancellor who for nearly thirty years had
treated him as negligible and imposed on Germany policies
directly antagonistic to his, he wrote him the most high-
minded and cordial letter confirming him in his office. To
do otherwise would have been to throw the Government

---

* Ponsonby, *Letters of Empress Frederick*, p. 281.
† *Letters III*, i. p. 390.

into endless confusion and difficulty, for the sake of a personal revenge altogether unworthy of him. It was too late to institute a different regime : health and strength and the expectation of active years were needful, and all he could look forward to was the release from his dumb and intolerable existence. The more patriotic course was to retain Bismarck in power rather than to imperil the stability of the State by attempting reforms which must so soon be abandoned again. Sometimes the Empress tried to cling to her belief that some measure of recovery was still possible, but she realised that in truth she and her husband were 'a mere passing shadow soon to be replaced by reality in the shape of William.' Bismarck was 'civil and nice' ; no doubt he was sorry for the woman whose husband was under sentence of death.*

The relations between the new Crown Prince William and his mother remained deplorable. As the Emperor's strength ebbed, she more strenuously than ever kept from him all that might worry or excite him, and she did her best to prevent William from seeing his father at all. Then once again there came up the question of the marriage of her youngest daughter, Princess Victoria, to Prince Alexander of Battenberg, which had already caused bitter feeling between William and his parents. While Alexander had been reigning Prince of Bulgaria, Bismarck, with William on his side, had induced the old Emperor to refuse his consent. Such a marriage, he considered, was a *mésalliance* for the daughter of the future German Emperor, and there were political reasons against it as well. For, though the Prince had been Tsar Alexander II's nominee for the throne of Bulgaria, he had proved himself far too independent to suit his taste, and the Tsar would have considered it an unfriendly

* Ponsonby, *Letters of Empress Frederick*, p. 293.

act if the German Emperor's granddaughter had married him. Queen Victoria (so, at any rate, it was believed in Germany) had approved of the proposed marriage, regarding it as a love-match, and it was supposed in Bismarckian circles that she had suggested it. Her support was attributed to a desire to make bad blood between Russia and Germany.* Certainly she took a great interest in the Battenbergs : Alexander's elder brother had married Princess Victoria of Hesse, the Queen's granddaughter, and his younger brother, Henry, in 1885 had married her youngest daughter, Princess Beatrice. Prince Alexander, the next year, had been forced to abdicate and was now living in retirement with his cousins in Darmstadt, and the danger of his marriage provoking international friction between Russia and Germany had therefore vanished, for he was no longer a reigning prince and this marriage would have been void of political significance. But now the Queen, for very wise reasons, was strongly against the marriage. William was still violently opposed to it, and now within a few months at the most he would become Emperor of Germany, and would certainly refuse his consent, even as his grandfather had done. Moreover Prince Alexander himself no longer desired it. He was no longer reigning Prince of Bulgaria, and therefore politically it would be of no value to him, and his affections were now with an opera singer, Fräulein Loisinger, whom he married within a year.

The Queen was spending her spring holiday of 1888 at the Villa Palmieri at Florence, and she intended to go to Berlin on her way home to see the dying Emperor for the last time. Lord Salisbury, her Prime Minister, did not like the idea at all, for he had heard from the British Ambassador that Prince Alexander had been invited there by the Emperor, in order that the betrothal should take place, and that

* Busch, *Bismarck*, iii. pp. 171, 174, 181.

Bismarck, who still believed that the Queen, firm in her 'Battenbergery,' * approved it, had threatened to resign if it did. Lord Salisbury therefore advised the Queen to give up her visit, rather than be involved in such an embroilment ; Bismarck in his present mood might show temper, and she might be received in Berlin with some hostile demonstration. The Queen was extremely angry : that Russia could possibly make objections to the marriage of her granddaughter to a private person was impertinent and ridiculous and preposterous : it was a purely family matter. But that was not her main point. William was opposed to it, and she had already telegraphed to the Empress Frederick not to allow the engagement unless he gave his full consent.

Lord Salisbury, reassured as to that, was still far from easy. He wrote again, telling the Queen that there was a good deal of anxiety in high circles at Berlin about any meeting between Crown Prince William and his grandmother. His head seemed to have been turned by the thought of all that must so soon be his, and high circles were afraid that 'if any thorny subject came up in conversation the Prince might say something that would not reflect credit on him, and that if he acted so as to draw any reproof from Your Majesty, he might take it ill, and a feeling would rankle in his mind which might hinder the good relations between the two nations.' Lord Salisbury even reminded her that 'everything that is said to him must be very carefully weighed.' † This was very tactfully put ; one can imagine him coining these elegant paraphrases, when all he wanted to say was 'William might be rude to you, ma'am, and then you might be rude to him.' But in spite of this elegance, it must have astonished the Queen to be told how to treat William ! She did not answer the letter, and off she went to Berlin.

* Sir J. Rennell Rodd, *Social and Diplomatic Memoirs*, i. pp. 134–137.
† *Letters III*, i. pp. 398, 399.

It was indeed a tragic household which she found at Charlottenburg. The Empress was worn out with constant attendance on her husband, William was daily getting more imperial and irritating his mother beyond endurance, and now, recognising the inevitable, she knew that her husband's life could not be prolonged for many weeks more : Mackenzie himself admitted that. But the Queen's presence was an enormous comfort to her, and there were rough places which no one could smooth out as well as she. Bismarck asked for an interview, which she most readily granted. He still supposed that she was in favour of the Battenberg marriage, and though, when she was in England, he could make mock of her as a match-making old lady who would bring the parson with her in her bag and the bridegroom in her trunk and have it celebrated out of hand,* he found it a very different matter when he was about to talk to her alone. He was shaking with nervous agitation, he wanted to know where she would be in the Presence Chamber, and whether she would be sitting or standing. He looked forward to a formidable half-hour, and it was a most agreeable surprise to find that she now agreed with him. The interview was cordial to the point of friendliness. She asked him that as long as the Emperor lived William should not be appointed Regent, and he promised. He promised also to stand by the Empress, and they agreed that William was most inexperienced and knew nothing — in spite of his work in the Foreign Office — about international relations. Then she saw William, and the result of that interview was that for the time she made reconciliation between him and his mother.† As for Lord Salisbury's apprehensions that there might be hostile demonstrations against her in the streets of Berlin, they melted away before the beam of her

* Busch, *Bismarck*, iii. p. 174.   † *Ibid.* p. 188.

prestige, and she was received everywhere with enthusiastic welcome.

But such a truce could only be temporary, for all the causes of hostility remained, and even the question of the Victoria-Alexander marriage was to have a recrudescence. The animosities between the doctors in charge of the Emperor grew bitter again. The surgeon, Professor Bergmann, in changing the canula in the Emperor's throat through which he breathed, managed this perfectly simple adjustment with such awkwardness that he caused him extreme suffering. Mackenzie said that he could not continue in attendance if Bergmann was allowed to touch the patient's throat again. Bergmann resigned, and William showed his sympathy by asking him to dinner. The German Press resounded with new invectives against the English doctors, and now the English and French Press retorted. William, enraged at Bismarck's refusal to appoint him Regent, began to criticise the Chancellor's foreign policy. He put ludicrous notes of censure on the margins of documents sent him only for perusal, signing them 'William, Crown Prince of the German Empire and of Prussia,' until the Chancellor asked him to refrain, for what he wrote had to be registered, and that was a waste of time. Sometimes the Emperor had comparatively good days : he went in to Berlin and was greeted by the crowds, and on May 24, though scarcely able to stand, he attended the marriage of his second son Prince Henry to Princess Irene of Hesse, the daughter of Princess Alice of England. The Second Guards Infantry Brigade, led by William, marched past him : this gave him, William recorded, his last great joy on earth.*

But whether he was seen or not seen, his appearance or his absence was fashioned into sensational calumnies against his

---

* William II, *My Memoirs*, p. 20.

wife. If unseen he was supposed to have died and his death
to be concealed by her : if he drove into Berlin it was she
who had insisted, plying him with stimulants to brace him
to it, and it was she who had forced him to attend the wedding of his own son.* Never had a devoted wife, watching
by the death-bed of her husband, been assailed with such
incessant malice, and well she knew that at his death these
assaults would be doubled in violence. But now his vitality
was on the swift ebb, and early in June he was moved from
Charlottenburg to the New Palace at Potsdam where he had
been born, where he had passed the early years of his married
life, and where he wished to die. He could no longer articu-
late a syllable, but he wrote on a sheet of paper that he re-
christened the palace 'Friedrichskron.' It bore its new title
for only a fortnight.

Once more, as when the three trunks of the Emperor's
private papers were deposited just a year ago in Buckingham
Palace for safer custody than would be theirs in Germany,
the determination to make sure that justice should be done
some day to him and to her seized the Empress, and, on the
day before he died, she sent for a Mr. Inman Bernard, Special
Correspondent of the *New York Herald* : perhaps he was
known to her or to Morell Mackenzie. In her presence
Mackenzie entrusted him with a parcel which, he was told,
contained the Emperor's Diary for the last ten years. Mr.
Bernard was bidden to convey this to the British Embassy at
Berlin with instructions to Sir Edward Malet to send it by
the Military Attaché to the Queen at Windsor. So sensational a 'scoop' needs confirmation, but that is not lacking,
for two days after the Emperor's death the Queen recorded
in her Diary that she received from the British Embassy at
Berlin papers of the Emperor Frederick which were sent her

* Ludwig, *Kaiser Wilhelm II*, pp. 50, 52.

for safe keeping.* Two consignments therefore of the Emperor's papers were now in England, namely, those which he had brought with him on his visit in 1887 for the Queen's Jubilee, and this record of the last ten years. That such precautions were justified was very soon apparent.†

On the same day Bismarck came to inquire at Friedrichskron, and the Empress took him to see her husband for the last time. He knew that the Chancellor had promised Queen Victoria to stand by his wife, and now, unable to speak, he took her hand and laid it in his, and his eyes looked from one to the other and back again, reminding him of his promise, and telling him that, with his death, the long enmity between them of thirty years was over.

Bismarck left them. They understood one another : it was not to William that the Emperor had committed her but to Bismarck, for with him lay the better chance, slender though it might be, of her receiving sympathy and consideration. The palace that night was full of stealthy movement : officers, newly drafted in, were receiving whispered orders and detailed instructions, and secret dispositions were being made. As the last hours dripped away, while the Empress watched by her husband, all was made ready for the great transformation scene of the morrow.

* Esmé Howard, *Theatre of Life*, p. 332 ; *Letters III*, i. p. 417.

† Sir Frederick Ponsonby (*Letters of Empress Frederick*, pp. 339–341) says that the War Diary of the Crown Prince Frederick, dealing with the Franco-German War of 1870, was also sent to England for safe keeping from San Remo. This does not tally with the account given to Sir Rennell Rodd (Lord Rennell) by the Empress Frederick herself. It seems clear from what she told him that this War Diary never left Germany at all. (Sir Rennell Rodd, *Social and Diplomatic Memoirs*, i. p. 157.)

CHAPTER V

THE Emperor died next morning, June 15, 1888, having reigned for ninety-eight days. The moment his death was announced, all the preparations for it, carefully and minutely planned the night before, were carried out. Companies of hussars instantly surrounded the palace, and the entrances into the park were guarded. No one, not even members of the family, were allowed to leave the precincts without a signed permit, no letters could be sent without the stamp of the censor, and all outgoing parcels were examined. Search-parties ransacked the palace for papers belonging to the late Emperor, and his son, dressed in the red uniform of his hussars with a sabre in his hand, himself searched his mother's room. Perhaps he hoped to find there his father's Diary of the last ten years, but it was already on its way to Windsor. While he lived his father was at liberty to deposit his private papers where he pleased, and he had chosen on two occasions to send relays of them to England, fearing that they were not safe from theft if they remained here, but with his death they passed, unless he had made special provision, to his son, who now ransacked the palace for them with such indecent haste.

In all things he showed a callous unconcern for his mother's feelings. At the request of the German doctors he permitted Professor Virchow to conduct a post-mortem on his father's body. As it was no longer in dispute that he had died of cancer, the only object can have been publicly to emphasize the fact that they had been right when they had diagnosed his illness as such and had recommended an operation which might have extirpated the growth, had not Mackenzie, with the backing of the Crown Princess, intervened. The palace which, a fortnight ago, had been christened Friedrichskron by his father reverted by the Emperor's orders to its former title, the New Palace. His father's will, executed on April 12, was brought to him, and in it he read words addressed to himself : 'I wish to have it set in evidence as my unbiased personal opinion that I entirely acquiesce in the betrothal of your second sister with Prince Alexander of Battenberg. I charge you as a filial duty with the accomplishment of this my desire.' Before his father was buried, William wrote to Prince Alexander saying that he forbade the match, owing to 'the profound conviction previously held by my late deceased grandfather and father.' * It was his intention, as it was also Bismarck's, to obliterate his father's brief reign and all that appertained to it.

The Prince of Wales, accompanied by his wife and his eldest son, came to Berlin for the funeral, which took place on June 18 : it was only three weeks since he had been there for the marriage of his nephew and niece, Prince Henry of Prussia and Princess Irene of Hesse. An untoward incident occurred which in its sequel vastly increased the mutual dislike between William and his uncle. The Prince of Wales well knew how his brother-in-law had detested the blood-and-iron policy of Bismarck, and in their conversations when, after the Franco-German War, the Crown Prince and Princess paid a long visit to Queen Victoria he had formed the impression that, on his succession to the throne of Germany, he would be inclined to restore to France some part,

---

* Ludwig, *Kaiser Wilhelm II*, p. 56. Bismarck asserted that the Emperor Frederick, like himself, regarded the match as a *mésalliance*, but had yielded to his wife's insistence. Busch, *Bismarck*, iii. p. 185.

at any rate, of the provinces of Alsace and Lorraine. The Prince now asked Count Herbert Bismarck whether the Emperor Frederick, if he had lived, would have done so. The question was unwise and tactless. He would certainly have been very angry if, immediately after his own accession, the heir apparent of Germany had asked one of his Ministers whether Queen Victoria had ever considered giving back to the Boers some part of the Transvaal. Count Herbert gave a non-committal reply, and, as was perfectly proper, told the Chancellor about this meddlesome inquiry. He in turn (probably after the Prince's departure) passed it on to the Emperor, with some of those dry, decorative comments in the fashioning of which he was so deft a master. There for the moment the matter lay incubating, like some germ-culture, and developed a peculiar virulence.

Mingled with the Empress Frederick's overwhelming desolation at her husband's death was the knowledge that the whole aim and purpose of her life had perished. For thirty years it had been shaped towards one end to be attained when he should be Emperor, and her task, now incapable of accomplishment, was buried with him. That future, towards which the aspirations of her power-loving nature had been incessantly directed, had resolved itself into three months of waiting not for its fruition but for its close by the merciful hand of death. For her there was scarcely a note of sympathy : as for him, the whole Bismarckian Press exhibited a shrugging contempt for the unavailing visionary whose dreams had come to nothing. He was dead and could no longer be an obstacle to the free development of Germany according to Bismarck's and the young Emperor's ideas. Sometimes her profound personal grief possessed her, sometimes there swept over it this sense of the complete annihilation of all the noble ambitions that had underlain her impetuosity. But, from whichever outlook she surveyed the future, she knew that William had no spark of true feeling for her, for his father's death caused him no twinge of personal sorrow, and indeed only cleared the way for him. Her double loss as wife and Empress was to him a double gain, and bereavement which, working on affection, often makes for reconciliation, only widened the breach between them. In every regard she was sundered from him, and she made no attempt to bridge the gap. Her pride forbade her to hazard an approach to one whom she held in contempt. All she was capable of was 'to close eyes and ears to the official world, and find it the only way not to feel the profoundest irritation against William.' But even that she found impossible, and she keenly observed and bitterly resented the oblivion in the circles of the new Court into which not only her husband but herself had been relegated. She would have saved years of misery and of a hostility which greatly reacted on the relations between England and Germany, whom it had been her mission to unite in ties of interest and friendship, if she had carried out the intention she had expressed some years before to her son. 'If your father,' she told him, 'should die before I do, I shall leave at once. I will not stay in a country where I have had nothing but hatred and not a spark of affection.' * But that was exactly what she could not bring herself to do. Her pride that forbade her to run away — so she termed it to herself — and leave her enemies in the field, her sense of extinction that tortured her by gazing on all she had missed, forced her to remain, and she began at once to look out for a place of her own where she could make her home in Germany.

The Queen had seen from the first that death would widen rather than close the estrangement that existed between her daughter and her grandson, and only a fortnight after the Emperor's death she wrote him a very wise letter. She

* Ludwig, *Kaiser Wilhelm II*, p. 15.

urged him to meet his mother's wishes in every way as to providing a suitable home for her, and, knowing them both very well, she realised that his mother was not making it very easy for him. She wrote :

'Let me also ask you to bear with poor Mama if she is sometimes irritated and excited. She does not mean it so : think what months of agony and suspense and watching with broken and sleepless nights she has gone through, and *don't mind it*. I am so anxious that all should go smoothly, that I write thus openly in the interests of you both.' *

William replied that he was doing his best to meet his mother's wishes, and that was probably true. However callously he had behaved during those first few days, he was now trying to conduct himself with great consideration towards her, and when late in the summer his aunt, Princess Christian, was in Berlin, she believed that, as far as intention went, he was very pleasant to her. He did much that hurt her ; 'but,' wrote the Princess, 'I really think that he does this out of thoughtlessness, and certainly *not* from premeditation.' † Both now and hereafter the Empress Frederick was too prone to construe into personal and intentional slights the changes in her position which her widowhood rendered inevitable. She was reigning Empress no longer, and she blamed her son and his wife for much of the suffering which destiny had brought on her. For years she and William, strong-willed and autocratic, had been in constant antagonism, and the tragedy of her future life, partly self-inflicted in that she clasped it and clung to it, was by no means entirely of his making.

The Queen had written to William on another topic in this same letter. She had heard that he was about to pay

---

* *Letters III*, i. pp. 423–425.
† Ponsonby, *Letters of Empress Frederick*, p. 328.

visits to other sovereigns, and begged him to wait until his father's death was less recent. There was not a word to suggest, as he subsequently stated,* that she thought that his first visit ought to be to her, or that he was planning to go to St. Petersburg first in order to vex his mother. The Queen merely asked him to postpone all visits for the present. But she seemed hardly to realise, he thought, that she was giving advice to an Emperor, and he felt compelled to write to her as her Royal Brother, putting her, kindly but firmly, in her place.

'At the end of this month [July] I shall inspect the fleet and take a trip in the Baltic, when I shall hope to meet the Emperor of Russia, which will be of good effect for the peace of Europe and for the rest and quiet of my Allies. I would have gone later if possible, but State interest goes before personal feelings, and the fate which sometimes hangs over nations does not wait till the etiquette of Court mournings has been fulfilled. And as I am quite *d'accord* with Prince Bismarck, I hope and trust that much good will come of the proposed meeting ; as I deem it necessary that monarchs should meet often and confer together to look out for dangers which threaten the monarchial principle from democratical and republican parties in all parts of the world. It is far better that we Emperors keep firm together. . .' †

This judicious letter, the Emperor recorded later, had a very salutary effect on his grandmother, who acknowledged that he was right and thereafter treated him as a Sovereign of equal rank. That was a delusion : the actual effect on the Queen was that she at once sent a very lucid telegram to Lord Salisbury saying : 'Trust that we shall be *very cool*, though civil, in our communications with my grandson and Prince Bismarck, who are bent on a return to the oldest times

* William II, *My Memoirs*, p. 25.   † *Letters III*, i. p. 425.

of government.' * Such frigidity in these early days promised inclement weather.

A blizzard quickly followed. The Prince of Wales's inquiry as to whether the Emperor Frederick would have wished to restore part of the provinces to France, had been incubating, and now Bismarck communicated with Lord Salisbury on the Emperor's behalf, making three formal complaints against the Prince :

(1) That the Prince had told a Russian Grand Duke — who had passed it on to the Tsar — that if the Emperor Frederick had lived he would have restored part of Alsace to France, of Schleswig to Denmark and of Hanover to the Duke of Cumberland.

(2) That the Prince and Princess of Wales had spoken to Bismarck himself about the restoration of part of Hanover.

(3) That the Prince treated William as an uncle treats a nephew and forgot that the nephew was an Emperor.†

Simultaneously the Emperor expressed himself. He unveiled, in August, a monument to his cousin Prince Frederick Charles, who had held important commands in the Franco-German War, and in his public speech at the unveiling he said:

'There are those people who have the audacity to maintain that my father was willing to part with what he, in conjunction with the late Prince, gained on the battlefield. We, who knew him so well, cannot quietly tolerate, even for a single moment, such an insult to his memory. He assuredly cherished the same idea as we do, namely that nothing should be surrendered of what had been gained in those great days. . . On this point there can only be one opinion, namely that we would rather sacrifice our eighteen army corps and our forty-two millions of inhabitants on the field

* Letters III, i. p. 429.   † Ibid. p. 439.

THE KAISER AND BISMARCK

of battle than surrender a single stone of what my father and Prince Frederick Charles gained. . .' To make the allusion to the 'audacious folk' quite unmistakable, he turned to General Blumenthal at the end of his speech and said, 'I hope my uncle, the Prince of Wales, will understand that.' *

The Emperor gave further expression to his high displeasure in the rudest possible manner. The Prince of Wales was to stay with the Emperor of Austria in September, and, hearing that nephew William was going there about the same time, he wrote to him, the day before this speech was delivered, thanking him for the hospitable welcome some English officers had received at the German summer manœuvres, and hoped that they would shortly meet at Vienna. He got no reply, and found on his arrival there that the British Ambassador was charged to tell him that William did not wish to meet him. To save his host from the slight embarrassment of having under his roof an Emperor and an heir apparent who turned their backs on each other (their suites presumably following their example), the Prince, boiling with fury, went to stay with the King of Rumania while his nephew was at Vienna, and returned after he had left to thank the Emperor of Austria for his pleasant visit.

Meantime Lord Salisbury had forwarded to the Queen Bismarck's bill of indictment against her son. She reserved judgment on the first and second counts till she had seen him, but dealt summarily with the third. She wrote to her Prime Minister : 'This is really too *vulgar* and too absurd, as well as untrue, almost to be believed (*sic*). We have always been very intimate with our grandson and nephew, and to pretend that he is to be treated in *private* as well as in public as "his imperial Majesty" is *perfect madness*. He has been

---

* Lee, *King Edward VII*, i. p. 648 ; Ponsonby, *Letters of Empress Frederick,* p. 336.

treated just as we should have treated his beloved father and even grandfather and as the Queen *herself* was always treated by her dear Uncle Leopold. *If* he has *such* notions he had better *never* come *here*. The Queen will not swallow this affront. . . He had also said to the Crown Prince [Rudolph of Austria] that if his uncle wrote him a very kind letter, he *might perhaps answer it*. All this shows a very unhealthy and unnatural state of mind ; and he *must* be made to feel that his grandmother and uncle will not stand such insolence.' *

That seemed to dispose of the third count. The Prince came home, and went straight up to Balmoral to see his mother about the others. All he would admit was that he had asked Count Herbert Bismarck whether the Emperor Frederick would have 'wished' to give back some part of the provinces to France ; the rest was lies. Lord Salisbury had intimated to the German Ambassador, on the strength of the Queen's summary judgment, that she would not let William come to England as long as his rudeness to his uncle remained unexplained, but Count Hatzfeldt had been far too frightened to deliver the message, and the Prime Minister was nervous that he might propose a visit to his grandmother himself and be told that he must not come. That would be awkward. Now he also learned that the Queen had asked the Empress Frederick to stay with her for several months during the winter of 1888–89. Considering the unhappy relations between mother and son, this would make a fresh cause for friction, and he suggested to the Queen that this visit had better be cancelled. He got a withering refusal. It would be impossible and heartless and cruel to stop her coming : besides, it would only 'encourage' the Emperor and the Bismarcks. 'You all seem frightened of them,' so ran this energetic telegram, 'which is not the way to make them

* *Letters III*, i. pp. 440, 441.

better.' She did not wish the subject to be mentioned again.*

When the Queen expressed herself like that, there was nothing more to be said, and she compounded a drastic prescription of her own to make the Bismarcks better. She sent the Prince of Wales across to Flushing in the *Victoria and Albert* to meet his sister, and went down in person with a galaxy of the family to welcome her on landing at Port Victoria. On the Empress's birthday, November 21, she received the whole of the German Embassy, headed by Count Hatzfeldt, at Windsor, and afterwards the English Court was formally presented to her. That was the way to teach William : not a word to him personally, but the spectacle of how his grandmother honoured his mother would convey the lesson. The Empress remained with her for three months, and even then the Queen was still determined that William should not visit her yet, for he must learn his lesson thoroughly, and she wrote to the Prince of Wales : 'William must *not* come *this* year. You could not meet him and I could *not,* after all he has said and done.' †
But, behind these salutary domestic dealings so firmly handled, there was a good deal of anxiety. The Queen was a strong believer in the potent effect which the relations between royal families exercised on their realms both for good and ill, and she was also aware that Lord Salisbury thought she had been injudicious in so pointedly making much of her daughter : William, though this treatment was designed to make him better, would not like his medicine, and that would be bad for international relations. She had already told her Prime Minister :

'As regards the political relations of the two Governments, the Queen quite agrees that it should not be affected (if possible) by these miserable personal quarrels, but the Queen

* *Letters III*, i. p. 443.   † *Ibid.* p. 467.

much *fears* that with such a hot-headed, conceited and wrong-headed young man, devoid of all feeling, that may at ANY moment become impossible.' *

But perhaps it was as well not to be too severe, so when Colonel Swaine, Military Attaché at Berlin, intimated to Lord Salisbury that the Emperor much wanted to be taken into favour again, she changed her mind about letting him come to Osborne, and said that he might visit her in the summer. But the Shah of Persia was coming also, and the date of his visit must be fixed first — it would do William good to know that.

Then there was still the Prince of Wales to settle with. He said that if William came to Osborne without having apologised for his odious rudeness at Vienna, he would not consent to meet him. So Prince Christian, who was going to Berlin, was commissioned to secure this important concession. The Emperor, who throughout his life was constitutionally incapable of saying he was in the wrong, took the easiest way out of the difficulty (for he wanted to go to Osborne) by declaring that there had been no Vienna incident, and that he was guiltless of any discourtesy to his uncle. That was untrue, but, since it would not mend matters to tell him that he lied, the Queen and the Prince accepted this staggering statement. In fact the Prince was sacrificed to political expediency, and he did not love his nephew any the more for that. Then, since William was forgiven, it was best to make a handsome job of it, and the Queen created him Admiral of the British Fleet, and the date of his visit was fixed to follow that of the Shah. He was delighted with this honour : to wear the same uniform as Nelson, he said, was enough to make him quite giddy, and he told the British Ambassador in Berlin that he felt as Macbeth must have felt when the witches cried : 'All hail,

* *Letters III*, i. p. 441.

who art Thane of Glamis and Cawdor too.' Having got over his giddiness, he applied himself very conscientiously to the discharge of his new office, and sent his grandmother many pieces of advice about her fleet. She ought to have more ships in Mediterranean waters ; the Naval Vote of £21,000,000, to be spread over the next four years, seemed to him adequate : later he thought it should be trebled, to counter American navy-building.*

The Emperor arrived at Osborne in the most amiable temper, and nobody could be pleasanter than he when he liked. He brought an escort of twelve ships of war to show that Germany had naval aspirations : indeed, one of his objects was to make a very thorough inspection of the British fleet, which was assembled in considerable force for the review in his honour, and he was good enough to tell his grandmother's other admirals and captains a great deal about guns and naval armaments. As regards the restoration of family cordialities, all past dissensions were swept away in a spate of gifts and decorations. The new Admiral of the British Fleet made his grandmother Colonel-in-Chief of his 1st Dragoon Guards, henceforth to be known as 'The Queen of England's Own' : he had selected this regiment because his father had served in it. He gave her a bust of himself in a helmet by Begas, and conferred the Order of the Black Eagle on his cousin, Prince George of Wales. The Queen invested Prince Henry of Prussia with the Garter, she gave Count Herbert Bismarck 'a beautiful box,' and sent his father a copy of von Angeli's portrait of herself. The Emperor breakfasted and dined with his grandmother, and spent the days with his uncle. The Cowes Regatta was going on, and the Prince made him a member of the Royal Yacht Squadron.

Certainly he was a pleasant guest, though possibly fatigu-

* *Letters III*, i. pp. 456, 500, 504, 575 ; Lee, *King Edward VII*, i. pp. 654, 658.

ing, for the Queen, on the morning after his departure, noted in her Diary that it was 'such a contrast' to have breakfast quietly again with her daughter and son-in-law. Lord Salisbury considered the visit a notable success ; it would, he hoped, efface past estrangements, and restore family affection and peace : for once he was over-optimistic. As for the Emperor himself, he abounded in gratitude and happy auguries for the future, and mentioned that he would be delighted to come to Osborne again next year. His letter to his grandmother from Bayreuth contained interesting passages :

'. . . my warmest thanks for the quite unexampled honour which you conferred on me with the commission as Admiral of the Fleet. It really gave me such an immense pleasure that I now am able to feel and take interest in your fleet as if it was my own, and with keenest sympathy shall I watch every phase of its further development, knowing that the British ironclads, coupled with mine and my army, are the strongest guarantees of peace which Heaven may (*sic*) help us to preserve ! Should, however, the Will of Providence lay the heavy burden on us of fighting for our homes and destinies, then may the British fleet be seen forging ahead, side by side with the German, and the "Red Coat" marching to victory with the Pomeranian Grenadier !' *

These very handsome expressions bore out exactly what Lord Salisbury had conjectured. He thought from the first that one of the reasons which made the Emperor so very anxious to be taken into favour again in England was that he had begun to distrust the solidity of Russia's friendship for Germany † and looked with strong suspicion on her growing attraction towards France. This letter bears it out : he definitely suggests that alliance between Germany and England is the surest guarantee for peace and the most

* *Letters III*, i. pp. 520–527. † *Ibid*. p. 477.

favourable arrangement — for Germany at any rate — in case of war. This was the first but far from the last of the Emperor's efforts to secure an understanding with England. That, in spite of all apparent evidence to the contrary, was the aim that he set before him for many years to come. He usually managed to defeat it himself by some outrageous and, to him, irresistible piece of duplicity or cantankerous behaviour. But there was nothing dearer to his heart than friendship with England.

A second point of interest is that the idea of building a powerful German navy was already rooted in his mind. One of his earliest acts after his accession had been to create a separate Admiralty Department in his Government : hitherto it had only been an annexe of the War Office. He seems here, prophetically, to see his fleet on a par with the British : his ironclads and theirs forge ahead together. As Admiral of the British Fleet he can now take the same interest in it as in his own, and sympathetically ('competitively' would perhaps have rendered the meaning with equal precision) watch every phase of its development. This national ambition of his was already recognised in England, and although some regarded the little German fleet as a joke, and the Emperor in his Admiral's uniform, giving peripatetic instruction to British naval officers on guns and armaments, as purely comic, others seriously questioned whether it was wise so guilelessly to let him see all he wanted.

During this visit the Queen talked to William about his treatment of his mother. Though deeply sympathetic with her, she knew that the Empress Frederick was over-eager to find fault with him, and she understood the discord between the two all the more clearly because she had been through oddly similar experiences in her girlhood, when, after her accession, she was in just the same position as William was now. Her own mother, the Duchess of Kent, an alien in a foreign land like the Empress Frederick, had failed to establish any real bond of affection and sympathy with her, and by tactless behaviour had antagonized the two sovereigns of the Queen's minority, George IV and William IV, much as the Empress Frederick had antagonized her father-in-law. Those early years of strict maternal rule had rankled in the Queen's mind, and when, at the age of eighteen, she came to the throne, she treated her mother very ruthlessly. She cut her off from all intimacy, and it was not until Prince Albert took the unhappy situation in hand that she mended her ways. Pangs of bitterest sorrow visited her after her mother's death, when the reading of the Duchess's private papers revealed the unsuspected love and tenderness which her mother had always felt for her.

William's case strongly resembled her own. For some ten years before his accession he had been on very discordant terms with his mother, who had been strict and domineering with him and far too censorious. Then he came to the throne, and his grandmother, in a way, could sympathise with him, for from her own experience she knew how tempting it was for young folk, who like herself and him were suddenly whisked up to the dizziest eminence, to assert their independence of those who had held them under extreme subjection, with cruel thoughtlessness. Her own experience cannot fail to have been in her mind when she enlarged to William on the Fifth Commandment. And her daughter, she knew, was listening too much to talebearers, who brought her news of William's and his wife's indifference to her feelings. She remembered what mischief had been wrought between her mother and herself by the spiteful garrulity of her old governess Lehzen, and advised her not to listen to any stories of the kind.*

* Ponsonby, *Letters of Empress Frederick,* p. 384 ; *Letters I,* iii. p. 439.

Back in Berlin again, the Emperor surrounded himself with men who sedulously fed his appetite for omnipotence, but there was one among them who had no proper respect for it. For over twenty years now, Bismarck's authority had been supreme. The Emperor William I had put himself completely in his hands, and, as the Empress Frederick observed, it was really true that the power of the Constitution and the Crown had been suspended. Bismarck had been a very useful friend to William during these years ; he had encouraged him in those principles which were in flat opposition to all that his father and mother had fruitlessly worked for, but the young man had been little more than the tool that he was sharpening for his own purposes, and he no doubt looked forward to a continuance of his own autocracy. But during this winter of 1889–90 there were constant collisions between them. The Emperor, for instance, wanted Germany to strengthen the hands of Austria in dealing with those ever-recurring Balkan questions, while Bismarck, still seeking friendship with Russia, encouraged her protecting influence over the Slav populations which by blood were her kindred. More acute was their dissension over internal Socialist problems ; Bismarck stood for the most rigorous repression of riots and disturbances ; the Emperor, more liberal than he, was for removing the causes of Socialism by remedying the just grievances of the employed against employers. Such collisions were bound to result in rupture. As long as Bismarck remained Chancellor the Emperor had not any real control over his Government, for it consisted not of his Ministers but of Bismarck's : while, with William asserting himself as Emperor, Bismarck found himself perpetually checked, and after a quarter of a century's autocracy any control at all was intolerable to him. Twice he threatened to resign, but the Emperor still had need of him to get certain military votes through the Reichstag. He was, however, determined to get rid of him as soon as he could screw up his courage, for he would never be able to realise that magic-lantern ideal of himself while Bismarck's huge figure cast its shadow on the screen. His officers and Ministers were as keen for the Chancellor's fall as he. They could manage the Emperor, though powerless against Bismarck, and they plied him with subtle suggestions. 'Frederick,' hinted Waldersee, 'would never have become the Great, if on his accession he had found and retained in power a Minister of Bismarck's authority and prestige.' *

The Emperor was still pluming himself on the success of his English visit, and, to keep cordiality warm, he invited his uncle and his second son Prince George to return it in March 1890. The Prince of Wales had not been to Berlin since his accession except for the funeral of the Emperor Frederick, and the occasion was to be celebrated with the utmost splendour : the death of William's grandmother, the Empress Augusta, in January was to be no obstacle. It can hardly have been a coincidence that on the day before the Prince started from England William sent a message to Bismarck demanding his resignation. A striking dramatic effect ! The Prince arrived in Berlin knowing nothing of it, and found that his nephew reigned indeed.

The psychological effect of the Emperor's *coup d'état* — for it was no less than that — on himself was immense. For years, looking in his mind-mirror, he had been making tentative sketches of his own image, as he saw it. For properties and costume there were a helmet, a sceptre, shining armour and the will of God ; for background, Europe regarding him from somewhere far below with upturned eyes of expectation, but as yet the sole and supreme figure eluded his imaginative pencil. Now with this dismissal of Bis-

* Ludwig, *Kaiser Wilhelm II*, p. 80.

marck he began the limning of it in strong strokes, for the
great deed was done, and he saw himself more clearly. Yet
even at the moment of its accomplishment his essential timidity was terrified at his own audacity and he abounded in
justification for himself. Russia would be loth to lose her
ally, and William telegraphed to the Tsar's brother that he
felt as sad as on the day his grandfather had died, but it was
God's will * — he often put the blame of possible disaster
elsewhere — that the Chancellor should go. To the Tsar
he said that Bismarck refused to obey his orders, and the
Tsar (according to William's account) warmly shook him
by the hand and said he could not have done differently,
adding, 'As for me I always mistrusted him and I never believed a word of what he told me.' † Sir Edward Malet received a different version. The Emperor told him that
Bismarck was so violent at his interviews that he was afraid
he would throw the inkstand at his head. He had therefore to think of his own dignity. To his grandmother in
England he said that they had parted with tears and embraces, but Bismarck would have infallibly died of apoplexy
if he had continued working. Bismarck was a victim of
insomnia and all its enervating effects : he had fits of cry-
ing when they were discussing affairs of State, and out of
compassion he had dismissed him in order to preserve his
life. These versions did not quite tally with the Prince of
Wales's impressions, for he went to see Bismarck before he
left Berlin, and found him robust enough to abuse William
in the most savage manner, and in excellent health. As for
the Empress Frederick, she discarded all these versions and
told her mother that William got rid of him because he
wanted his Ministers to obey him and carry out the orders
he gave. He was a 'most thorough despot,' and, cordially as
she had detested Bismarck as Germany's evil genius, she

---

* Ludwig, *Kaiser Wilhelm II*, p. 103.   † William II, *My Memoirs*, p. 18.

thought everything would be much worse than it was before.* She deplored the event which at any moment during the last thirty years she would have hailed with paeans of joy. One thing, however, was quite clear. The Emperor desired friendship with England far more than with Russia, and though he asserted that Bismarck's retirement made no difference to German friendship with Russia, the treaty which Bismarck was negotiating was never concluded. William treated his uncle on this visit to Berlin with honours usually accorded only to reigning monarchs, he appeared at the state banquet in the uniform of Nelson, and in proposing the Prince's health publicly repeated what he had written to his grandmother, that he hoped that 'the English fleet would co-operate with the German army in keeping the peace.' †

Lord Salisbury, though doubtful of the permanent value of such expressions, thought it well to make the most of them for the advantage of both countries, and he now devised the cession of Heligoland to Germany in exchange for the protectorate of Zanzibar, Witu and Somaliland in East Africa. Six years ago the project had been supported by Count Münster, the German Ambassador in London, but it had been abandoned : this seemed an excellent opportunity for its revival. ‡ Heligoland was of no sort of use to England unless it was strongly fortified, whereas Germany looked on it with covetous eyes as a protective station for the Kiel Canal now in construction. On the other hand, the protectorate of Zanzibar, situated between the Cape and Egypt, was likely to be very valuable to England in view of colonial expansions, while Germany was finding endless difficulties in her administration there. The Queen looked on the proposal with strong disfavour when it was first put

---

* *Letters III*, i. pp. 587, 590 ; Ponsonby, *Letters of Empress Frederick*, p. 412.
† Ludwig, p. 108.　　　　　　　　　　　‡ Lee, *King Edward VII*, i. p. 663.

to her, and the fact that William would be pleased made no appeal to her. The people of Heligoland had been very loyal and it 'was a shame to hand them over to an unscrupulous despotic power like Germany without first consulting them.' Moreover, her imperialistic instincts were suspicious of such a transaction. She wrote : 'The next thing will be to give up Gibraltar, and soon nothing will be secure, and all our colonies will wish to be free. . .' Lord Salisbury treated these far-reaching scruples with due gravity. He did not think it would be wise to take a plebiscite of the 2000 inhabitants of Heligoland, for that would be a most dangerous precedent : Gibraltar or Cyprus might demand a plebiscite too, and who could tell what would happen ? He assured her also that the cession of Heligoland should not constitute a precedent, but he omitted to explain what prevented any future government from regarding it as such. His judicious handling quieted her fears and, knowing that her Prime Minister was fully as imperialistic as herself, she consented.*

The Emperor was in ecstasies. He had not the smallest difficulty in persuading himself that the idea of this exchange had originated with him : it had long been his firm resolve to get back Heligoland for Germany, for in British hands it was 'a constant menace to Hamburg and Bremen and rendered futile any project for building a navy.' And how cunningly he had outwitted greedy and acquisitive England by his sagacity and foresight, for he had previously ascertained that, with the development of other ports on the East African coast, Zanzibar would soon be of no importance at all, and he chuckled to himself at having passed off this valueless bartering counter in payment for so desirable an acquisition.† Lord Salisbury was quite content to leave it at that, and the Bill for the exchange went through both

---

* *Letters III*, i. pp. 612, 615, 621.   † William II, *My Memoirs*, pp. 53, 54.

Houses almost without opposition, and received the Queen's consent on August 4, 1890.

That same day the Emperor arrived on his promised visit to Osborne, and there was never a more cordial meeting. From Cowes he went home *via* Heligoland, and welcomed its inhabitants to their citizenship in the German Empire. 'Without a battle,' said the exultant War Lord, 'without a tear this beautiful island has passed into my possession. We have acquired it by a treaty freely concluded with a country to which we are related by blood. I drink to the illustrious lady to whom we are indebted for the transfer.' * The moral lesson to be drawn from this most desirable addition to the Empire was clear to see. Blood and iron had been the technique of the discarded Chancellor, and here was William showing a better way and reaping with the sickle of consummate diplomacy the fruits of his peaceful harvesting. He remembered with pride that Bismarck had once said of him, 'Some day that man will be his own Chancellor.'

* Lee, *King Edward VII*, i. p. 666.

CHAPTER VI

MEANTIME the Emperor's relations with his mother had become altogether past mending. Acute collisions did not occur, because on the rare occasions of their meeting the Empress Frederick spoke to him only of uncontroversial matters, but the condition had become chronic and incurable. She no longer sought to influence him, but she could not live up to her expressed resolve to retire mentally from the arena where she had hoped to be so active and beneficent a force, and everything he did provoked her bitter criticism. Ever since his accession her constant letters to the Queen had been reiterated catalogues of the insults which he had permitted to be showered on her, of his pompousness, his ignorance, of his callousness and want of dutiful feeling : sometimes she thought that he was definitely insane. He was like a child who pulls off a fly's wings out of sheer thoughtlessness ; he was green and suspicious and prejudiced ; he thought all women were 'dolts or idiots.' The unhappy woman had indeed many grounds for complaint, but she kept alive her own misery by multiplying them. William's wife, whose marriage with him she had approved and strongly advocated, came under the ban. She had no sense of gratitude towards her mother-in-law ; her head was turned by her position, she put on grand, condescending airs, and (perhaps this was the chief offence) she was convinced that

everything that William did was perfect.* The Empress
clung to her grief and her inconsolable loss ; if she lunched
or dined with them it was terrible to visit those scenes, and
no one knew or cared what she suffered. Constantly had
she regretted the bitterness of the English Press towards
Germany, but now when *The Times* adopted a more
friendly tone and spoke with approval of her son, she
thought it 'curious' : she feared it would encourage him to
believe himself infallible. She had been the victim of venomous and absolutely unfounded attacks, William had
behaved sometimes brutally to her and often most thought-
lessly, and he became to her the compendium and person-
ification of those who now slighted and neglected her. Her
idea of leaving Germany had long been abandoned, and
she bought an estate at Cronberg and built herself a house
which she named 'Friedrichshof,' where she intended to
live in complete retirement. But it was impossible for so
active-minded and restless a woman, only just fifty years
old, to obliterate the political interests which had engrossed
her so long, or patiently to see her son, whose ideas and
ideals were so utterly opposed to hers, in possession of all
that, but for her husband's premature death, she would
have shared with him. Even if William and her daughter-
in-law had behaved to her with the most delicate consideration, she would still have been desperately unhappy, and
have felt herself ill-used.

Next year (1891), instead of the Emperor coming to
Cowes for the holiday which he said that he enjoyed more
than anything in the whole year (his uncle did not rate
it so highly), he and the Empress paid their first state visit
to the Queen at Windsor. It was an occasion that war-
ranted some slight uneasiness, for, only the month before,

* Ponsonby, *Letters of Empress Frederick,* pp. 400, 410.

the Prince of Wales had been involved in a very disagreeable *cause célèbre* arising out of what happened at a house-party at Tranby Croft. There is no use in going into the details of a scandal already stale and too thoroughly explored. Briefly, a member of this party indulging in the simple and entertaining game called baccarat was believed to have cheated. An incredibly stupid species of court-martial was held, at which the Prince, who should never have been brought into it at all, presided ; and the accused promised that he would never play cards for money again, on the condition that the members of the court-martial never divulged these proceedings. The secret leaked (or rather spouted) out, he brought an action for libel against certain of his accusers, and the Prince was summoned as a witness. While the trial lasted, the Press abstained from comment : the moment it was over, a tempest of abuse assailed him. All he was actually guilty of was that he had played baccarat, but that was sufficient excuse to unloose this tornado of invective : it was if it was he who had been suspected of cheating. For years the Prince's hedonistic manner of life, his associates, his sedulous attendance at race-meetings, his supposed extravagance and debts had given rise to widespread disapproval, and now owing to the trial all this had become relevant matter for public comment.

The Emperor could not resist such an opportunity. He wrote a letter of avuncular reproof to his uncle, telling him how unsuitable it was that a man of his position and age should gamble for substantial stakes with subalterns. Anything more gratuitously impertinent could scarcely be imagined, and it was in accordance with William's chosen demeanour towards the Prince. But the visit went off very decently : possibly there were some nips of domestic frigidity, when his uncle advised him to mind his own business, for William wrote afterwards to his grandmother, briefly alluding to the 'disagreeable moments' that he had experienced. Four days at Windsor were succeeded by a week at Buckingham Palace, and he laid great stress on the friendly welcome which he had received. He always took the most optimistic view of his popularity in London (the wish being father to the thought), and a man waving his hat and shouting ' 'Ullo, Kaiser !' made his eye glow with pleasure. The English, he wrote to the Queen, desired to make him feel quite at home : well they might, for he was so much of an Englishman himself. 'All thinking people' approved of his unwearied efforts 'for the maintenance of peace and the development of goodwill amongst all nations — *nota bene* as far as it is possible. . . I hope to be able to pursue my way, which Providence has marked down, and continue to strive for the fulfilment of those great problems which were so ably begun by dear Grandpapa Albert.' *

The Queen with her unrivalled common sense had by this time formed a very correct estimate of William, *qua* Emperor, and, discounting the mutual dislike with which he and his uncle regarded each other, she had no doubt whatever that William sincerely wished to be friends with England. But why that '*nota bene*' warning ? It may be assumed that she guessed the answer to that, for she had observed also that William already wanted to have England all to himself. No true friend of Germany should look for friends elsewhere. He did not approve of England, or indeed any nation, being on warmer terms than distrustful caution with other Powers, and there had been manifestations of goodwill among them which distressed him. The French fleet, under Admiral Gervais, had been paying a visit to Russia, where Tsar Alexander III had given it a welcome that might almost be taken as an unfriendly act towards Germany. Now, on the fleet's return to France, the British

* *Letters III,* ii. p. 51.

Government invited it to put in at Portsmouth, and a programme had been drawn up which roused the Emperor's suspicions. The French officers were to dine with the Queen, and she intended to review the French fleet and her own at Spithead. This was rather awkward, for her two grandchildren, Prince Henry of Prussia, the Emperor's sailor brother, and his wife Princess Irene of Hesse, would be staying at Osborne when the French fleet arrived. It would be a matter of the deepest offence to William if Prince Henry's visit was postponed, and, on the other hand, French sensibilities would be much offended if a German prince took any part in the reception of the French fleet. The Queen referred this difficult conundrum to Lord Salisbury, who could only suggest that, when the French dined with her, her German grandchildren should have dinner in another room, and of course they would not accompany her to the review. But a more ingenious plan was evolved, and it was settled that they should go for a cruise down the Channel in the Prince of Wales's yacht, the *Aline,* while the Queen was engaged with her French visitors. They set off before the enemy arrived and, returning next day when the review was over, had the tact not to ask their grandmother what she had been doing with herself. They would not have liked it, for at dinner, after the health of the President of the Republic had been proposed, the band played the *Marseillaise,* and the Queen stood up during it. That gesture gave supreme satisfaction to the French, but the Queen did not much relish doing it herself, and the Empress Frederick strongly remonstrated. She reminded her mother that the 'horrid' *Marseillaise* was a hymn of revolution, 'and was used by the Socialists as the symbol of violence and all their mad Labour principles. A respectable government, such as a peace- and order-loving republic ought to be, does not choose as its national anthem a melody so closely asso-

ciated with the massacre of kings, aristocrats and priests.' *
She always disliked the French, and her feelings were extremely bitter just now, for earlier in the year she had paid
a visit to Paris, and had so hostile a reception from the
French Press, who deemed her visit an insult, that she cut
it short and crossed to England.

The Emperor then did not approve of the civilities paid
to France by the Tsar, since that looked as if they were becoming friends, nor of their endorsement on the part of
England by his grandmother.   The *idée fixe* that all Europe
was engaged in a conspiracy under the general chairmanship of his wicked uncle to encircle Germany was already
beginning to outline itself in his mind, and his method of
defeating that was not to do his best to form a solid alliance,
based on good faith and community of interests, with any
of these nations, but to sow discord between any two of
them.   Bismarck, it is true, had often used that method, but
even he with his experience and his statesmanlike grasp of
affairs had not made very much of it, and in his pupil's
hands it became one of ludicrous pettiness, as of some jealous
woman who, in the patter of social intercourse, strives to in-
gratiate herself with one friend by running down another.
Such a method is very liable to detection, for it so often
happens that the two exchange notes, and find that the
mutual friend has been crabbing each to the other.   Where
friendships between nations are concerned similar consequences are apt to follow, and by constantly pursuing this
policy the Emperor managed to acquire the deepening distrust of every nation with whom he wished to be friends.
At this particular juncture he reasoned that the cordialities
between France and Russia on the one side and France and
England on the other might lead to a further and thoroughly undesirable cordiality between Russia and England.

* *Letters III*, ii. pp. 61–68 ; Ponsonby, *Letters of Empress Frederick*, p. 426.

It was therefore in accordance with his methods that he wrote to the Queen in December 1891, on the occasion of the engagement of Princess Victoria Mary of Teck to Prince Albert Victor of Wales. There was a sympathetic preamble ; he was delighted at it ; it would make a joyful and merry Christmas for England, and he was glad for Uncle Bertie's sake. Also he had been to see his mother's new house at Cronberg, a miracle of good taste, all her own, within, and of skilful landscape gardening, all her own, without. Then came the real point of the letter, namely, the worthlessness of Russia as an ally. To begin with, Tsar Alexander III had been very rude to him : he had passed through Prussia on his return from the family gathering at Copenhagen without paying him a call. William felt that this was intended as a snub and was a violation of the politeness customary between sovereigns. And what a pack of troubles Russia was in ! Crops had failed, the loan which her government had tried to raise for the relief of agrarian famine had not realised a half of the sum required. 'A great financial crisis,' he went on, 'is looming in the background, and the throng of famished peasants is growing daily. . . I think this fearful calamity will with God's help for some time to come keep the Russians from making war on their unsuspecting neighbours. This, of course, would keep the "Johnny Crapauds" [the French], as your sailors call them, quiet, and if they keep quiet everybody else is quiet. So that on the whole the outlook for the end of the year is a good one.' *

That was typical : Russia's troubles made the future brighter than it would otherwise have been, and with Russia financially crippled and threatened by famine, the Johnny Crapauds (the Emperor's version of 'Froggies') would not be able to do much encircling. So much seems certain, but

* *Letters III*, ii. pp. 82–84.

the Emperor's habit of expressing diametrically opposite opinions simultaneously on the same subject makes it difficult always to follow him.   He wrote, for instance, in his *Memoirs* that, as long as Tsar Alexander III was alive, Germany was safe from any attack from Russia, but a few months only after this letter to the Queen he told her that Russia was busy preparing for an invasion of Germany, was massing troops on the frontier of Eastern Prussia, and that a Russian general lately at Warsaw had proudly remarked, 'Je suis la poing de la Russie sur le poitrine de l'Allemagne ; un mot du Tsar et je l'enfonce.' *   Steadfast, however, was his desire to keep on good terms with his grandmother, and again he proposed himself for a private visit to Osborne during the next Cowes week.   This time the Queen was far from enthusiastic : she could hardly prevent his coming when he was now a member of the Royal Yacht Squadron, but she told him that she would not be able to house him and his suite ; he must live on his yacht, and he could come and lunch or dine with her occasionally.   Unknown to him, she was even less encouraging, for she privately instructed her secretary to ask the British Ambassador at Berlin if he could not throw out a hint to William 'that these regular annual visits are not desirable.' †   This year (1892) there could be no political discussions at all during the Emperor's visit, for, though Lord Salisbury was at Osborne, the Conservative Government had just been heavily defeated by the Liberals, and his resignation was imminent.   The Queen, sorely against her inclination, was obliged to ask Mr. Gladstone to form a Ministry, but she felt it was terribly dangerous to entrust the Empire 'to the shaking hand of an old, wild and incomprehensible man of 82½.' ‡   The only con-

* William II, *My Memoirs*, p. 19 ; *Letters III*, ii. p. 116.
† *Letters III*, ii. p. 107, note.
‡ Guedalla, *The Queen and Mr. Gladstone*, ii. p. 70.

solation was that Lord Rosebery was induced reluctantly to accept the post of Foreign Minister. That might steady the shaking hand, for his foreign policy was that of Lord Salisbury, and he fully appreciated the need for caution in dealings with the Emperor. Both of them were strongly in favour of being on the best of terms with Germany, but neither of them desired to form any closer tie. England still kept herself aloof from alliances of all sorts : not since the Crimean War had she ranged herself with any European Power.

The Queen's hopes that Sir Edward Malet might hint to her grandson that she was prepared to forgo the pleasure of his annual visits to Cowes met with no immediate fulfilment. She did not want to tell him so herself, and Sir Edward could not screw himself up to deliver this austere message, or, if he did, the Emperor could not believe his ears, for he continued to pay them for three more years yet. To establish a formal and ratified treaty with England was certainly his paramount ambition, and when next he came over, in the summer of 1893, he was getting very anxious about the isolation of Germany, for France and Russia were forming a friendship which seemed highly ominous and encircling, and the welcome given to the French fleet at Cronstadt, which he had found so disagreeable, had been echoed by the enthusiastic popular reception given to the Russian fleet at Toulon. He did not like it at all ; but, on the other hand, he had high hopes that England might be equally uneasy about her isolation, for Russia in the Pamirs and the Balkans, and France in Egypt and on the Congo, were pursuing very provocative anti-British policies. That was to the good.

This year, for the first time, the Emperor brought with him in his suite Count Philip von Eulenburg, a man twelve

years older than himself, and now his Minister at Munich.
He had first met Eulenburg in 1886, when he was twenty-
seven years old, and a very intimate relation, reeking of
romance and sentimentality and artistic aspirations, had at
once sprung up between the two. Prince William had
poured into it that side of his nature which had long been
repressed by his stern upbringing, and which in a more
happily constituted man would have ripened in friendship
with his wife or with other women. But Dona never could
be his intellectual or artistic comrade, since she was quite
destitute of the endowments from which such comradeship
could spring, and he found his domestic life extremely bor-
ing. In public he would speak of her as the paragon of
wives who made it possible for him to support the tremendous burden of empire, and, visiting with her the Borussian
Corps at Bonn, to which he had belonged as a university
student, he told them that the smile she had bestowed on
them that day had ennobled their lives. But in private she
did not ennoble his, nor did she exist for him except as a
dignified but tedious presence who sat sewing after dinner
till he asked her whether she was going to stop there all
night.* Emotionally, indeed, women made no appeal to
him, any more than to his grandfather, the Prince Consort,
and as intimate companions he vastly preferred the unmixed
society of his own sex. He had inherited from his mother
and grandfather vivid artistic tastes, and he frankly adored
this large, soft, witty and highly cultivated Count Eulenburg, who wrote Nordic sagas, which he set to music and
sang in his agreeable baritone voice, while William, sitting
by the piano, turned over the pages in rapt enchantment.
They went together to the Wagner festival at Bayreuth, and
planned to get the master's operas properly given at Berlin.
Eulenburg dedicated a volume of ballads to him ; he sent

* Ludwig, *Kaiser Wilhelm II*, p. 146.

him his *Nordic Battle Song,* and hoped that the brass band of the Hussars, supplemented by bugles, would be able to render it worthily. When they met at shooting parties they made woodland trysts, and William quoted to him stanzas of his own Nordic lays, and confided to him the flatness of his domestic life. Eulenburg sent him a Tyrolean rustic knife with the carved motto 'Das Leben ohne Freut ist wohl ein Traurigkeit,' and commented that it was right to 'stab anyone with it who disturbs our joy,' and he contrasted their intimate communion of deep friendship with the pretentious glitter of Court functions. How it made him suffer to think that 'the social abyss between us, bridged by our friendship, must inevitably widen more and more when the Imperial Crown is on your head,' and he signed himself 'in unchangeable affection and faith.'

This tie was far the most intimate the Prince William had ever formed with any human being, and he did not permit the social abyss to widen when he became Emperor. He drank brotherhood with his friend, he addressed him with a kinsman's 'Du,' and he allowed 'my bosom friend Philip Eulenburg, the only one I have,' a freedom of speech and an immunity from his appalling practical jokes which he granted to no other. He regarded him as his good genius, and telegraphed to him : 'May your person, with its striving after ideals, always be preserved to fortify my strivings.' He respected as well as loved him : and indeed Eulenburg was very far from being only the yodelling troubadour which *Kladderadatsch* represented him. He was an extremely able diplomatist, and his devotion to his young friend, though probably reinforced by the sense that it earned him large dividends in power and influence, would appear to have been quite genuine, and he often used the Emperor's affection for him to admirable purpose. He gave him good advice, he warned him with great tact to be more sparing of his God-given eloquence in public speeches which often had so deplorable an effect. 'If your Majesty,' he wrote to him, 'would be more economical of such a gift, it would be a hundred times more efficacious.' When the Emperor wrote his name in the 'Golden Book' at Munich, and appended the bombastic sentiment 'Regis voluntas suprema lex,' Eulenburg did not hesitate to tell him that he had made a monstrous *gaffe,* for to Bavarians 'regis voluntas' connoted the disordered whims and sensualities of insane kings ; moreover, people thought that he implied that his will overrode that of the Bavarian Government. When in answer to these frank observations the Emperor telegraphed to him *en clair* about idiotic Bavarian loyalists, and the incredible folly of these good people, Eulenburg reminded him that they had a private cipher of their own and begged him to use it for such indiscreet communications. He told him that his subjects did not approve of his incessant travelling tours ; when a critical debate in the Reichstag on Army Estimates was approaching, and the Emperor intended to remain in Rome during it, Eulenburg wrote to him to say he must come home, for Germany would resent his not being on the spot, and back he came. When, on a Norwegian cruise, the Emperor drafted a very ill-advised despatch on foreign relations, and gave it to Eulenburg, who was representing the Foreign Office, for transmission, Eulenburg refused to send it. No one but the Queen ever ventured to speak to him with such uncompromising frankness or with better effect, and never once did the Emperor resent his plain speaking. All this was to the good ; what was not so salutary was that intrigue was as native to Eulenburg as his romantic and artistic tastes, and to his influence may reasonably be attributed much of the Emperor's tortuous and insincere dealings. Loyalty to him was a meaningless term ; times without number he belittled his friends to the

Emperor with deft feminine touches while to them he professed the warmest affection. He wanted him to have no
other friends except himself — again a typical characteristic
of the Emperor's — and, though by no means a place-
seeker, he was jealous of any possible influence that might
supplant his own, and thus he raised for himself a host
of enemies eager for revenge. Of his homosexual propen-
sities, over which subsequently so ruinous a scandal arose, it
is possible that the Emperor knew nothing, though, considering their long intimacy, this does not seem very probable.*

Such in outline was this brilliant and brittle person who
for many years had an influence with the Emperor far ex-
ceeding that of any other of his intimates, and who in 1893
accompanied him to Cowes. Shortly before their arrival
a situation had arisen between England and France which
threatened, unless handled with tact and firmness, to become very dangerous. The French had unwarrantably occupied territory adjacent to Siam and were blockading
Bangkok. Their object was to obtain a coterminous frontier
with India, and Lord Rosebery's object, as Foreign Secretary, was to secure a buffer state between the frontiers. The
Queen, seriously alarmed, recommended him to get the support of the Triple Alliance ; he, on the other hand, thought
it more consonant with England's prestige to settle the matter without its backing. On the day after the Emperor's
arrival he telegraphed grave news to Osborne, for the French
persisted in the blockade, though Siam had tendered un-
qualified submission, and requested the English gunboats
to leave. He asked that the German Ambassador, Count
Hatzfeldt, who was in attendance on the Emperor, should
come to see him at once, in order that he might talk over

* Haller, *Philip Eulenburg*, i. pp. 41–213 ; Ludwig, *Kaiser Wilhelm II*, pp. 29,
31 ; Bülow, *Memoirs*, 1897–1903, p. 218.

the situation with him and sound the views of the predominant partner in the Triple Alliance. That evening the Emperor was dining on the Prince of Wales's yacht, and the Queen sent across her secretary, Sir Henry Ponsonby, who reported to the party what had happened and showed him Lord Rosebery's decoded telegram. The Emperor was in high spirits that night ; these high spirits were sometimes very embarrassing. He read the telegram and, observing the grave faces round him, broke out into hearty laughter. He slapped his uncle on the back, and said he would soon be seeing active service in India.

The party broke up after that, and the Emperor went back to the *Hohenzollern* with Eulenburg. He began to appreciate the seriousness of the situation, and at once construed Lord Rosebery's desire to see the German Ambassador into an invitation to Germany to associate herself with England in a protest to France and, if necessary, in action against her, and at last that bright dream of his political ambition seemed likely to be fulfilled ! But instead of exultation it was panic that surged up within him. That deep-rooted timidity, that conviction of inferiority, which he so often strove to hearten with bombast and bragging, asserted themselves and utterly overwhelmed him. As if war was already declared between Germany and England on the one side of France and Russia on the other, he cowered before the frightful prospect, bewailing himself that Germany would not be able to withstand the combined Russian and French forces on land, and that the English fleet, even if reinforced by his own, was not equal to the fleets of the enemy. That was terribly humiliating to him personally, for he had been very eloquent lately on the magnificent growth of his young navy. Eulenburg administered consolation : he told him that probably the dispute would be settled amicably. Then, since Count Hatzfeldt was prevented by illness from going to see Lord

Rosebery, the Emperor sent for Count Metternich, Chancellor of the German Embassy, and told him to go up to London next morning in his place and make himself extremely cordial. Suddenly the crisis calmed down, and, before Metternich could reach London, Lord Rosebery telegraphed again to say that the French had agreed to the constitution of a neutral zone, which was all that was required : details to be settled in due course.*

An immense relief : the mercurial Emperor instantly recovered his spirits and devoted himself to sport. He had entered his yacht the *Meteor* against his uncle's newly built *Britannia,* for the Queen's Cup. He remained on deck the whole time in ceaseless activity, now at the wheel, now hauling on the sheets : rather risky, thought his uncle, for a man with only one serviceable arm. Eulenburg spent some hours during the race with the Prince of Wales, and in his Diary wrote a detailed account of the long *tête-à-tête* conversations which they held. They talked of the Siamese crisis now happily over : the Prince considered that France had been instigated by Russia, 'which,' he said, 'is explicable by the antipathy of the Tsar to my nephew Willy.' They talked of German colonial expansion. The Prince could not understand the Emperor's 'colonial game.' He could not get colonies of any importance, and had better give it up. They talked of the German naval programme : surely, said Eulenburg, that ought not to disturb mighty Albion, especially since Germany had not renewed the secret treaty with Russia, and was looking towards England with the eyes of friendship. They talked of the German Ambassador Count Hatzfeldt, who, the Prince said, was quite out of touch with the Court and with influential circles.

* *Letters III,* ii. pp. 284–292 ; Lee, *King Edward VII,* i. p. 669, note ; Haller, *Philip Eulenburg,* i. pp. 142–144 ; Eckardstein, *Ten Years at the Court of St. James's,* p. 56.

Now it is true that the Prince was not always a model of discretion, but it seems unlikely to the point of impossibility that he should have been so unguarded with a man whom as yet he barely knew, but who was his nephew's most intimate friend, and who (as immediately happened) would be certain to tell him what he and the Prince had talked about. Eulenburg's Diary, in fact, must be taken to be an account of what he told the Emperor that the Prince had said rather than of what the Prince did say. Eulenburg affirms that in these hours he got to know the Prince 'thoroughly'; he considered him crafty, malicious and sinister and emphatically no friend to Germany. Now and for ten years yet his influence over the Emperor was very strong, and we may safely conclude that he used it to intensify his dislike and distrust for his uncle.*

The Emperor had the pleasure of defeating the *Britannia* and lifting the Queen's Cup and in reaction from his abject collapse the night before, and in relief at the solution of the Siamese crisis, his exuberance soared. Next day the *Britannia* raced the American yacht *Satanita,* and the Emperor followed in the victorious *Meteor.* The wind dropped, and, since the Queen was giving a state dinner that night in honour of her grandson, the Prince signalled to him that the race must be abandoned in order that they should get back in time. The Emperor objected; the programme, he signalled back, should be carried out. In consequence the two reached Osborne when dinner was over, and their hostess was not pleased.† Altogether this was not a very happy family gathering, and the Emperor sent neither letter nor telegram to his grandmother to say how much he had enjoyed himself. Probably he had not done so. True, he

* Haller, *Philip Eulenburg*, pp. 144–147.

† Lee, *King Edward VII*, i. p. 672 ; but the statement that this race, of which the course was the circuit of the Isle of Wight, did not start till 8 P.M. is scarcely credible.

had won the Queen's Cup, and it was pleasant to have defeated Uncle Bertie and to have been so rude to him. But it was a horrid moment when he thought that his dream of procuring an alliance with England might involve a conflict with Russia and France. It required a great deal of bawling and self-assertion to fortify himself against that internal conviction of inferiority. Not otherwise does some small, timorous boy whistle loudly to keep up his courage when he crosses a churchyard in the gloaming.

Off he went to more congenial gatherings with his chosen friends (no woman among them) for imperial romps and shooting parties, where every schoolboy prank of his was hailed as a masterpiece of humour. When cruising on his yacht he made obese and elderly generals do physical drill on deck to keep them fit. Sometimes he joined them, weight-lifting with his powerful right arm, but more often he was puckishly inclined, and, as these panting and perspiring gentlemen were squatting with bent knees and arms extended, he came behind them and pushed them over. There was music in the evening or conjuring tricks or variety entertainments : Count Goerz was always popular with his famous imitations of animal noises, and he and Kiderlen acted the Siamese twins connected by an enormous sausage, and when the fun was at its height he turned all lights off, to the Emperor's huge delight. But every Sunday morning he preached to the ship's company; this sermon, he told Archbishop Davidson, was mainly written for him by his chaplain, but he revised it, 'leaving out all dogmatic trash.' *
Or there was a shooting party at the Wusterhausen Palace of Frederick William I, where, in pious memory of his stern ancestor, the Emperor and his guests sat on hard wooden chairs when the day's slaughter was over and smoked clay pipes. As master-costumier to his intimate circle he de-

* Bell, *Randall Davidson*, i. p. 240.

signed and prescribed a pretty shooting uniform for himself and his guests ; its most striking features were a coat with high military collar and brown jockey boots with silver spurs. Thus clad the party stood in a compact circle round their loaders facing towards all points of the compass, while deer, hares and rabbits were driven into an enclosure from which there was no escape and shot down as they crouched huddling against the palisade. Or there was a pheasant-shoot, and it was a memorable day when the Emperor sanctioned the erection of a block of granite in the preserves of Prince Donnersmarck on which was to be inscribed in letters of gold : 'Here His Majesty William II brought down His Most High's fifty-thousandth animal, a white cock-pheasant.' Or he would spend a week at Liebenberg with the friend of his heart. All the female members of Eulenburg's family absented themselves for his visit, and there was shooting during the day, and rich programmes for the evening. Eulenburg promised 'to sing some of his loveliest songs,' and Lieutenant von Chelius played to them in the evening, and Captain Count Moltke ('Beloved Kuno,' as 'Phili' termed him) played also, and Lieutenant von Hülsen was deft with conjuring tricks, and Count Kalnein made puns, and Herr Varnbüler drew caricatures, and the Troubadour sang his ballads sitting at his piano in those tall brown boots with silver spurs. Despatches arrived daily from the Foreign Office at Berlin, but the All Highest dealt with those very summarily : marginal comments such as 'Liar' : 'Rubbish' : 'The man's a scoundrel' : 'Those mutton-heads in my Reichstag,' were sufficient, and in this graceful company he could lay down the burden of his omnipotence and his haunting sense of fear.*

* Ludwig, *Kaiser Wilhelm II*, pp. 143–144 ; Haller, *Philip Eulenburg*, i. pp. 81, 82, 189–191.

CHAPTER VII

THE Emperor was to celebrate his thirty-fifth birthday on January 27, 1894 : he had been given his commission in the 1st Regiment of the Guards on his tenth birthday, and this was his Military Jubilee and a very special occasion. There was one distinction which he much coveted — namely, to hold rank in the British Army. As Admiral in the British fleet he could wear the uniform of Nelson, which made him dizzy with pride, but that was not enough : he wanted to be dizzy on land as well as at sea. He had always had a passion, he wrote to his grandmother, for 'H.M. Redcoats,' and he set about achieving his ambition by asking her if, as Chief of his Dragoon Guards (an honour he had bestowed on her at Osborne in 1891), she would allow him to place Uncle Bertie *à la suite* of the Queen's Own German Regiment. Simultaneously he told Colonel Swaine, the British Military Attaché at Berlin, that he himself would like nothing better than to be made honorary colonel of a Highland regiment. Colonel Swaine transmitted this desire, but unfortunately there seemed to be nothing that the Queen liked less, and she was very firm about it. She wrote to her secretary : 'This would never do, and he is an Admiral. The Queen thinks he is far too much spoilt already.'

The Prince of Wales joined in. The Queen had told him of William's wish to appoint him *à la suite* of her German Dragoon Guards, and he felt very much flattered, and hoped she would allow him to accept the honour, for he, like his nephew, had a huge appetite for new uniforms. And would she not return this compliment by making William a British General on the occasion of his Jubilee ? No foreigner had ever before been made an honorary colonel of an individual British regiment, but to make him a General in the Army would be easy, and would please William immensely. But the Queen still disliked any notion of the sort, and with true impartiality said that 'this fishing for uniforms on both sides is regrettable.' In any case the Duke of Cambridge, as Commander-in-Chief, the Duke of Connaught and the Secretary for War, Mr. Campbell-Bannerman,* must be consulted first. Meantime she had to answer the Emperor's offer to appoint the Prince of Wales *à la suite* in her German regiment, and she telegraphed to her Ambassador in Berlin that her son was much gratified by this kind wish, but that it would not be possible to appoint the Emperor honorary colonel in any regiment of her Army.

The affair was now becoming truly momentous. Colonel Swaine told the Emperor how delighted his uncle was, but omitted to say that the Queen considered the idea of making him an honorary colonel quite impossible. The Prince, who had got his new uniform, thought this unfair : William certainly ought to be given one too : and he returned to the attack. He wrote not to his mother (perhaps he had heard her strictures about this fishing for uniforms) but to her secretary, complaining that she had asked for his opinion, but when he gave it, listened to somebody else who knew nothing about the passion in Germany (as well as England) for uniforms. He now thought that the Emperor ought to be made a Field-Marshal. The objection that the Emperors of Austria and Russia would then want to be made Field-

* Later Sir Henry Campbell-Bannerman.

Marshals also 'wouldn't wash for a moment.' William was the Queen's eldest grandson, and that was reason enough for making him anything. Meantime the Duke of Cambridge had signified his strong approval of this step, and the Queen appealed to Lord Salisbury, her late Prime Minister, to know whether the Emperor had not been made an Admiral in order to avoid giving him military rank. Lord Salisbury couldn't remember hearing anything about that, but with bland detachment he suggested that *if* the foreign policy of the present Government was to keep on good terms with Germany, it would be wise to gratify him. That hint from the Opposition evidently had its effect on the Queen : she thought William must be made Something, for, rather fussed, she wrote to her secretary : 'What is to be done about this hateful business of Hon. General or Field-Marshal ?' And how tiresome that Lord Salisbury couldn't remember !

Finally Lord Rosebery joined in. Lord Salisbury's little sarcasm about the foreign policy of the present Government had reached him, and it was evident that the late Prime Minister did not quite understand the question and must be instructed. Germany, he explained, was very jealous of England and would strongly resent the Emperor receiving any favour from her. Such an appointment would prevent rather than promote good feeling between the nations, and he considered that the Queen's veto was based on sound judgment.

The Queen had now consulted everybody whose opinion she valued, two of her sons, the Commander-in-Chief, her Ambassador and her Military Attaché in Berlin, her late Prime Minister, the Secretary for War and the Secretary for Foreign Affairs. She did not consult her present Prime Minister, Mr. Gladstone, because she did not value his opinion. But even now she could not make up her mind.*

* *Letters III*, ii. pp. 344–355.

The Emperor's birthday in January, commemorating his Military Jubilee, for which this distinction had been designed as a present from his grandmother, went by, February and March went by also, and still nothing was done : it really looked as if no distinction was to be granted him. The Queen gave her Prussian Dragoons a set of kettledrums, and it seemed as if he would have to be content with that *Ueberraschung*. But in the middle of April Lord Rosebery once more wrote to her on the subject. The Prince of Wales and the Duke of Cambridge had been pressing him again about it. But he stuck to his previously expressed opinion. The Queen had already given her grandson the highest possible distinction in making him an Admiral of her fleet, and if this was added 'there will be nothing left to give, and it will simply leave the German Emperor unsatiated while yet young.'

The Queen received this letter in Florence : she was about to start for Coburg to attend the marriage of two grandchildren, the Grand Duke Ernest of Hesse-Darmstadt, son of Princess Alice, and Princess Victoria Melita of Coburg, daughter of the Duke of Edinburgh, who had now succeeded to the throne of Coburg. The Emperor was to be present, and he had the pretty thought of sending to Coburg a squadron of the Queen's Prussian Dragoons to meet and salute her with the National Anthem and a roll of their new kettledrums. Perhaps this little attention did the trick ; in any case before he left she made him Honorary Colonel of the 1st Royal Dragoons, which she had previously declared to be quite impossible. This joyful surprise overwhelmed him : 'I am moved, deeply moved,' he wrote, 'at the idea that I now too can wear beside the Naval uniform the traditional British "Redcoat." ' He looked forward impatiently to meeting his brother officers, and, in spite of the awkward happenings last summer, would much like to come to Osborne again for Cowes week.*

Considering the extreme reluctance of the Queen to grant him any military rank in her Army, the conclusions that the Emperor, looking back on the past from the tranquillity of Doorn, drew about the wisdom and far-sightedness of her action are truly amazing. 'It is a very extraordinary fact,' he wrote, 'that British Statesmen never realised what a happy combination Providence had procured for them in placing the eldest grandson of the great Queen Victoria on the throne of Germany. Her Majesty did so ! By investing me with the rank of Admiral of the Fleet and granting me the Honorary Colonelcy of the splendid Regiment of the Royals, she intended to create relations with our forces for the benefit of both.' † English statesmen, it is true, had not always been enthusiastically grateful to Providence for placing him on the German throne, but it was a singular delusion to suppose that the Queen indulged his passion for uniforms in order to create amicable relations between the armies of England and Germany.

A matter of no less importance than William's British uniform had occupied the Queen's attention at this great royal gathering at Coburg. One morning the young Tsarevitch Nicholas had come to her room hand in hand with yet another of her grandchildren, Princess Alix, sister of the Grand Duke of Hesse, and she learned that they were engaged to be married. Though she said she was 'quite thunderstruck' the news did not really surprise her, for she knew of the young man's attachment, and there can never have been a more agreeable thunderbolt. The Tsarevitch was first cousin to the Duke of York, now heir presumptive to the English throne, on his mother's side, and the future

---

* Letters III, ii. pp. 391–396.   † Waters, Potsdam and Doorn, p. 96.

Tsarina was his first cousin on his father's side. Instantly the Queen took them both under her matriarchal wing, for this would be a family alliance of the greatest magnificence. Princess Alix, hitherto quite negligible and barely mentioned in the Queen's Diary, suddenly became a most important personage. She inspired her grandmother with the warmest affection ; never again is she spoken of without the most endearing epithets, and mingled with that warmth was an almost reverential regard, for would not darling Alicky, 'gentle little simple Alicky,' become the 'Great Empress of Russia' ? She and her future husband paid the Queen a visit of many weeks in the following June and July, and Alicky pledged herself to pay another during the winter. Her necessary change of religion into the Russian Church, the remoteness of her future home and other considerations, which at first had seemed drawbacks, sank into nothingness. Relations with Russia, which had often given cause for anxiety before now and had brought the two nations to the brink of war, were quite certain to improve. Even Lord Rosebery, who was slightly heretical about the value of these royal alliances, thought that this one would have a good effect on the peace of Europe.*

The Emperor came to Cowes again this year (1894) only a week after Princess Alix had left, and made his first call on his grandmother dressed in his new English uniform. There was a military review in his honour at Aldershot, he led a squadron of his new regiment, and felt himself, he said, indeed to belong to 'the thin Red Line of England,' as well as to his own thicker one. This time he enjoyed himself enormously, and wrote an ecstatic letter to his grandmother telling her that the Cowes week was his real holiday, and that he hoped to come again next August 'and be able to bear home that only trophy that I really covet and I

* *Letters III*, ii. p. 400.

work for through the whole of the year, "Her Majesty's Cup." ' How he adored dear old Osborne, 'which my *entourage* has come to love as much as I do, fascinated by the kind and benevolent *accueil* of the much revered Queen !' What a success the review was, the charming pavilion, the perfect arrangements, the splendid view, kind Uncle Arthur (the Prince of Wales did not attend this function), the attractive field-day, the splendid Royals, the nice comrades in arms, who looked upon him as one of themselves ! . . .

Certainly a most gushing and affectionate preamble, but that was not all he had to tell the Queen. He knew what a long stay the Tsarevitch and his affianced had made in England, and nothing could be more disagreeable than the notion of amity between England and Russia. He would not have been true to his own nature if he did not give his unsuspecting grandmother a word of warning. The Tsar, he told her, was suffering from Bright's disease. Cholera was raging in Western Russia. Troops were being massed on the eastern frontier of Germany, and by next year there would be ten army corps and eight cavalry divisions stationed there. This was very ominous : it was believed in Germany that Russia was intending to strike some unexpected blow in the East, and in order to prevent Germany 'from helping anybody they are going to attack, they have marshalled the enormous forces on our frontier.' * This was truly characteristic, for the coming marriage was likely to draw England and Russia closer together, and so it was his duty to warn the Queen what Russia was about. She was a treacherous nation not to be trusted : it would never do for England to make friends with her.

The Prince of Wales fully shared his mother's views as to the political value of his niece's engagement, and within a few months a chance presented itself to him personally of

* *Letters III*, ii. pp. 423-424.

assisting in the improvement of Anglo-Russian relations. During October Tsar Alexander III became desperately ill, and the Tsarina, the Princess of Wales's sister, begged her and the Prince to come out to her. They started at once for Livadia in the Crimea, but the Tsar was dead before they got there. Princess Alix was at once received into the Orthodox Church, and then the portentous funeral journey to St. Petersburg began. Swathed in crape and flags and glittering with royal insignia, the imperial train started on the first stage to Moscow, taking three days in transit, and passing from the warmth and sunshine of the south into the bitter cold of Central Russia. Every day it halted for intercessions for the dead, and then moved solemnly on past stations crowded with kneeling townsfolk and peasants from the country round, and at night it was guarded by a cordon of troops. There was a state service in the Archangel Church in the Kremlin, and once more the train continued its journey to St. Petersburg, where, after eleven days of continuous obsequies, the interment took place in the Cathedral of St. Peter and St. Paul. Always by the side of the new Tsar Nicholas was the Prince of Wales, and for the final ceremony the Duke of York came out from England to join his father. Then there was the Tsar's marriage to follow. According to Russian ecclesiastical use it could not take place between Christmas and Easter, and so a week later mourning was suspended and it was celebrated in the chapel of the Winter Palace. The Prince had ascertained that the Tsar, like the Kaiser, would appreciate being appointed honorary colonel of a British regiment : to this the Queen at once assented without any demur, and on his wedding day he was made Colonel-in-Chief of the Scots Greys.*

This was all very disagreeable for the Emperor. He had warned his grandmother that treacherous Russia was medi-

* Lee, *King Edward VII*, i. pp. 689–690.

tating hostile action to England in the East, and had massed troops on the German frontier so that he could not come to the rescue, but she had not paid the slightest attention, and now his uncle, that insidious, encircling man, was spending a solid month in Russia, *en famille* with the new Tsar, masking under the guise of sympathy and support his political plans for an English *rapprochement*. An added sting, superficial but intensely irritating, lay in the fact that he himself had particularly wanted the colonelcy of a Scottish regiment, and what had been denied him, in spite of his tincture of Stuart blood, had been accorded to tinctureless Nicky. On his way home the Prince broke his journey to stay with his sister, the Empress Frederick, at her new house at Cronberg, and William went there to greet his presence in Germany. But it may be presumed that it was an invincible curiosity as to what had been going on during this month of highly undesirable intimacy rather than cordiality that took him there.

The Emperor's suspicions as to the real reason for his uncle's prolonged stay in Russia were quite justified. Neither the death of his wife's brother-in-law nor the subsequent marriage of his niece would have induced him to endure those weeks of mourning and requiem and funeral bakemeats, followed by that brief flash of barbarically splendid nuptials, unless he had been firmly convinced that he was rendering his country a service of which nobody else was capable. The theory that friendly and consanguine kings produced co-operative peoples was a matter of faith to him, and in this instance it was shared by English Ministers. Lord Rosebery wrote to him that he had done wonders for England, Russia and the cause of peace throughout the world. Sir William Harcourt forecast that the intimate and friendly relation which he had established had reversed the previous mutual hostility between the countries, and the

Press endorsed that verdict. To the Emperor the prospect of friendship between England and Russia was a fresh link in that encirclement of Germany which, he was convinced, was his uncle's chief political aim. He was still most anxious to procure the friendship of England, but, as always, a necessary condition was that she should not be friends with any other nation.*

What was to be done, and how ? To supplant the wicked uncle in the confidence and affection of the Tsar and instal himself there in his place was the end in view, and he started that remarkable correspondence which continued till the eve of the Great War. He told the Tsar that he had begun very well. Democratic deputations had presented addresses to him demanding reforms : he replied that these were 'unrealisable imaginings,' and that he would unflinchingly maintain the principles of autocracy. 'A capital speech,' wrote William, 'it made a deep impression everywhere.' †

His next approach was characteristic. He had written not so long ago to his beloved grandmother warning her of Russian designs in the East, and telling her that he was powerless to check them owing to the massed forces on his frontier. He now constructed a brilliant inversion of the same theme, turning it upside-down, and he wrote to Nicky as his devoted and affectionate friend : 'I shall certainly do all in my power to keep Europe quiet, and also guard the rear of Russia, so that nobody shall hamper your action towards the far East.' . . . Could they not meet on their yachts in the Baltic during the summer, 'and have a quiet little chat' ? ‡

That would do for a beginning, and William turned his

---

* Lee, *King Edward VII*, i. p. 691.
† *The Kaiser's Letter to the Tsar*, p. 8. These are subsequently referred to as *Willy-Nicky Letters*.
‡ *Ibid*. pp. 10, 11.

eye elsewhere. A bright spot was the tension between England and France. France was known to be planning an expedition from the west coast of Africa across the continent into the Upper Nile valley, which since the fall of Khartoum had remained in the hands of the Mahdi and his spiritual successor the Khalifa. Sir Edward Grey, early in 1895, stated in the House of Commons that such an expedition into Egyptian territory would be regarded in England as an 'unfriendly act,' and the hostility of the French Press was so violent that the Queen doubted whether it would be advisable for her to travel through France and spend her spring holiday at Cimiez.* A second bright spot was that there might be trouble ahead for England in South Africa. The English Uitlanders in the gold-mining district of the Witwatersrand were bitterly complaining of their unfranchised status, and President Kruger had sent a telegram to the Emperor on the occasion of his birthday in January, hoping that the Transvaal and Germany would form ties of the closest friendship. A third bright spot was that the friendly relations lately established between England and Russia by his encircling uncle were not developing in the way he had feared. Very violent Anglophobe articles had been appearing in the Russian Press, and it was supposed that they were written by a man with whom the Tsar was on most friendly terms. They had produced so bad an impression in England that the Queen wrote privately to the Tsar hoping that he would let it be known that he disapproved of them. These possible sources of trouble for England, it must be understood, were agreeable to the Emperor, only because they threatened the cordiality of her relations with other countries. On the other hand, it was disagreeable that Lord Salisbury had again become Prime Minister, for he put a positively derisory price on the value of an alliance with

* *Letters III,* ii. pp. 462, 474.

Germany : in fact he put no price on it at all. But the Emperor wrote to the Queen wishing her joy on his return to power, and looked forward to much joy of his own in his coming visit to Cowes in the summer of 1895 ; it was always the zenith of his holiday, he said, to visit her in her 'quiet comfy old house.' *

It proved to be another species of zenith. He brought with him among his escorting ships two new cruisers, the *Weissenburg* and the *Wörth,* named after Prussian victories over France in the war of 1870. The day after his arrival was the anniversary of the battle of Wörth (August 6), in which his father had inflicted a heavy defeat on Marshal MacMahon. That morning he went across to this ship and made a speech to the officers and crew on the invincibility of the German army. Perhaps he intended this to be a tactful hint to his English hosts that Germany was their true friend, but more obvious was the extreme offensiveness of such a proceeding, and the Prince of Wales was furious. Later on the same day was the race for the Queen's Cup, in which the Emperor's *Meteor* was to sail against the Prince's *Britannia.* When the handicaps were announced the Emperor telegraphed to the Royal Yacht Club : 'Your handicaps are perfectly appalling,' and scratched the *Meteor.*

The first day therefore of this visit seemed to reach the zenith of infelicity, but in fact the zenith was not nearly yet attained. Next morning the English Press took up that deplorable speech the Emperor had made on the *Wörth,* strongly condemning it. Nothing could have been in worse taste, was the general view, than to make these insolent allusions, while he was a guest in English territorial waters, to a nation with whom England was on friendly terms, and an article in the *Standard* frankly recommended him to get back to his own dominions before issuing any fresh insults.

* *Letters III,* ii. pp. 508, 535.

Meantime the Queen had consulted the Emperor as to the successor of Sir Edward Malet as British Ambassador in Berlin, and, perhaps rather incautiously, she had suggested that Lord Wolseley might be appointed. This was incautious because the Prime Minister had told her that it was felt that he would be the most suitable man to succeed the Duke of Cambridge, lately resigned, as Commander-in-Chief : it was therefore possible that he would prefer that to any diplomatic appointment. The Emperor, as his grandmother said, had 'jumped at' the chance of having so distinguished a soldier as ambassador, and she realised that William would be grievously disappointed if he was not sent. The choice of the two posts was then offered to Lord Wolseley, and he accepted that of Commander-in-Chief without a moment's hesitation. It was awkward : and in the rather thundery atmosphere which had now developed the Queen thought it wiser not to tell William that Lord Wolseley had declined Berlin till his visit was over, and then wrote him a long, careful letter from Balmoral explaining that she had done her best, but that Lord Wolseley had preferred the post of Commander-in-Chief. She was very sorry.*

A further incident, the most infelicitous of all, is related in detail by Baron Eckardstein. It never had any existence in fact, but, since Eckardstein's account has been often quoted and has passed into historical currency, it is perhaps worth while to show that it is a fantasy of his own. He tells us that Lord Salisbury, then Prime Minister, desired to discuss the Eastern question personally with the Emperor and to propose to him the partition of the Ottoman Empire between England, Germany and Austria. An interview was arranged on board the *Hohenzollern* for August 8, but the launch which was to have conveyed Lord Salisbury broke down and he was an hour late. He came panting up the

* *Letters III*, ii. pp. 545, 547, 549, 561.

companion-ladder full of apologies, but found the Emperor in so bad a temper at having been kept waiting that, when he brought forward his proposals, which must have led to England joining the Triple Alliance, there was only a 'heated altercation,' and the opportunity was lost for ever.*

This account is a tissue of impossibilities. It states that Lord Salisbury was anxious to make an alliance with Germany, whereas throughout his holding of office, though wishing to be on good terms with her, he consistently disapproved of any binding relations. It states that he intended personally to open a discussion about the partition of the Ottoman Empire with a man whom he radically distrusted, instead of first employing the constitutional channels of Foreign Office communication between Ministers. It implies that the partition was to be arranged without consulting either Russia or France. If it had been carried through it must have led to war. As a minor point, Eckardstein states that this interview took place on August 8 : Lord Salisbury had gone back to London on August 7.

What really took place was as follows. Lord Salisbury had already had an interview with the Emperor of a friendly and complimentary kind on his arrival on August 5. He made no such proposals as Eckardstein attributes to him. Next morning he wrote his name in the Emperor's visiting book on the *Hohenzollern*. At 3.30 P.M. that day he received a telephone message from the yacht that the Emperor would see him at 4 P.M. He supposed that this was a mere civility in response to his call that morning, and replied that he was to have audience with the Queen at that hour and could therefore not attend, and in the evening he wrote to the German Ambassador making his apologies. He went back to London next morning, and on the following day

---

* Eckardstein, *Ten Years at the Court of St. James's*, pp. 57–60 ; Lee, *King Edward VII*, i. pp. 670, 671.

(August 8) the Queen telegraphed to him that 'William is a little sore' at having waited for him for some hours, supposing that he would have come when his audience with her was over. She suggested that he should explain this to Hatzfeldt : he had already done so, but did it again. Lord Salisbury was not therefore late for this momentous interview, nor was he received by an exasperated Emperor whose loss of temper made discussion impossible, for he had not appeared at all, and there was no such interview. Doubtless Eckardstein had heard that there had been a misunderstanding about Lord Salisbury seeing the Emperor on August 6 : the rest was all his own.*

This ghastly visit lasted for six days. The Emperor had deeply offended public opinion in England, and in private, on the social side, he was guilty of such rudeness to the Prince of Wales as could hardly have been forgiven in an ill-bred boy who, it might be hoped, would learn decent manners before he became a man. Unfortunately the Emperor was thirty-six, and clearly he had not learned them yet. At the Royal Yacht Club he behaved as if all the functions of the Commodore and committee were vested in him ; on the *Hohenzollern,* with English guests present, he alluded to his uncle as 'the old peacock.'

The Prince had tried to get on with his nephew, but he had long disliked him and was continually offended by his rudeness and arrogance. He was very quick-tempered himself, and it is idle to suppose that he always maintained an attitude of impenetrable cordiality. In addition to this natural antipathy between the two, the Emperor was extremely jealous of the man who was so genial and whom everybody liked, and for the sake of indulging this jealousy he committed these quaint stupidities. If his object had been to pick a quarrel with England and to render any future *rap-*

* *Letters III,* ii. pp. 547, 548. Private information.

proachement more difficult, he could not have behaved himself in a way better calculated to attain that end, and yet all the time his real aim was precisely the opposite. Then, feeling himself unappreciated and misunderstood, he left these ungracious shores, and, as if following the advice of the *Standard,* that he should launch any further insults against the French from his own territory, he went a tour with the Empress to the battlefields of Alsace and Lorraine. In order to remind the French that his speech to the sailors on his cruiser was a reasoned performance, he unveiled a statue of his father at Wörth, and declared that the provinces were part of the German Empire for ever. The ironical dispositions of destiny decreed that twenty-three years later he and they were simultaneously severed from it, he by his self-sought exile in Holland, and the provinces by their reunion with France.

CHAPTER VIII

THE Emperor was addressing his young soldiers : 'There is but one law,' he said, 'and that is my Will.' Ample justification for this claim was forthcoming : 'I am the instrument of the Most High.' At the swearing-in of recruits he told them that they must be prepared to shoot down their fathers and mothers if he bade them so to do. He often made similar announcements in official speeches, delivered with remarkable eloquence in that forced, harsh voice.

Those confident assertions of his own omnipotence gave comfort to that inferiority complex, his from birth, but they had established, by constant repetition, a hold of their own, and we must figure these two extreme convictions as co-existing in that brilliant and unstable mind and simultaneously functioning there. At one end of his psychological spectrum lay so august a sense of his own importance that conceit is no term to apply to it : at the other a panic fear that all the world was conspiring against him. He invariably suspected others of designs corresponding to his own. Just now, as Lord Salisbury noticed with a sort of detached interest, he was under the curious delusion that the British Government were engaged in anti-German intrigues with Russia.* It might therefore be conjectured, as a working hypothesis, that the Emperor was busy on precisely analogous adventures. That hypothesis soon justified itself.

* *Letters III*, ii. p. 586.

Throughout the year 1895 it had seemed likely that trouble was brewing in the Transvaal over the franchise which the Uitlanders reasonably demanded and which President Kruger refused to grant. Before the year was over the storm broke. Dr. Jameson, the Administrator of Rhodesia, collected five hundred irregular troops and, on December 30, crossed the frontier of the Transvaal in the expectation that the Uitlanders would rise. The moment the news reached the Colonial Office Mr. Chamberlain telegraphed to the Cape that Jameson must be recalled, and officially repudiated the raid. Jameson disregarded the order, the Uitlanders did not support him, and on January 1, 1896, his force surrendered to the Boers.

It was a great opportunity for the Emperor to intervene with his usual recklessness. He had already been interesting himself in Transvaal affairs, for Dr. Leyds, Secretary of State to Kruger's Government, was in Berlin, and both the Emperor and his Chancellor had been in conference with him, while out at Pretoria the German Consul, Herr von Herff, had the ear of the President and did all in his power to stiffen the Boer Government against granting the British demands.* Despite Chamberlain's official repudiation and the personal assurance of Sir Frank Lascelles, the newly appointed Ambassador in Berlin, that the raid was a complete surprise to the British Government, the Emperor wrote to the Tsar : 'Now suddenly the Transvaal Republic has been attacked in a most foul way, as it seems not without England's knowledge. I have used very severe language in London, and have opened communications with Paris for common defence of our endangered interests, as French and German colonists have immediately joined hands of their own accord to help the outraged Boers. I hope you will also kindly consider the question, as it is one of upholding treaties

* Lee, *King Edward VII*, i. p. 719, note.

once concluded. I hope all will come right, but come what may, I never shall allow the British to stamp out the Transvaal.' *

These sentiments merit consideration. It must be conceded that the phrase 'not without England's knowledge' had some justification, for, though the British Government at home had no previous knowledge about the raid, it is certain that Mr. Cecil Rhodes, Prime Minister at the Cape, knew that something of the sort was on foot, and gave it the sanction of his silence. But why should the Emperor, given that he desired to be friends with England, appeal to France and Russia to join him in the defence of their endangered interests ? Partly, no doubt, it was his passion for flamboyant gesture, but below that ran the tortuous policy which he adopted four years later during the South African War. Now, as then, he hoped that these two allied countries, whose friendship was such a source of uneasiness to him, would by their threatening language towards England drive her into the Triple Alliance. Now, as then, neither France nor Russia was disposed to threaten.†

Next day (January 3, 1896) the news came to Berlin that the raid had failed and that the raiders had been made prisoners. The Emperor summoned an Imperial Conference, at which were present his Chancellor, Prince Hohenlohe ; the Foreign Secretary, Baron Marschall von Biberstein ; Admiral Hollman, and Herr Kayser, the Colonial Secretary. Holstein, Political Director of the Foreign Office, who would never meet the Emperor if he could possibly avoid it, sat in an adjoining room. The accounts of what took place differ in many details, but the vital points are manifest.

The Emperor, in a frenzy of excitement and impetuosity,

---

* *Willy-Nicky Letters*, p. 30.
† Eckardstein, *Ten Years at the Court of St. James's*, pp. 85, 86.

opened the proceedings by proposing to declare a German
protectorate over the Transvaal. Troops must be landed in
Delagoa Bay (Portuguese territory) and sent to Pretoria. It
was a slight shock to him when the Chancellor said : 'That
would mean war with England.'

The instrument of the Most High had never thought of
that, and there was nothing he desired less. A bright idea
struck him and he instantly replied : 'Yes, but only on land.'

Exactly what he meant by that nobody has been able to
explain. Would he tell England (of whose fleet he was an
Admiral) that she must keep her Navy at home, and not
interfere with his troopships ? She might refuse : and his
proposal fell to the ground. But something must be done
to calm his frenzy, thought his Ministers, some piece of
sensationalism must be devised to satisfy his craving for self-
assertion : something characteristic and dramatic, but nothing that could conceivably produce a rupture. The ingenious Herr Kayser had a bright idea : how about sending a
telegram to Kruger congratulating him on having captured
the raiders ? A capital notion : the Emperor approved, and
Marschall drafted it :

'I sincerely congratulate you that you and your people
have succeeded, by your own energetic action and without
appealing for help to friendly Powers, in restoring order
against the armed bands that broke into your country as dis-
turbers of the peace, and in safeguarding the dignity of your
Government from attacks from without.'

This was an anticlimax after the Emperor's first proposal,
but it served to satiate him. He substituted for the phrase
'the dignity of your Government' the stronger expression 'the
independence of your Government.' He had some faint
foreboding that his grandmother would not be pleased, for,
as he signed the telegram and passed the pen to Marschall
for his signature, he very sensibly observed : 'You have put

an end to my visits to Cowes.' But, when the publication of this message was hailed by a tremendous chorus of approbation from the Anglophobe German Press, the Emperor said it was entirely his own idea.* He continued, intermittently, to think well of it, and ten years later he told Mr. Frederick Whitridge that he had convinced Cecil Rhodes that it was the only honourable course for him to take. Rhodes pounded the table with his fist and cried : 'If I had been in your place, I, too, should have sent that telegram to Kruger.' † Later the Emperor changed his mind, and we find in his *Memoirs* that, instead of claiming the merit of it, he asserts that he was forced by his Ministers to sign it against his will.

In his official capacity, the Emperor never did a sillier thing than this ; it was of the same *genre* as, in private life, his ill-bred impertinence towards his uncle, when, all the time, he wanted to be friends with England. It raised a storm of indignation there, which, since the telegram was signed by him, was quite properly directed against him personally. More dangerous was his proposal, which was taken up by the German Government, to order a cruiser to proceed to Delagoa Bay and land colonial troops to march through Portuguese territory to Pretoria. This came to nothing, for the Portuguese Government at once stated that no German troops would be allowed to land.

There was still this preposterous telegram to be dealt with. As the Emperor had signed it personally and dealings with him might be personal also, who could possibly be so competent to conduct these as his grandmother ? She drafted her letter to him on the very day that he sent his telegram :

---

* Ludwig, *Kaiser Wilhelm II*, pp. 173–175 ; Lee, *King Edward VII*, i. pp. 721–722 ; Waters, *Potsdam and Doorn*, p. 138.

† Private Diary of Mr. Frederick Whitridge.

'MY DEAR WILLIAM,

'As your Grandmother to whom you have always shown so much affection and of whose example you have always spoken with so much respect, I feel I cannot refrain from expressing my deep regret at the telegram you sent President Kruger. It is considered very unfriendly towards this country, which I am sure it is not intended to be, and has, I grieve to say, made a very painful impression here. The action of Dr. Jameson was of course very wrong and totally unwarranted ; but considering the very peculiar position in which the Transvaal stands to Great Britain, I think it would have been far better to have said nothing. Our great wish has always been to keep on the best of terms with Germany, but I fear your Agents in the Colonies do the very reverse, which deeply grieves us. Let me hope that you will try and check this. . .

'I hope you will take my remarks in good part as they are entirely dictated by my desire for your good.

'VICTORIA, R.I.' *

A kinder, wiser and more withering letter could hardly have been devised. As a sister Sovereign the Queen told him — she did not argue — that he had, no doubt unintentionally, been very unfriendly to her people ; and his grandmother added that she was writing thus for his good. With the most violent vituperations going on in the English Press at the telegram, and whoops of frantic applause in the German Press, a 'good snub,' such as the Prince of Wales begged his mother to administer to William, might have produced disastrous results. She knew that William was genuinely fond of her and that at heart there was nothing he desired more than to be friends with England, and her letter was one that must certainly cause him to pause and think before

* Letters III, iii. pp. 8, 9.

committing himself to any further folly. The result of what he had done was to inflame public opinion, as voiced in the Press, to a very dangerous pitch, and it was of the highest importance that he should keep quiet and let it cool down. The Queen was quite as angry with him as was his uncle, but the 'good snub' would have been almost as injudicious as the telegram itself. 'Those sharp cutting answers,' she told the Prince, 'only irritate and do harm, and in Sovereigns and Princes should be most carefully guarded against. William's faults come from impetuousness (as well as conceit) ; and calmness and firmness are the most powerful weapons in such cases.' *

The Queen's letter had the desired effect. It deflated William. It brought him to his senses, and in his answer to his grandmother, flying to the opposite extreme, he adopted a tone of misunderstood benevolence. His motives, he wrote, had been of the most exalted nature. Though a week before he had told the Tsar that the raid had been made 'not without England's knowledge' and had asked for his co-operation with France and Germany to uphold the independence of the Transvaal, he now said that he knew that the British Government had done all they could to stop the raiders. The raiders were rebels. He proceeded :

'Now to me Rebels against the will of Her Most Gracious Majesty the Queen are to me the most execrable beings in the world, and I was so incensed at the idea of your orders being disobeyed, and thereby Peace and the security of my subjects being endangered, that I thought it necessary to show that publicly. It has, I am sorry to say, been totally misunderstood by the British press. I was standing up for law, order and obedience to a Sovereign whom I revere and adore, and whom to obey I thought paramount for her subjects. Those were my motives and I challenge anybody

* *Letters III*, iii. p. 20.

who is a Gentleman to point out where there is anything hostile to England in this.' *

Indeed, his defence of his telegram was almost as silly as the telegram itself, and his own later account of the meeting at which it was compiled and signed and sent gives the lie to it. He there maintained that his Chancellor insisted on its being sent, because his subjects were murmuring that he had secret sympathies with England, that he was the tool of his grandmother, that he obeyed her dictation. He was told that he must make an end of all that and, by this telegram, assert his independence.† He yielded, he said, very reluctantly ; yet at the time he told the Queen that he sent this same telegram in order to show his indignant sympathy with her ! If he had been so aghast and horrified at those execrable rebels, would he not have expressed his sentiments to her directly and at once instead of congratulating Kruger ?

The Queen, herself the most truthful of women, was really sorry that William should be like that. Such explanations, to put it as mildly as possible, were 'lame and illogical' ; in effect he said 'What I have written I have not written.' She sent his letter to Lord Salisbury, who agreed and respectfully advised her 'fully to accept all his explanations without enquiring too narrowly into the truth of them.' He stuck to his opinion that the Emperor had been trying for six months to frighten England into joining the Triple Alliance, and there was now fresh evidence for that, for Count Hatzfeldt had just proposed a secret agreement between Germany and England, and had given him many warnings 'of the danger of isolation.' What the Emperor himself really feared was the isolation of Germany. ‡

---

* Lee, *King Edward VII*, i. p. 726.   † William II, *My Memoirs*, p. 81.
    ‡ *Letters III*, iii. pp. 20, 21 ; Eckardstein, pp. 82–84 ; Ludwig, *Ex-Kaiser Wilhelm*, pp. 173–177.

Meantime the hope that the Prince of Wales's visit to Russia would prove the foundation of a better understanding between the two countries had quite dried up. It was a feeble growth at the best, and the death of M. de Giers, the Russian Foreign Minister, and the appointment in his place of the notorious Anglophobe Prince Lobanoff swept the withered stalks away. In the spring of 1896 the start of the British expedition up the Nile for the reconquest of the Sudan, which had been in the hands of the dervishes since 1885, caused the old ill-feeling to flare up again. A convenient opportunity for this start was found in the fact that an Italian force had been defeated by the Abyssinians at Adowa, and their base at Kassala was threatened : an advance therefore by English and Egyptian troops into the Sudan as far as Dongola would relieve the pressure on the Italian base. The Queen was most discreet over this : she telegraphed to Lord Salisbury that she highly approved of this kind plan 'to help the poor Italians' ; * but they both knew that the ultimate object of the crusade was the recapture of the Sudan. Unluckily Russia and France were equally aware of the English intentions — it would be an insult to their intelligence to suppose otherwise — and France had already issued a permit from the Colonial Office for an expedition under Captain Marchand to cross Africa eastwards from the French Congo and, with the design of forestalling the English, to plant the French flag at some point on the White Nile in the Southern Sudan. With an Anglophobe Foreign Minister in Russia the jealous animosity of the two allied countries was in full blast again, and the German Emperor had been busy in his secret correspondence with the Tsar with further tortuous devices for shepherding England into the fold of the Triple Alliance by encouraging Russian mis-

* *Letters III*, iii. p. 33.

trust. The English fleet, he told him, was sulking (skulking ?) in a suspicious manner round the Dardanelles : probably England meant to seize Constantinople and put an end to Russia's supreme ambition : and once more he reminded him that if Russia meditated an advance to the East, he would keep Europe quiet. Then, turning to another quarter that gave him uneasiness, he uttered a very solemn warning on the impossibility of the Tsar ever being *intime* with France. Republican France, still stained with the blood of its King and Queen, was an enemy to Christian kings and emperors. 'Nicky, take my word on it, the curse of God has stricken that People for ever. . .' * As always, a psychical transfusion of bad blood into the veins of other nations was his prescription for procuring their friendship with Germany.

After the Kruger telegram it was impossible that the Emperor should pay any visit to England in 1896, but the Queen still clung to the value of intimacy between related royal families in promoting the friendliness of nations, and asked the Tsar and his wife with their baby daughter to pay her a long informal visit, *en famille,* at Balmoral in September. So informal was it to be that at first she did not mean to have any Minister there, nor even the Russian Ambassador, M. de Staal, unless the Tsar wished it : the visit was to be a private one to the Empress's grandmother.† But it was felt that if the Prime Minister did not meet the Tsar the visit would have a bad rather than a good effect, for it would look as if, though he was an affectionate grandson, political relations were strained ; and so Lord Salisbury was bidden. It was privacy and intimacy, however, which she hoped would be fruitful, and the conditions were very propitious. The Anglophobe Prince Lobanoff had died very suddenly three

* *Willy-Nicky Letters*, pp. 25, 26. † *Letters III*, iii. pp. 63, 64.

weeks before, the day after her grandchildren arrived marked the longest reign of any British sovereign, and the Queen thought it 'most satisfactory' that news had just arrived from the Sirdar that Dongola had been captured — though, since Russia looked very coldly on this expedition up the Nile, there was possibly another side to that. . . Tenderly and constantly she embraced her grandchildren : Nicky was all amiability and affection, Alicky was darling and sweet and simple, and dear baby Olga was a beautiful big child. They had drives, and teas in bothies, and large family parties, and a cinematograph record was taken of the matriarch in her bath-chair with the clan of children and grandchildren moving about the terrace ; commemorative trees were planted, and the two Sovereigns had cosy talks together. Never had a reigning monarch made so long and intimate a visit to the Queen ; but when it came to business, to ascertaining what the Tsar really thought about the causes of international dissensions, and how he was prepared to act, she could get nothing out of him. She spoke of the possibility of deposing the Sultan, but Nicky would say no more than that he thought it would be a risky business. She asked him whether this 'apparent great friendship' between Russia and France was a defensive move against the Triple Alliance, and he assented : Russia and France both felt themselves isolated. She spoke of his coming visit to Paris, wanting to get at his political attitude towards the French, but had no better luck. He 'did not relish the French' ; he was much shocked at their irreligious spirit, he intended to visit Notre-Dame as soon as he got to Paris and give an interview to the Archbishop. That was all very proper ; the Prince Consort had just the same feeling about the French, but it had no relevance to what she wanted to know. He would not talk about the Sudanese expedition, 'but seemed to have no objection,' and 'he seemed to regret William's injudicious policy and Germany's inimicality' towards England. His affectionate gentleness, his drifting instability, as of thistledown, was even more baffling than William's truculence, for the Queen rightly conjectured that behind that was a real desire to be on good terms with England, whereas it was impossible to tell what lay behind this vague amiability. Lord Salisbury fared no better : he understood the Tsar to say that he had no objection to England's remaining in Egypt, but then he broke off and changed the subject 'as though he felt that he was committing an imprudence.' So dissatisfied was the Queen with the result of these talks that she wrote to the Tsar, not forty-eight hours after he had left for Paris, asking him to show the French that he disapproved of their continual hostility to England. But he gave her no assurance as to that, and the Tsarina in a brief telegram from Darmstadt merely sent tender love and said that Willie had lunched with them. No doubt the thistledown received some vigorous puffs.*

The Queen's Diamond Jubilee was to be celebrated in June 1897, and, six months before, she caused it to be announced that no crowned heads were to be bidden : the King of Siam said he was coming, and he had to be told that he was mistaken, and all ambassadors were informed. But the German Emperor, who had declared after the last visit to Cowes that he had done with England, began to fear that England had done with him, and, though knowing that no sovereigns were to be asked, he wrote to the Queen to inquire whether she would wish him and his wife and some of their children to attend ; in that case they would lay their plans for the summer accordingly. He also got his mother to write an intercessory letter for him to the Prince of Wales, who was horrified at the prospect. With bitter memories of holidays at Cowes in his mind, when William had con-

* Letters III, iii. pp. 68–103 ; Willy-Nicky Letters, pp. 37, 38.

stituted himself 'Boss,' he felt sure that the Queen would much regret it if she allowed him to come. 'He would arrive also,' he said, 'with an enormous suite and would try to arrange things himself, and endless trouble would arise.' But he need not have disquieted himself, and he was assured that there was not the slightest fear of her permitting it. 'It would *never* do for many reasons, and the Queen is surprised that the Empress should urge it.' *

The Empress Frederick would surely not have urged it a month later, for another reason against it had been added to the many that the Queen had in mind. Crete, whose inhabitants were in the main Greek and Christian, formed part of the Ottoman Empire, and now, when they appealed to the Greek Government to free them from that yoke and annex the island, King George yielded to the popular enthusiasm and permitted the landing of Greek troops in Crete, who attacked the Turkish garrisons : these, on the advice of the Powers, had been much reduced in the previous autumn. Probably King George would have been deposed if he had refused ; possibly also he trusted too much to the value of royal relationships, for the Greek dynasty was very well connected. He himself was the son of the King of Denmark, and brother of the Tsar's mother and of the Princess of Wales : his wife, Queen Olga, was the Tsar's aunt, and the Crown Prince Constantine had married Princess Sophy, sister of the German Emperor and granddaughter of Queen Victoria. But it would have been wiser of him to risk abdication and trust to so many royal families for his reinstatement. Instead he consented to an act of war on Turkey, and this the Powers could not possibly tolerate. Again, if they allowed Crete to sever herself from Turkey, other Christian states of the Ottoman Empire, notably Macedonia,

* *Letters III*, iii. pp. 116–127.

would rely on their benevolence and dismember it them-selves, producing a situation which the Powers had always feared to face. The most that they could do was to get the Sultan to grant autonomy to Crete under Turkish suzerainty, and to couple with this the order to Greece that her troops should instantly evacuate the island. Greece refused, and for the moment the six Powers, as the Emperor remarked, became *les six impuissances*. Not content with this most imprudent persistence, Greece encouraged her countrymen in Macedonia to revolt, and on April 17, 1897, Turkey de-clared war on her. There was no serious fighting, for the Greek armies melted away before the Turks, and in three weeks the whole of Thessaly from Mount Olympus to the port of Volo was in their hands and the way was open to them to reconquer the entire kingdom.

This again was impermissible, but as yet the Powers could not arrive at any joint intervention. At one time it seemed possible that Russia, France and England would come to-gether, but Russia backed out, and without her France re-fused to act with England, while England alone was per-fectly powerless to influence the Sultan, who regarded her as his bitterest enemy. Russia's withdrawal had been due to German pressure, and now the Emperor, backed up by the Tsar on one side and Austria on the other, commanded the situation.* 'We Emperors,' as he had once told his grand-mother, were keeping firm together, he was in control, and was quite determined to make no intervention till all Greek troops had left Crete. Personal feelings stiffened him, for he detested the King of Greece, he had quarrelled with his sister Sophy because on her marriage she had been received into the Greek Church, and he was quite callous as to the fate of king and kingdom. Harsh and vindictive as was his attitude, he was certainly right in principle, for if Greece

* *Letters III*, iii. pp. 156, 161.

to her, and she only paid an indemnity of £4,000,000 to
Turkey. Subsequently Prince George of Greece, the King's
second son, was appointed Governor of Crete.

In June of this year (1897) Count Bernhard von Bülow
became Secretary of State in the Foreign Office at Berlin
in place of Baron Marschall, and, later, succeeded Prince
Hohenlohe as Imperial Chancellor. He had a great personal affection for the Emperor, he appreciated the quickness with which he grasped salient points in politics, but he
was alive to the harm done by his indiscreet and bombastic
utterances. He recognised in these the dope the Emperor
administered to his own internal quakings. Like the
Queen, Bülow deplored the antagonism between him and
his uncle, as being likely to become a real source of danger
in the future. Trained in the school of Bismarck, he was
eager to restore the ancient amity between Germany and
Russia, but he deprecated the Emperor's view that this was
desirable because it would make the English 'burst with
envy.' To spite one nation was not, he told him, the object
of making friends with another, but never could he drive
out of the Emperor's system that pleasure of giving annoyance to others by some successful stroke, which was so characteristic of his warped mind. In those intimate conversations which the Emperor held with his new Foreign
Secretary about the navy which he was set on building, that
difference between them came out strongly. To Bülow's
way of thinking, a large navy was necessary to Germany for
the protection of her vastly increased trade and commerce
overseas, but to the Emperor, though he still cherished the
dream of a solid alliance with England, the idea of rivalling
her navy and of the perturbation this would cause her was
an ingredient in his enthusiasm for building his own. He
could not view the growing might and prosperity of his Em-

pire save in terms of the relative declension of other Powers, and, though this was partly due to his conviction that there was a general European conspiracy to encircle Germany with foes, he took a definite pleasure in the set-backs of others. Fearfully jealous himself, he loved to inspire jealousy and by the light of personal experience picture to himself the sufferer's pangs.*

Yet, by another of the strange contradictions in his most exasperating character, there existed, side by side with his intimations of omnipotence and his incurable inferiority complex, a childlike eagerness to be appreciated, and he did not resent the most unpalatable truths being told him about the performances of which he was most proud, provided this was done with a certain tact and friendliness. Eulenburg discovered this long ago, and passed on the hint to Bülow when first he took office as Foreign Secretary, with some other discerning observations. If you have a policy to recommend of which he disapproves — so ran this counsel — he will act on it if you can make him fancy that he thought of it himself. You can get your way with him if you mingle appreciation with your criticism : with this sauce he will swallow with avidity what he would otherwise reject : he is like a child, who must occasionally be praised for his efforts or else he will be discouraged and show temper. This was perfectly true, and even where the Emperor's personal talents were concerned he did not mind the most withering condemnation provided that it contained some small tribute to his genius. When, for instance, this passion for building a navy took hold on him, it could be easily foreseen that he would be bound to design a battleship himself which would render obsolete all else that sailed the seas. He set to work on his plans, he furnished this vessel of the future with en-

* Bülow, *Memoirs,* 1897–1903, pp. 56, 338, 440, etc.

KAISER WILLIAM II

gines of incomparable speed and guns of unheard-of range, and he sent the unique design, when complete, to Admiral Brin, Italian Minister of Marine, who, till the Emperor took the field, was supposedly the foremost of naval architects. Admiral Brin reported on it as follows :

'The ship which your Majesty has designed would be the mightiest, the most terrible, and also the loveliest battleship ever seen. She would surpass anything now afloat, her masts would be the tallest in the world, her guns would out-range all others. And the inner appointments are so well arranged that for the whole crew from the captain down to the cabin-boy, it would be a real pleasure to sail on her. This wonderful vessel has only one fault ; if she were put on the water she would sink like a lump of lead.' *

Criticisms like this, as Bülow said, the Emperor never re-sented. Though his ship would sink like a stone, it was otherwise immeasurably magnificent, and the cabin-boys would be comfortable. That was a tribute to his genius ; and, above all, this criticism was private : nobody (except perhaps Admiral Brin) would laugh at him. But he writhed under public censure and ridicule, and the English Press had, since the Kruger telegram, been discharging broadsides of both at him : indeed, he had requested his grandmother to stop the publication of *Punch*. She did not think that was quite within her province, but she felt very keenly that these ceaseless attacks on him and his nation were dangerous and inflammatory stuff, and she asked her old friend Sir Theodore Martin, who had written the monu-mental biography of the Prince Consort, to interview pri-vately, but in her name, the editors of the leading English papers, and beg them to stop this baiting.† The Emperor was much gratified at its cessation, but, having found out

* Bülow, *Memoirs*, 1897–1903, pp. 3, 66. † *Letters III*, iii. p. 224.

that the Queen had used her influence, he wrote witheringly
to the Tsar of the so-called 'Free Press' in England.*

This English olive branch, however, was a little blighted
by a fresh scrap between him and his uncle. Admiral Baron
von Senden und Bibran, the Emperor's elderly naval aide-
de-camp, who had always been with him at Cowes, often
came to England as his private messenger, carrying letters
to his grandmother and picking up bits of news for his
master. He was an adept in tactlessness, and held forth, in
such London clubs as made him an honorary member, about
the immense fleet Germany was building. One morning
the Prince of Wales found him in the equerries' room at
Marlborough House, and, being busy, had not much to say
to him : probably he was rather curt. So the Admiral on
his return told the Emperor that the Prince had been deliberately rude to the All-Highest's messenger and therefore, vicariously, to the All-Highest. The Emperor instantly
made a formal complaint to the British Ambassador, and
requested him to inform Lord Salisbury of his uncle's insults. The Prince was furious : he denied having been rude
at all, and said that such an accusation was an insult to
him. He wished the Admiral to be told that he wanted
never to see him again. This energetic reply was a slight
shock, and the Emperor made the very original suggestion
that his grandmother should act as arbitrator between them.
Such quarrels between grown-up men would be purely
ludicrous if they were private persons ; as it was, it was a
real hindrance to the establishment of good relations between the countries that the ruler of one should be perpetually showing his teeth to the heir apparent of the other.†

The quarrel blew over without any domestic arbitration,
the Emperor recovered his temper, and in April 1898 he sent
a congratulatory telegram to the Queen on Kitchener's vic-

* *Willy-Nicky Letters*, p. 53.   † Lee, *King Edward VII*, i. pp. 734, 735.

tory on the Atbara. Conversations took place just at that time between Mr. Chamberlain, the Colonial Secretary, and Count Hatzfeldt, German Ambassador in London, on the subject of Germany's desire for colonial expansion and coaling stations for her mercantile marine. Hatzfeldt's report of these made a favourable impression on the Emperor, his passion for original diplomacy, winging itself with imagination, soared like an eagle, and a month after he wrote to the Tsar a fantastic history of what had passed. As testimonial to his own profound sagacity he told him that the cessation of the attacks on him in the English Press had made him think that something was in the air, and here it was, an offer of a 'treaty of alliance with England.' This offer was *urgently* renewed,' but 'by his commands coolly and dilatorily answered in a colourless manner.' For the third time (all this apparently taking place within a month) the proposal was made, 'putting a *certain short term* to my definite answer, and accompanied by such enormous offers showing a wide and great future opening for my country that I think it my duty to Germany duly to reflect before I answer.'

A slight qualm of dizziness is excusable. Chamberlain's conversations with Hatzfeldt were merely exploratory, but the Emperor solemnly informed the Tsar that the Colonial Secretary had made offers of an alliance to the German Ambassador on his own initiative and twice urgently renewed them with magnificent promises of colonial concessions and a request for an immediate reply. He knew this was not true, and what could have been the object of so fantastic a fairy-tale ? We find the answer towards the end of this remarkable letter. He wrote :

'What the tendence (sic) of this Alliance is, you will well understand, as I am informed that the Alliance is to be with the Triple Alliance and with the addition of Japan and

America, with whom pourparlers have already been opened ! What the chances are for us in refusing or accepting you may calculate yourself !

'Now as my old and trusted friend *I beg you to tell me what you can offer me and will do if I refuse.* Before I take my final decision and send my answer in this difficult position I must be able to see clearly, and clear and open without any back thoughts must your proposal be. . . But time is pressing, so please answer soon.' *

Here then is the explanation. The Emperor represented to the Tsar that a splendid offer of alliance with England had been made him, in order to see what bid the Tsar would make for his refusal of it. But no bid came, since Russia, very sensibly, did not believe there was anything to bid against.

The Emperor, undiscouraged, returned to this offer of alliance from England. Actually there had been none, and so he began to make proposals himself. He got his mother to write to the Queen. 'I do know for a fact,' she said, 'that William *is most* anxious for a *rapprochement* with England and *hopes* with all his heart that England *will* COME forward in some sort of way, and meet him half-way.' This was a rather different aspect of what was going on from the account that the Emperor had given to the Tsar. William's proposals arrived, but the British Government considered the territorial demands to be excessive and rejected them. The Emperor, deeply offended, declared that his efforts had been treated with 'something between a joke and a snub.' † Then he had to explain to the Tsar why this splendid treaty of alliance with England, so urgently pressed on him, for his refusal of which he had been prepared to bargain, had come to nothing, and again the aid of imagination must be invoked, for how could a self-

---

* *Willy-Nicky Letters*, pp. 53, 54.   † *Letters III*, iii. pp. 258, 262.

respecting Emperor explain that no such alliance had ever been offered him ? He wrote :

'England has still now and then reopened negotiations with us but has never quite uncovered its hand : they are trying hard as far as I can make out, to find a continental army to fight for their interests ! But I fancy they won't easily find one, at least not *mine* ! Their newest move is the wish to gain France over from you, and they in consequence have suddenly decided to send the Duke of Connaught to the French Army Manœuvres. . .' *

Overwhelming evidence ! And how characteristic was this final touch ! All his diplomatic efforts had failed, but he could at least warn the Tsar that England was trying to detach France from Russia. Possibly the Tsar might believe that. It was worth trying.

* *Willy-Nicky Letters*, pp. 57, 58.

CHAPTER IX

THE Emperor continued to find ample opportunities for the exercise of his diplomatic gifts : no pie was complete without his finger. He prided himself on having learned his statecraft from Bismarck, but he cannot have been a very attentive pupil. Bismarck is credited with having said that telling the truth is a valuable device for a diplomatist who wishes to camouflage his real design, because his opponent often draws the conclusion that under cover of apparent frankness he is telling lies : in any case it sets him guessing. The Emperor misapplied this maxim, and seemed to hope that by telling lies he might induce people to think that he was telling the truth, which they seldom did. He did not attempt to frame any constructive policy for his own country ; his notion of constructiveness was, by making mischief between other countries, to wreck any constructive policy of theirs. That Germany should stand secure and foursquare amid the ruins of Europe was the ultimate Utopia.

In September 1898 came the news that Kitchener had annihilated the dervish armies at Omdurman, and the Sudan once more was in Anglo-Egyptian hands. Instantly the Emperor telegraphed to his grandmother his warmest congratulations : 'I was able to announce the joyous tidings to the regiments assembled at the foot of the Waterloo Column on the Place d'Armes of Hanover, who gave three cheers for you and their brave British comrades.' * Im-

* *Letters III*, iii. p. 274.

mediately afterwards the Sirdar came upon the minute
French expeditionary force under Captain Marchand, which
had reached Fashoda in the summer and had hoisted the
French flag on the Upper Nile. The French refused to
haul it down, and for the next six weeks the situation required delicate handling. The chance of serious developments suited the Emperor's ideas very well, for it was most
desirable that France and England should quarrel. Luckily,
M. Delcassé, the keystone of whose policy for the next seven
years was to establish good relations with England, had
lately become French Foreign Minister. He was quite
determined that the dispute should be amicably settled, and
gave that assurance to the British Government. Eventually
he and Lord Salisbury found a formula which would enable
France to evacuate without humiliation, and the Emperor,
since that chance was over, seized the opportunity for making trouble between France and Russia. He had heard that
Count Muravieff had counselled the French to withdraw,
and so he wrote to the Tsar that Russia had given her
'*friends and allies* a mortal blow and brought down their
ancient prestige never to rise again.' The Moslem population (he was touring in Palestine) called this withdrawal
France's second Sedan : 'France will never forget that piece
of friendship,' he said, 'nor will she ever feel very grateful
for it. . .' Then followed some discouraging observations
on the condition of France generally. The Dreyfus case
was in the courts, and in what a quagmire France was floun-
dering ! 'The whole of Europe reeks with the stench !
Shewing how far the corruption, lying and dishonour has
already gained in the nation and above all in the army.'
In the East France was looked upon as a dying nation, and
the friendship of a dying people was no use to Russia. His
own reception there, however, had been astounding : 'never
had a Christian — Giaour — Monarch been fêted and re-

ceived with such unbounded enthusiasm,' while the hatred
for the English was growing more and more intense. As
for England's conduct in Crete, 'a certain power was using
us all as catspaw to help her to get Crete or Suda Bay.' *
That would do : he had told Nicky that Russia had deeply
offended France ; that France was looked on in the East
as a moribund nation ; that England was detested there,
and that never had a Christian king been received with such
enthusiasm as himself. Nicky would surely see where his
true interests lay.

But nobody was yet aware of the Emperor's tone towards
England in this instructive correspondence with the Tsar,
and he had been making himself very agreeable to his English relations. He had twice congratulated the Queen on
the success of the Sudanese campaign, and he had been most
enthusiastic about the ships of the Mediterranean squadron,
which he had visited at Malta. Nearly three years had
elapsed since that deplorable telegram to Kruger, during
which time he had never been asked to England, and in the
autumn of 1898 the Queen consulted Lord Salisbury about
inviting him again. He was in favour of it, for England's
isolation was becoming almost too splendid, and, with
France still dangerously bitter about the Marchand affair,
'it was desirable,' he thought, 'that the world should believe
in an understanding between Germany and England.' He
therefore advised that if the Emperor showed any wish to
be asked, the Queen should indulge him.†

She went cautiously about this (for had not William declared that he would never set foot in England again ?),
and sounded him through his mother and the British Ambassador in Berlin, and a hint also was conveyed to him
that his uncle had spoken nicely about him. The Queen
did not want him for the celebration of her eightieth birth-

* *Willy-Nicky Letters*, pp. 60, 68, 69.　　　　† *Letters III*, iii. p. 312.

day in May, nor did anybody want him to come to Cowes again for the regatta, but she said she would be very glad to see him at Osborne some time in the summer. He jumped at the idea, he was all eagerness, and in his Christmas letter to her, with thanks for the pretty flower-pot she had sent him, of course he told her, as he had told the Tsar, in what a deplorable state of corruption were the French army and the French Government. Russia, he assured her, was no better : she was on the verge of a financial collapse, for during the last fifteen years she had been keeping her troops on the Prussian frontier almost at war strength, and the country was in the grip of famine and typhus : it was easy to see why the Tsar had asked the Powers to join in a peace conference ! 'Anyhow,' he concluded, 'our relations are now so clearly defined, and the necessity for respecting our mutual interests and the possibility of mutual help are gaining more and more on our subjects, that I look out with absolute confidence into the coming year.' So much for the Tsar as soon as England beckoned again ! *

He was forty years old on January 27, 1899, and his grandmother wished 'he was more prudent and less impulsive at such an age.' In answer to her birthday letter, he recalled with sentimental flutings how dear Grandpapa Albert used to swing the 'tiny weeny little brat' in a table-napkin, and she to nurse him. God had enabled him to bear this heavy burden of sovereignty. Moreover, he had 'the happy knowledge that you observe and follow my career with the love of a very, very kind Grandmother. And I venture to believe that when the Sovereign will sometimes shake her wise head over the tricks of her queer and impetuous colleague, the good and genial heart of my Grandmother will step in and show that, if he sometimes fails, it is never from want of goodwill, honesty or truthfulness, and thus mitigate the

* *Letters III*, iii. pp. 312–324.

shake of the head by a genial smile of warm sympathy and interest ! ' *

The Queen must have wondered at so curious a selection of the qualities he claimed for himself, and have faintly recalled the goodwill of the Kruger telegram and the honesty and truthfulness of his explanation of it. But presently her shakings of the head were unmitigated by any semblance of a smile, for William became more cantankerous and unreasonable than perhaps ever before.

Trouble began in February. The Duke of Coburg, Prince Alfred, lost his only son, and the question of his successor had to be settled. The next in order of birth of the Prince Consort's sons was the Duke of Connaught, and after him his son Prince Arthur. The Queen was quite determined that the Duke should not give up his military career in England, while if Prince Arthur was to inherit, it would be only reasonable that he should finish his education in Germany. He had no intention of taking up this inheritance, but he could not renounce his rights till he was twenty-one. He was then quite certain to do so, and thus his education in England would have been broken to no purpose.† The duchies accepted the Duke of Connaught as his brother's successor, and he, being abroad and not knowing what his mother felt about his acceptance, informed the Coburg Government that 'He and his house are prepared to fulfil their duties towards the Duchies.' ‡ Unfortunately the Emperor had not been consulted, and in consequence he flew into a violent rage and threatened that the Reichstag should veto the appointment. That roused the Queen, for she held that the succession was a matter for her, as head of the family, to settle, and that the Emperor had got nothing to do with it. Legally she may have been right, but as Saxe-Coburg was part of Confederated Germany it would have been very awkward if she nominated the Duke and the Emperor refused to accept him. However, as she was quite determined not to allow the Duke to succeed, and as his son was equally determined to renounce his rights when he came of age, there was no difficulty in his withdrawing, and this suited everybody. The young Duke of Albany, son of Prince Leopold, took up the succession, and the Emperor approved. He had asserted himself : he had shown he would stand no opposition to his will.

Meanwhile he had been pursuing that jungle-path which he continued to believe had been blazed for him by Bismarck, and which he hoped might render Russia and England permanently antagonistic. He had already done his best to sow distrust of England in the minds of the Tsar and his Ministers, and now, abandoning this correspondence for a while,* he took up the complementary task of inducing England to believe that Russia was engaged in sinister designs against her. He plied Sir Frank Lascelles, British Ambassador in Berlin, with tales of secret Russian intrigues in the East, which Sir Frank duly communicated to the British Government. The Queen did not believe them, but from her knowledge of William she drew the very plausible deduction that he was pouring into the ears of the Tsar and his Ambassador at Berlin, Count Osten-Sacken, the same type of tale about England as he was telling Sir Frank Lascelles about Russia. In fact she deduced the essential spirit of the Willy-Nicky letters. It seemed a case where she might do well to intervene directly, instead of employing diplomatic channels.

But where was the use of writing to William as she had

* From December 1898 till June 1900.

done after the Kruger telegram ? He would only exhibit a tissue of fulsome explanations or denials which nobody could believe. So she wrote to the Tsar instead :

'I feel I must write and tell you something which you ought to know and perhaps do not. It is, I am sorry to say, that William takes every opportunity of impressing upon Sir F. Lascelles that Russia is doing all in her power to work against us ; that she offers alliances to other Powers, and has made one with the Ameer of Afghanistan against us. I need not say that I do not believe a word of this, neither do Lord Salisbury nor Sir F. Lascelles.

'But I am afraid William may go and tell things against us to you, just as he does about you to us. If so, pray tell me openly and confidentially. It is so important that we should understand each other, and that such mischievous unstraightforward proceedings should be put a stop to. You are so true yourself that I am sure you will be shocked at this.' *

That was the simplest plan : whatever the Tsar's private answer was, her letter bore good fruit a little later, and she went off to Cimiez for her spring holiday, Lord Salisbury being there at the same time. It had been noticed that the Emperor was particularly prone to take offence when his grandmother was in France, suspecting Anglo-French machinations, and his ill-humour this year was intensified by the disturbance about the Coburg succession, and by the fact that she had refused to let him come to England with his younger children for her eightieth birthday on May 24. She was quite firm about that, for she did not want him any more than she wanted him at her Diamond Jubilee. She meant serenely to enjoy this ripe anniversary without the risk of those disturbing elements which William was apt to introduce into the bosom of the family. Four days after

* Lee, *King Edward VII*, i. pp. 741, 742, note.

this peaceful birthday she received a truly astonishing letter from him. He enumerated the benefits he had showered on England : how, as Colonel in the British Army, he and his troops around the Waterloo Column at Hanover had cheered her and their British brothers-in-arms after the victory at Omdurman ; how as Admiral of the British Fleet he had visited Malta as a sign of his affectionate interest in her Navy ; how he had defied public opinion in Germany by receiving Cecil Rhodes ; and in return for all this, Lord Salisbury, always the villain of the piece in the Emperor's eyes, had treated Germany in the dispute now going on about Samoa with utter disregard of the rules of civility between great Powers. He cared no more for Germany than for 'Portugal, Chile or the Patagonians,' and Germany was very bitter about it. His own honest labour to make the two countries understand each other had been thrown away, his arduous work of years had been destroyed ; shame and pain and a heart bleeding in silence had been his personal lot. . .

And then came the real point of the letter. The Queen had not let him and his children come to England for her birthday. Germany, he said, would have understood that such was the dutiful visit of a grandson to his grandmother, but in the fever of public opinion against England it would be utterly impossible for him to come there on a mere pleasure trip to Cowes. He could not therefore come to England at all.*

This letter had contained a schedule of Lord Salisbury's offences about Samoa, and before answering it the Queen sent it to him for inquiries. He returned a categorical refutation of all the Emperor's complaints : there was not a word of truth in any of them. She enclosed Lord Salisbury's memorandum in her reply to William, which was in

* *Letters III*, iii. pp. 376-378.

her very finest style : 'Your letter, I must say, has *greatly astonished* me. The tone in which you write about Lord Salisbury I can only attribute to a temporary irritation on your part, as I do not think you would otherwise have written in such a manner, and I doubt whether any Sovereign, ever wrote in such terms to another Sovereign and that Sovereign his own Grandmother, about their Prime Minister. I should never do such a thing, and I never personally attacked or complained of Prince Bismarck, though I knew well what a bitter enemy he was to England and all the harm he did. . .*

'Your visit to *Osborne*, not to *Cowes*, I looked on as a visit for my *birthday*, as I was not able to receive you on the day itself. I can only repeat that if you are able to come, I shall be happy to receive you at the end of July or August.' †

What was to be done ? William saw that his grandmother was very much vexed with him, and that must be put right. Anxiously he read her letter again, and noticed that she said that a visit in the summer would count as a birthday visit. It would be 'for' her birthday, and Germany would understand why he went. So, though he had just asserted that any visit this year was impossible, he found it could be managed, and a date was fixed for July : owing to an accident to the Empress the visit was postponed till November. The Queen most cordially hoped that nothing would prevent it.

During the summer of 1899 relations between England and the Transvaal grew critical. President Kruger still refused to give the Uitlanders any effective measure of franchise, though the taxes of the Transvaal were mainly borne

---

* This was not strictly correct. The Queen, appealing to King William I of Prussia to avert war with Austria in 1866, told him he was being deceived by one man (Bismarck).

† *Letters III*, iii. pp. 381, 382.

by them, and after weeks of increasing tension and repeated warnings the British Government decided in September to send out troops from India and artillery and cavalry from England, to meet the menace of the Boers, who were massing troops on the Natal frontier. The situation was watched very jealously by France and Germany, for their colonial interests were expanding and those of England crossed them at many points.* President Kruger no doubt trusted that they would intervene on behalf of the Boers ; it became evident that he had no intention of granting the reforms demanded by the British Government, and that his real design was to set up a South African Republic. In order to anticipate the arrival of troops from England Kruger issued an ultimatum on October 9, 1899, that, unless all English troops sent out since June were recalled and no fresh troops were landed in South Africa, a state of war would exist as from October 11. This ultimatum remained, of course, unanswered.

The war, therefore, had been in progress some six weeks when the German Royal Family, Emperor and Empress and two of their sons, were due at Windsor on November 20. The Samoan dispute had been settled some ten days before, and the Queen and her grandson exchanged most cordial telegrams of mutual satisfaction and expressed the customary hopes and wishes for national friendliness. But simultaneously there occurred yet another of those personal scraps between the Emperor and the Prince of Wales which threatened the cancellation of the visit altogether, and it looked as if the Queen's hope that nothing would prevent it would be unfulfilled. The Prince found that his nephew intended to bring in his suite Admiral von Senden und Bibran, with whom he had quarrelled two years ago for having carried false tales to the Emperor of his uncle's rude

* *Ibid.* p. 392.

treatment of him, and the Prince had sent a message to the British Ambassador in Berlin that he wished to have nothing more to do with the Admiral. Up flared the venerable quarrel again ; the Prince said he would not meet such a *'potin,'* and Eckardstein was entrusted with the mission of seeing what could be done about it in Berlin. He interviewed the Foreign Secretary, the Lord Chamberlain, and finally the Emperor, who only said 'If I go to England at all this autumn, I shall take whom I like with me.' The thwarted diplomatist hurried back to London, and, after calling in the friendly offices of the Duchess of Devonshire, he drafted a proposed treaty of peace by which the Prince consented to meet the Admiral on condition that (i) he apologised, (ii) he did not stay at Windsor, but only attended the state banquet there, (iii) he should not accompany the Emperor on his subsequent visit to Sandringham. Berlin refused to accept the second clause and insisted that the Admiral should stay at Windsor. London yielded, and the incident was closed. The cancelling of the Emperor's visit would have had a most disastrous effect, but it hung in the balance until ambassadors and high officers of State succeeded in inducing the Prince of Wales to sleep under the same roof as a member of his nephew's staff.*

The visit went off without further imperilments of international relations. Count Bülow, the German Foreign Secretary, accompanied the Emperor, and, in the absence of Lord Salisbury owing to the death of his wife, talked over the political situation with Mr. Balfour and Mr. Chamberlain. He and the Emperor had private conversations with the Queen and deplored the savage tone of the German Press, which they had agreed to attribute to the posthumous evil influence of Bismarck : it was safer to treat it as of ancient origin — the Danish war, the Austrian war,

* Eckardstein, *Ten Years at the Court of St. James's*, pp. 123, 124.

but nothing recent. All controversial topics were avoided, and the Emperor was full of carefully selected early memories of Windsor : how, at the age of four, he attended Uncle Bertie's wedding and toddled along the corridor holding his mother's hand. He shot over the Windsor covers with his uncle, he rode before breakfast in the English mode, and, pointing to the Round Tower, he exclaimed, 'From this Tower the world is ruled,' to the intense irritation of the military members of his staff, and he continued to repeat to his grandmother the assurance of his goodwill. After five days at Windsor there was a three days' visit to Sandringham, and the same conversational precautions were observed. The Empress was unwilling to go to Sandringham at all, for she thoroughly disliked and disapproved of her host, but her self-control was impeccable.*

The total result of this family party was just about what Lord Salisbury had hoped from it : it gave the impression that an understanding existed between England and Germany. Mr. Chamberlain, however, who was less practised in the correct valuation of the Emperor's amiability, was far more optimistic. The cordiality seemed to him so genuine and so solidly based that in a speech at Leicester immediately afterwards he pronounced that Germany and England were natural allies, that every cause of difference had been eliminated, and that the way was clear for an Anglo-American-Teutonic *entente*. Certainly now, as always, the Emperor wished for the closest and friendliest relations between England and Germany, but Mr. Chamberlain did not yet know the obstacles which he seemed doomed to erect between himself and his heart's desire by his appetite for those futile intrigues which he hoped would be the means of attaining it.†

* Bülow, *Memoirs*, 1897–1903, pp. 301–305 ; *Letters III*, iii. pp. 421, 423.
† Lee, *King Edward VII*, i. p. 748, note.

CHAPTER X

DURING December 1899 British arms in South Africa went through a very critical period. Three times in the Black Week they suffered serious reverses, at Stormberg, Magersfontein and Colenso. These only stiffened the determination of the British Government to go through with their task without interference from anybody. The Emperor wrote highly sympathetic letters to his grandmother and his uncle for Christmas, calling to mind the 'lovely days' he had spent at Windsor and Sandringham and lamenting that 'the message of the Angels of Peace on Earth and Goodwill to Man' was sadly far from fulfilment : in fact the New Year and the new century would be greeted by 'shrieks of dying men, killed and maimed by lyddite shells and balls from Quick-firers.' However, the British aristocracy had shown that they as well as the rank and file knew how to die.*

He himself greeted the New Year with an outburst of diplomatic activities, framed on the same lines as those he had indulged in over the Jameson Raid, and crowned with similar unsuccess. He sent for Count Osten-Sacken, Russian Ambassador in Berlin, and told him point-blank that, if the Tsar had a mind to advance towards India, he himself would mount guard over Russia's western frontier and undertake that none should stir in Europe. The astonished ambassador asked if the Emperor wished him to convey this

* *Letters III*, iii. p. 444.

message to the Tsar. The Emperor said that he did, and added : 'I have already given him this assurance more than once.' *

That was the case, for in the spring of 1895 he had written to him : 'I shall certainly do all in my power to keep Europe quiet and also guard the rear of Russia so that nobody shall hamper your action towards the Far East.' † He must also have repeated this encouragement quite lately, for the Tsar, immediately after the three reverses in December, instructed Sir Charles Scott, British Ambassador in St. Petersburg, to assure the Queen that 'he was animated by the most friendly feelings to us in this hour of trial, and that nothing was further from his thoughts than to take any advantage of our difficulties, or to countenance any step likely to increase them. He begged Her Majesty's Government to discredit entirely any reports of Russian projects likely to conflict in any way with our interests.' ‡ This message from the Tsar to the British Government points with certainty and precision to his having received further suggestions from the Emperor to embarrass England in the East. The Tsar wrote privately to the Queen as well, and from the tone of his message to her through the Government we may conjecture what he had to say.

As far as the Tsar then was concerned the Emperor's diplomacy (whatever was its ultimate object) had not been fruitful, and a further discomfiture awaited it. Count Osten-Sacken duly transmitted this New Year greeting to the Russian Foreign Minister, Count Muravieff, who circulated it among other Russian ambassadors, with an official note that Germany seemed to suggest that Russia and France should take concerted action against England under German initiative.§ It was thus reported to M. Delcassé, the

---

* Lee, *King Edward VII*, i. p. 763.   † *Willy-Nicky Letters*, p. 10.

‡ *Letters III*, iii. p. 439, note.   § Lee, *King Edward VII*, i. p. 765.

French Foreign Minister. For a moment he was puzzled. The two allies, Russia and France, could surely determine their policy towards England without putting themselves in committee under the Emperor's chairmanship, and that France should associate herself with Germany in any international question would be a very singular thing. Indeed the Emperor must have known that he was proposing an impossibility. What could there be at the bottom of it ? The light broke, and Delcassé saw that the answer to this grotesque riddle was exactly the same as that which Lord Salisbury had continually maintained was at the bottom of all the Emperor's diplomacy. England was in difficulties, and if France and Russia added to them she might at last be induced to join the Triple Alliance. There was nothing in the world that Delcassé feared more than that, and after the cordialities of the Emperor's recent visit to England it had seemed possible. He had telegraphed to Count Metternich when he left : 'Reception and atmosphere better than ever. The consequences for the future will in all human probability be very satisfactory and favourable.' * Moreover Mr. Chamberlain, in his speech at Leicester directly after the conclusion of his visit, had spoken of the undesirability of England's isolation and affirmed that Germany and England were natural allies. But ever since Delcassé had come into office his chief international aim had been to restore a better understanding between France and England, with a view eventually to an Anglo-French *entente,* and if he fell into this clumsy trap he would not only wreck that, but possibly drive England into the arms of Germany. There seems no doubt that this interpretation of the Emperor's intentions was correct, and France maintained her attitude of complete neutrality.

Versatile as ever, the Emperor had simultaneously been

* Bülow, *Memoirs,* 1897–1903, p. 341.

taking other steps to endear himself to England and procure an alliance. He enclosed in his Christmas letter to the Prince of Wales about lyddite and the shrieks of the dying a memorandum based on what was being said in German military circles concerning the war in South Africa up to date. It was a short document, just a prologue to prepare the way for a more elaborate table of 'Aphorisms' which soon followed. It was pessimistic in tone with purpose in its pessimism. At present (it pointed out) no English objective had been attained, and the failure had been very expensive. England needed far more troops, and these new troops would be unaccustomed to 'tropical warfare,' their officers would be inexperienced, and it was doubtful whether such would succeed when trained and seasoned troops had failed. Rebellion might not improbably break out in Cape Colony. . . The moral was easy to draw, and what was written between the lines was quite as much to the point as the lines themselves. England was in need of a friend, and, on the day that the Emperor wrote, the German Government sent a very sympathetic message to Lord Salisbury.*

The Emperor sent his uncle his second table of Aphorisms early in February 1900. They were lengthier and more explicit. He again reviewed the military operations, which now included the British reverse at Spion Kop, and advised that any plan for an offensive campaign ought to be postponed till adequate reinforcements had arrived and had got acclimatised. That would take time : perhaps in the autumn of 1900 the British might be ready for it. In the interval 'it would be wise policy to place such a *respite* for the Army *in absolute safety* against foreign Powers, the attainment of which in the present situation of the world appears somewhat doubtful. . . If therefore diplomacy *cannot guarantee* absolutely to secure the respite just referred to, it

* *Letters III*, iii. p. 445.

would certainly be better to bring matters to a settlement.'

The twenty-second and concluding paragraph of these Aphorisms ran as follows :

'Even the best football club, if it is beaten notwithstanding the most gallant defence, accepts finally its defeat with equanimity. Last year in the great cricket match of England *v.* Australia, the former took the victory of the latter quietly with chivalrous acknowledgment of her opponent.' *

A covering letter accompanied these advices, in which the Emperor hoped that they might be of practical use, and suggested that the Queen would be interested in them. Another person who would certainly have been interested in them was M. Delcassé, for they completely bore out his sagacious interpretation of the Emperor's willingness to be chairman of a committee of Germany, France and Russia to threaten joint action against England. The Emperor knew that nothing would induce England to make a settlement with the Boers at this stage of the war, for it would be tantamount to an acknowledgment of defeat. So he recommended it, unless she could find a friend who would guarantee her absolute security against foreign Powers while she was accumulating sufficient forces in South Africa. No invitation could have been more definite : the friend was ready. But even now he could not act straightly : he must always have some counter-strain of intrigue going on, for, as the Prince of Wales pointed out in his reply, Dr. Leyds, the Secretary of State for the Transvaal, was in Berlin and had been entertained by the German Chancellor on the Emperor's birthday. As for the last paragraph of the Aphorisms, the Prince merely remarked that a conflict in a cricket match and an acceptance of defeat could not be seriously compared with a conflict in which the British Empire was at stake.

* Lee, *King Edward VII*, i. pp. 805–810.

The Emperor, it must be acknowledged, had very bad luck in the timing of this last attempt to draw England into the embrace of the Triple Alliance. Hardly had he recommended a cessation of serious operations until the autumn, during which respite invidious foreign Powers must be held in check, when the tide of war turned. Lord Roberts and Lord Kitchener had been sent out to the Cape, and before the end of February, without any respite at all, Kimberley and Ladysmith had been relieved, and General Cronje had surrendered at Paardeberg on the anniversary of Majuba. Fervently did the Emperor shower felicitations on his uncle : what pleased him as much as anything was that Lord Roberts had acted in accordance with the principles laid down in Aphorisms, II. § 20, for the conduct of the war next autumn, and had concentrated all available forces at one point. A brave old soldier ! Valiant troops ! Effective commissariat ! He still feared that 'Sundry Peoples' were intriguing in other parts of the world against England. This he felt by instinct, and for himself : 'I want a strong unhampered England. It is eminently necessary for the Peace of Europe. . . With superhuman efforts Bülow and I slowly got the better of the German Press, swamped as it was with articles, news, canards and, last but not least, roubles and francs from both sides with a view to creating a so-called anti-English feeling.' Here surely is a resumption of what we may call the oblique approach, namely, the warning of hostile machinations by Russia and France, brought to the notice of England by her only true friend.

A few days afterwards the Emperor wrote again. His instinct that sundry peoples were intriguing had justified itself, for he reported that Count Muravieff had invited him to join with Russia and France to force England to make peace with the Boers, a course which he himself had recommended in the second set of Aphorisms, in case she could not find a friend in Europe. But here was the friend, pen in hand, and he had declined to have anything to do with the scheme. The Tsar, who had organised the European Peace Conference at The Hague, had better find out whether England felt disposed to accept his arbitration, but Germany would have nothing to do with it.*

This was an interesting letter. Only a few months ago the Emperor had proposed a combination of Germany, France and Russia ostensibly to embarrass England, and on that occasion he was to be the chairman of this hostile committee. That scheme had failed because Russia had repudiated it and Delcassé had seen that it only masked a design to entice England into the Triple Alliance. This was a variant of the same design but with the difference that Russia was now stated to have initiated it, and England's honest friend to have repudiated it. But Lord Salisbury could not believe that Muravieff's invitation had ever been approved by the Tsar, and on thinking it over he began to doubt whether the Emperor had ever received such an invitation at all.† Possibly he had invented it, but at any rate his motive in inventing it indicated his goodwill to England. Another oblique approach.

The Prince of Wales, on the other hand, believed that Muravieff had sent this invitation to the Emperor, and that William's repudiation of it showed his sincerity. He wrote to the Queen : 'William, I am sure, wishes to be our true friend, and he indeed deserves our thanks and confidence' ; and to William himself his thanks were of the warmest : 'You have no idea, my dear William, how all of us in England appreciate the loyal friendship which you manifest to us on every possible occasion. We hope always to look upon Germany as our best friend as long as you are at the

---

* Lee, *King Edward VII*, i. pp. 768, 769.   † *Letters III*, iii. pp. 503, 527.

helm.' * These were very handsome expressions, and the Queen endorsed them. She sent him a most cordial and grateful telegram, and repeated the same sentiments to the British Ambassador in Berlin. She also dealt with the suggestion of intervention on the part of 'Sundry Peoples' in her very firmest style without troubling the Foreign Office, and in her telegram to Sir Frank Lascelles she left no room for doubt about that matter. As Lord Salisbury gladly acknowledged, she could put the case with an uncompromising clarity which would not have been *convenable* if it came from her Ministers.

'Please convey to the Emperor,' she wrote, 'that my whole nation is with me in a fixed determination to see this through without intervention.

'The time for and the terms of peace must be left to our decision, and my country, which is suffering from so heavy a sacrifice of precious lives, will resist all interference.' †

It has been usual to represent the Emperor's attitude towards England during the whole of the South African War as that of a treacherous and crafty enemy masking his real purpose under sympathetic and friendly professions. But the documents, if fairly weighed, lead to precisely the opposite conclusion. He adopted the crookedest of methods, he appeared to devise hostile combinations of other Powers, he reared bogeys to terrify England, he used tricks to which no straightforward man would condescend, but these were in accordance with his diplomatic methods, and in every case they were devices to further the accomplishment of his sincere desire to be allied with England. The two most discerning statesmen of the day, M. Delcassé and Lord Salisbury, were agreed over that, and eventually his

* Lee, *King Edward VII*, i. p. 770.   † *Letters III*, iii. p. 509.

uncle, who habitually took the lowest view of his trustworthiness, came to the same conclusion. The Prince even desired to enter into personal relations with the Emperor again, and, regardless of the frenzy of irritation which intercourse with his nephew always aroused in him and of his registered and re-registered vows that William should never again come to England for Cowes week, he asked him to do so. The Emperor accepted this unlooked-for invitation, but perhaps it was as well that urgent affairs kept him at home, for indeed the less these two saw of each other the better.

The Boxer rising in China caused acute anxiety in Europe this summer : it was rumoured at the end of July that the foreign legations at Pekin had been captured and the staffs massacred. This turned out to be untrue, but an international force had to be sent out to restore order and affirm the prestige of civilisation. The Emperor was insistent that it should be put under the command of his Field-Marshal Count Waldersee, and this was done : Russian, German, English, Japanese and Americans were ingredients in this unique military *macédoine*. He was exuberantly conscious of being the instrument of the Most High with regard to this expedition ; he had lately declared that no important decision could be made in world politics without his personal approval, and he hurried to Bremerhaven, in an ecstasy of egotism, to see off a troopship of German soldiers. There was a lofty wooden erection on the quay : some thought it was a header-board for high diving, some that it was a tower from which fire brigades were to practise, some that the sailors were to perform acrobatic feats on it, but none guessed its real nature till the Emperor stalked on to the quay and made plain that it was a pulpit. On such an occasion he might be trusted not to be caught at anything commonplace. He climbed to the very top of it and addressed the embarking troops in his harsh, far-carrying voice. There came a remarkable passage :

'There will be no quarter,' he proclaimed, 'no prisoners will be taken. As a thousand years ago the Huns under King Attila gained for themselves a name which still stands for a terror in tradition and story, so may the name of Germany be impressed by you for a thousand years on China so thoroughly that never again shall a Chinese dare so much as to look askance at a German.' Then the reincarnation of King Attila descended from his pulpit, and with this benediction ringing in their ears his Huns set sail for China.

The aged Chancellor, Prince Hohenlohe and the Foreign Secretary had been looking at each other in blank dismay at these frightful sentiments, and Bülow, as was his wont when the Emperor made one of his greater *gaffes,* got hold of the newspaper reporters and ordered them not to write out their shorthand notes for publication, but wait for the version of the imperial speech which he would send them. The evening papers came in at dinner that night on the *Hohenzollern,* and the Emperor, to whom the joy of seeing his orations in print was ever new, pounced eagerly on them, but found that all the most magnificent passages had been omitted. His face expressed the bitterest chagrin, and, suspecting the identity of the censor, he said indignantly to Bülow, 'You have struck out the best bits of it.' Unfortunately there had been a reporter sitting on a house-roof apart from his colleagues whom Bülow had not nobbled, and later in the evening another paper was brought in which contained a verbatim report of the whole speech.* It was too late to stop it now, for it had already been telegraphed by the exultant editor to all the central news agencies of Europe, and it formed a valuable source of anti-German propaganda. The Emperor who was so fond of alluding

* Bülow, *Memoirs,* 1897–1903, pp. 356–358.

to his subjects as Christians and peace-loving folk, generous, humane and cultured, had bade them emulate a horde of heathen barbarians, while he, King Attila, waved them on to wholesale massacre. That speech was remembered and reprinted fourteen years later, and it was by the Emperor's own name for his troops that, under the same inspiration, they invaded Belgium.*

The speech made an extremely bad impression in England, for British troops were now under German supreme command, and such were the exhortations of the War Lord. England, like Germany, was a civilised and Christian nation, but what would have been the consternation if the Queen, bidding God-speed to her guard of Gordon Highlanders at Balmoral when leaving for South Africa, had exhorted them to live up to the glorious traditions of the Huns and kill all prisoners ? Indeed the Emperor had no more bitter enemy than his own undisciplined tongue. No one, not even himself, could tell what it would say next.

But below all his varying moods, that one basic desire of his, to remain on the best of terms with England, continued constant. He manifested it towards the close of the year in an unusually straightforward manner. President Kruger in November fled from the Transvaal with a very considerable luggage of bullion, and came to Europe to enlist sympathy and intervention. He was given an enthusiastic reception in France. President Loubet received him officially and the Chamber passed a unanimous vote of sympathy with the Boers. He was received equally warmly in Holland, and also at Cologne on his way to Berlin, where he hoped to have a personal interview with the Emperor. The Queen telegraphed to William that, for the sake of

---

* During the war the official bard of Germanised Turkey, Zija Gök Alp, wrote a stirring ode addressed to 'My Attila, my Huns,' which was popular in Prussia but really referred to the original King Attila.

the friendly relations so desirable between England and Germany, she trusted he would not receive the President, for it would arouse bitter ill-feeling in England. It was really difficult for him to refuse to do so, for popular sympathy for the Boers ran as high in Germany as it did in France. He sent for Bülow, who had lately become his Chancellor, and they settled that it was better to ignore popular feeling than to endanger friendly relations with England : possibly the fact that France had given the President such a welcome was a contributory reason why Germany should not. So Kruger was told that his proposed visit to Berlin would be fruitless, and he returned from Cologne to Holland.*

There had never been any human being for whom the Emperor felt such unvarying respect and affection as the Queen, nor any whose influence was more salutary in checking the 'impetuosity' she so often deplored. For the last six months her strength had been gradually failing, and late on January 17, 1901, Baron Eckardstein, acting as German Ambassador in London during Count Hatzfeldt's indisposition, telegraphed to the Emperor that the Queen was critically ill and might die any moment.† This was not quite the case, for the Duke of Connaught was staying with the Emperor in Berlin for the celebration of the bicentenary of the foundation of the Prussian Monarchy, and it is quite impossible that he should not have been summoned if his mother's condition was as critical as Eckardstein represented. But Eckardstein had political reasons for desiring the Emperor to come to England at once, and he knew that such a telegram would bring him, for his devotion to his grandmother was very sincere, and this gesture of breaking off these Prussian celebrations and hurrying to England would appeal to

* Bülow, Memoirs, 1897–1903, p. 467.
† Eckardstein, Ten Years at the Court of St. James's, p. 188.

his imagination. Eckardstein had lately held conversations with the Duke of Devonshire and Chamberlain which in his view promised well for an Anglo-German alliance, and the moment was propitious, for the Queen could certainly not live long, and the Prince of Wales was bitterly offended at the vituperative campaign against England in the French Press. It was an opportunity, and the Emperor on the receipt of this telegram quite grasped the possibilities. He made all travelling arrangements for himself and his uncle to start at once, and punctuated his journey with volleys of excited telegrams to Bülow.

Eckardstein met him on landing with the gratifying news that when it became known in London that he was on his way 'people wept for joy,' and the Emperor recorded how, when he drove with the Prince of Wales from Victoria to Buckingham Palace, where he stayed the night, a man stepped out of the silent crowd that lined the streets and, advancing to the side of the carriage, said 'Thank you, Kaiser.' Never, even on such an errand, could he get rid of the consciousness that all the world was a stage and he the only player. Next day he went down to Osborne, but it is doubtful if the Queen ever recognised him ; she seems to have mistaken him for his father.* She died on January 22, 1901.

* William II, *My Memoirs*, p. 98 ; Eckardstein, p. 189.

CHAPTER XI

THERE had been no stopping the Emperor from coming to England, but now arose the difficulty of getting him back to Germany again. Whether or not London had been as deeply moved at his arrival as he imagined, his abandonment of the celebrations in Germany and his instant departure had been much appreciated, and between King Edward's disgust at the scurrility of the French and the accounts Eckardstein gave the Emperor of the Chatsworth conversations he was more hopeful than ever before of bringing off the long-cherished scheme. The German Foreign Office, in terror of his talking with his usual flamboyant irresponsibility, telegraphed to the German Embassy in London that he must on no account be allowed to have private interviews with English Ministers, and Holstein, in his anxiety to get him home again, made the very original suggestion that his personal safety was in danger in London. The Empress, a convinced Anglophobe, who detested the new King, had strongly opposed his going to England at all, and as soon as the Queen's death was known she bombarded Chancellor Bülow with entreaties to make him return and not wait for the funeral. She was sure he would get very tired and exhausted : she thought it was 'particularly dangerous the way everyone — particularly the ladies — is trying to besiege his warm, friendly nature, and turn his head (they all, of course, want to win him for their own ends), for the Kaiser will get the impression that his presence is essential there.' Let his brother Henry go to the funeral, let Crown Prince William go, let them all go, as long as the Emperor returns. His mother was of the same mind : she thought he ought to come home, even if he returned for the funeral ; she was also terribly ill herself and wanted to see her son. But all entreaties were useless. The Emperor was far too busy and full of plans, and he would not budge. He told his wife that his aunts needed him : they treated him like a brother, and he must be on the spot with advice and support. Again the Empress wrote to Bülow, and her letter bristled with spite against King Edward. 'To crown everything else, the new English King has made the Emperor a Field-Marshal. If this is not an irony in the present circumstances, I do not know what is. It is supposed to be a gracious act, but I consider it tactless. The Kaiser of course has got to look pleased. I wrote and told him that I hoped he did not expect me to congratulate him on this occasion, it was supposed to be a gracious act but opinions could differ regarding it. I think the country will not like it either. Besides he will be celebrating his birthday abroad.' *

This outburst from a woman usually so self-contained was astonishing. The ladies were dangerous, the King was tactless, they all wanted to use the Emperor for their own ends, and he would wear himself out and not be at home for his birthday. What the poor lady was really afraid of was the rebuilding of the temple of family affection, and indeed she had cause for apprehension, for the Emperor had been at his very best during those first days at Osborne, full of sympathy and tact and helpfulness. The King created him, as we have seen, a Field-Marshal, and when Prince Henry and the Crown Prince William joined the gathering he created the one Vice-Admiral of the British Fleet, and invested the

* Bülow, *Memoirs*, 1897–1903, pp. 498–501.

other with the Order of the Garter. In the fortnight which intervened between the Queen's death and the interment in the Mausoleum at Frogmore, King and Emperor had long political talks together, and not a discordant point arose, for the King's displeasure with France was very much to his nephew's taste, and both looked with suspicion on the possible *rapprochement* between Russia and the United States of America. Though the German Foreign Office had been timorous as to what the Emperor might say if he had the chance of talking to any English Ministers, he had an interview with Lord Lansdowne, but the most correct discretion reigned. They spoke of the Balance of Power in Europe, but that subject was abandoned because, while Lord Lansdowne thought that the British fleet was the deciding factor, the Emperor had the impression that Germany's twenty-two army corps had something to do with it. England's isolation was spoken of : the Emperor said that she could no longer isolate herself, but must combine with 'the Continent.' As Russia and France were both out of favour, the meaning of 'the Continent' was not hard to seek, but nobody said 'Germany.' *

Before the Queen's coffin was finally deposited in the Mausoleum beside that of her husband the Emperor had been in England well over a fortnight. On the day of his return to Germany there was a lunch in his honour at Marlborough House, and, replying to his health proposed by the King, his discretion broke down and he made a very explicit statement :

'I believe there is a Providence which has decreed that two nations which have produced such men as Shakespeare, Schiller, Luther and Goethe must have a great future before them ; I believe that the two Teutonic nations will, bit by bit, learn to know each other better, and that they will stand

* Eckardstein, pp. 191, 192.

together to help in keeping the peace of the world. We ought to form an Anglo-Germanic alliance, you to keep the seas, while we would be responsible for the land ; with such an alliance, not a mouse could stir in Europe without our permission, and the nations would, in time, come to see the necessity of reducing their armaments.' *

Alas for the dashed hopes of the German Foreign Office ! It was just exactly this sort of thing that they dreaded his saying. He directly asked for an alliance with England ; he emphasised his sense of the effectiveness of the combination : not a mouse could stir without Anglo-German permission. He administered a direct snub to the Tsar, whose proposals at the Peace Conference last year for the reduction of armaments had been dropped without debate, by the implication that England and Germany together would be so strong that other nations might as well disarm. He had ranged himself in direct opposition to German national sentiment, which was very hostile to England, and to English national sentiment which fully reciprocated it. The only course was to prevent any publication of the speech, and this was done, to the Emperor's great chagrin, for he thought that it would have had an admirable effect.†

Indiscretion followed indiscretion in these last fervent moments. He decorated Lord Roberts with the Order of the Black Eagle, thus honouring with high official recognition the Commander-in-Chief of the British forces in South Africa in the Boer War. He could not have issued a more direct challenge to the violent anti-British feeling in France, Russia and his own country, and there was no suppressing this. Back he went to Germany radiant with personal success, and Caran d'Ache, the French caricaturist with the Russian *nom de crayon,* duly and dryly allegorised the complacent Sovereigns. The Emperor plumed up his mili-

---

* Lee, *King Edward VII,* ii. p. 11.   † William II, *My Memoirs,* p. 100.

tary moustache as the *Hohenzollern* steamed away from the white cliffs of Albion, and said 'J'ai foutu l'Angleterre dans ma poche,' and King Edward in his dressing-gown, with cigar in his smiling mouth, handled a despatch-case and murmured 'L'Allemagne est dans le sac.' * . . . Both these receptacles had holes in them.

The Emperor returned home more English than his uncle. Usually he lived in uniform, changing it half a dozen times a day to suit the character of his engagements : now he wore civilian clothes even when officers dined with him, and his tie-pin was of red enamel with his grandmother's cipher in diamonds. His talk, even as his mother's had been when first she came as a bride to Prussia, was a Hymn of Praise of all things English, and it had precisely the same unhappy effect as hers. So too had his decoration of Lord Roberts with the Order of the Black Eagle, for his subjects construed that as a deliberate rebuke to the national sympathy with the Boers. His wife, with her sensible bourgeois mind, had correctly conjectured what the effect of this long visit to England would have not only on the Emperor himself but on his people, whose Anglophobism was highly inflamed by his Anglophilism.

But, as usual, he never remained long in one stay, especially where friendly relations with his uncle were concerned. King Edward had arranged to come to Germany almost immediately to see his sister, the Empress Frederick, who was dying of cancer, and the Emperor insisted that he should stay with him at his Homburg palace. It was not fitted for winter habitation, for its heating apparatus was of the most elementary sort. A quantity of iron stoves were therefore installed which were so ardent and difficult to regulate that the heat in the rooms became tropical, and,

* Eckardstein, p. 196.

when windows were opened, arctic blasts poured in. The King therefore decided to stay with his sister at Friedrichshof, and the Emperor was so annoyed that the warmth of his sentiments not only to his uncle but to England was markedly chilled.*

While the King was there occurred that strange incident which eventually led to the publication of a selection from the long series of letters which the Empress had written to her mother during the forty-three years which had elapsed since she went as a young bride to Germany. They had been kept at Windsor, but after the Queen's death the Empress had asked that they should be returned to her for some purpose of her own, and they were now at Friedrichshof. She was kept much under morphia to deaden the agonies she was suffering, but there were clear intervals, and in one of these she sent for Sir Frederick Ponsonby, the King's equerry and her godson, and asked him to take her letters back to England with him. She explicitly told him that the Emperor must not get hold of them, and later that night she sent to his room two portmanteaux containing this bulky correspondence. Sir Frederick formed the very reasonable conclusion that she had sent for her letters originally to help her to compile from them a refutation of the monstrous slanders about her which had been published in Bismarck's *Memoirs,* especially those concerning the Emperor Frederick's illness : this conclusion is amply supported by passages in the letters themselves. They contained also the bitterest complaints about her son's treatment of her, and it was obvious that if he got hold of them he would destroy them. The strong presumption therefore was that she gave them to her godson in order that he might base on them some such publication as she had intended but was now unable to carry out. Sir Frederick accordingly

* Bülow, *Memoirs,* 1897–1903, pp. 502–503.

brought them back to England without the knowledge of the Emperor.*

The Emperor, of course, had always known of the existence of this correspondence, and he suspected that it had come into his mother's possession, for after her death in the ensuing summer Friedrichshof was instantly surrounded by troops, who, by his orders, allowed no package to go out without examination, and search was made for them. Without doubt he wanted to get hold of them and destroy them. A precisely parallel situation had arisen after his father's death in 1888. He had put the New Palace in a state of siege while he made search for his father's papers, and especially for his Diary during the last ten years. Then, as now, he could not find what he sought, for the day before his father's death it had been dispatched to England for safe keeping. For twenty-seven years Sir Frederick Ponsonby kept these letters, and then, judging that sufficient time had elapsed, followed out what he had every reason to believe fulfilled the Empress Frederick's intentions with regard to them, and published a selection of them.

So, for this reason and for that, for pique with his uncle, for that ever-recurring jealousy, for chagrin that when the All-Highest piped melodies in the English mode his subjects did not rise and dance, the warmth of the Emperor's sentiments towards England and his uncle suffered a wintry refrigeration. Chancellor Bülow, on the other hand, and Freiherr von Richthofen believed that his visit had made England far more friendly and that a defensive alliance might be arranged. But they regarded his speech at Marlborough House as a direct *invitation à la valse,* and it was for England to advance towards her beckoning partner. Bülow therefore instructed Eckardstein to report to Berlin any

* Ponsonby, *Letters of Empress Frederick,* pp. x–xiv.

promising conversations he held with British Ministers.*
He reported that Chamberlain had inquired whether Germany was seriously disposed to conclude an alliance of
some kind. Instantly the Emperor's essential timidity took
alarm : instantly also his suspicions of some dangerous design grew alert, and he must be very wary, on the look out
for traps. According to his own account he asked against
whom this proposed alliance was directed : it seemed to him
evident that England required the support of the German
armies to be at her disposal for some dark purpose of her
own. He fancied that Russia might be the menace which
she wanted to counter, fearing designs on India and on Constantinople. But the idea of offending Russia appalled him :
that would never do, for there had always been a 'traditional
brotherhood-in-arms' between Russian and German armies.
France might come in with Russia, and Germany might be
attacked on two fronts. The English fleet would then be
of little help ; or there might be a change of government in
England and the Houses of Parliament refuse to ratify the
alliance. Only a few weeks ago he had proclaimed (as indeed he had often done before) that the German army and
the English fleet between them could dictate to Europe, but
now, when the project seemed possibly realisable, he found
a score of reasons against it. He made the most of small
points at issue between Germany and England in China, and
told King Edward that the British Ministers were 'unmitigated noodles.' He did all he could, through timidity, suspicion and fractiousness, to barricade the road that might
have led to the goal which he desired.†

Two meetings took place this summer (1901) between
King Edward and the Emperor. The first was at the funeral of the Empress Frederick in the middle of August

---

* Bülow, *Memoirs*, 1897–1903, pp. 503, 504.
† William II, *My Memoirs*, pp. 100–103 ; Eckardstein, pp. 195, 216, 217.

when the Emperor, no doubt in order to impress his uncle, ordered an immense military display. At this meeting there was no serious discussion of political topics, but ten days later another took place at Wilhelmshöhe for that express purpose. An indication of the mood the Emperor was in may be gathered from a letter he wrote to Bülow just before, in which he said : 'The building of our great fleet must be expedited as quickly as possible. That will be a nice surprise for the English, and perhaps it is also aimed at them.' It was not therefore much to be wondered at that the meeting was a complete failure. There was not a single point on which they were at one : it was as if their object was to explore fresh avenues, which would render impossible the alliance or cordial understanding which they had met to discuss. They raked up irrelevant topics in order to differ about them. 'Why was the Tsar about to visit the French fleet ?' asked the King (as if the Emperor had arranged a proceeding which he disliked as much as anybody). 'Was not it equivalent to a demonstration against England ?' 'It might be taken in that light,' said the Emperor. 'Why was the Tsar so eager to see the German Chancellor ?' . . . 'Probably to discuss political questions.' . . . 'What about English dealings with Japan ?' asked the Emperor. He was told, and said that he considered them treacherous, and in the manner of 'perfidious Albion.' (Uproar.) To make matters even pleasanter than they were already, the Emperor remarked on the cordiality of the relations between Germany and France just now : German and French troops had served together under a German commander in the East, their economic interests harmonised : he wondered whether England was wise in maintaining, as she had hitherto done, her splendid isolation. How pleasant was the understanding between the European Powers ! The Tsar was to visit France, the Tsar was to talk to Bülow, Russia had a very clever Ambassador in the United

States, and England perhaps did not know how friendly their relations were becoming.* What was the Emperor's point in making all these exasperating observations ? Possibly, by pointing out how dangerous England's isolation was, he was making another approach, a shade more oblique than usual, to entice the poor lone sheep into the German fold : possibly he merely wanted to annoy his uncle : probably he was at last beginning to despair of ever inspiring confidence in the minds of such English statesmen as Lord Salisbury, who never believed a word he said. The effect, anyhow, on the King was that he got fussed and irritated over the talk, contributing discords, and went back to his cure at Homburg with no other trophies than the silver *épergne* which his nephew had designed and given him. Nobody could make out what the Emperor was after, and that was not surprising, for neither he nor Bülow nor Holstein, that curious mole-like worker in the earth who threw up soil at unexpected places from his underground burrowings in the hope that others might take his mounds to be mountains, had any definite policy, but were only engaged on mild flirtations with any Power who would whisper in a corner with them.

That certainly was becoming Mr. Chamberlain's view, and, being a very shrewd business man, he had no use for people who did not know their own minds, who would not talk straight, nor base their discussions on definite proposals. It was almost two years since he had made that speech at Leicester in which he had so strongly advocated a German alliance, and since then he had worked for it, though his policy of Tariff Reform, which was regarded in Germany as directly aimed at her growing industrial prosperity, made him the most detested of English statesmen. But now his enthusiasm was spent. He came to the conclusion that

* Lee, *King Edward VII*, pp. 126, 128–130.

there was nothing doing and swept the vague papers off his desk. Meantime the German Press was getting more offensive than ever over the conduct of the war in South Africa, reviling the English for their cruelty and severity. Hitherto Chamberlain had taken the correct view that no official notice should be taken of a scurrilous foreign Press (and for that matter the English Press was seeing to its being properly answered), but now, as Colonial Minister, he made a speech at Edinburgh in which he said that a nation which vilified the barbarity of British Generals in South Africa had better remember its own conduct of the Franco-German War.

That was a great mistake. Whether Mr. Chamberlain was right or not in implying that the Germans conducted the war in 1870 with unprecedented barbarity was beside the point. He had retorted officially to unofficial abuse and in a tone that could not fail to be considered insulting. Germany was compelled to take official notice of this, and Bülow, with pacific intention, first tried, through the British Ambassador, to induce Chamberlain to withdraw what he had said, or to explain, as the Emperor had done with the Kruger telegram, that he meant something quite different, or to say how much he admired the virility of the German army — anything would do. Otherwise his speech was sure to be brought up in the Reichstag, and the Chancellor would be compelled to defend the honour of the German army in suitable terms. Chamberlain refused either to retract or to explain.

King Edward did all that was possible to sandbag the tottering structure of international cordiality. Just one thing had to be made clear first. He had seen in some paper that the Emperor wished to come to England for the anniversary of his grandmother's death on January 22, 1902. That was impossible : Windsor and Buckingham Palace were in the hands of plumbers and decorators (of which they stood in sad need), and he could not receive people like Emperors.

Short of that, the King, oblivious of his last unprofitable conversation with his nephew, abounded in assurances of the usual kind : nothing was closer to his heart than the desire that Germany and England should see eye to eye on questions that importantly concerned them. Finally to dispose of the Emperor's desire to be at Windsor on January 22, the King suggested that the Prince of Wales should go to Berlin for the Emperor's birthday on January 27, and as a Christmas present he sent him yet another Highland costume which the Queen had given the Emperor's father, and which had come to light at Windsor in the excavations into the mass of mixed relics which for the last sixty years had been accumulating there. Crown Prince Frederick must have forgotten to have this packed — perhaps in 1864, perhaps in 1870 — and his son received it as 'a touching and splendid gift.' He outvied his uncle in perfervid expressions of amity, with an authoritative statement that God had entrusted the Teutonic races with the dissemination of culture in the world, and apart from the Eastern races there were none others through whom He could fulfil His designs. He himself had done all he could to suppress the bitterness of the German Press, which need not be taken too seriously, for he was 'the sole arbiter and master of German foreign policy.' He humbly offered to the master of the greatest Navy in the world the rank of Honorary Admiral in the newest.*

Then all these budding olive branches were stricken with black blight. A question was asked in the Reichstag at the Budget debate, in January 1902, about Mr. Chamberlain's Edinburgh speech, and Chancellor Bülow made a very moderate and dignified reply. He called it a 'crooked judgment,' and, as such, repudiated it. Germany, he said, was intimately knit up with her army and was indignant at this insult, but he took it for granted that Mr. Chamberlain had

* Lee, *King Edward VII*, ii. pp. 136, 137.

not intended to offend her. Germany had always tried to maintain friendly relations with England ; the reputation of her army was too bright to be tarnished by unjust attacks, and he recommended the Reichstag to take no further notice. Some member of the Reichstag expressed himself very strongly about Chamberlain and the British Army : instantly the Speaker of the Reichstag called him to order, and Bülow endorsed his censure in the most emphatic manner, and declared he would not allow himself to be forced into an unfriendly attitude towards England : Bülow, in fact, minimised the incident to the best of his power. But he might as well have tried to bridle Behemoth : the German Press went mad with rage, and military clubs resembled lunatic asylums. To make matters, if possible, worse, Chamberlain replied to this debate in the Reichstag by another speech refusing to withdraw or qualify anything he had said.*

The situation was almost as acute as that which followed on the Kruger telegram. The King wrote to his nephew to say that he thought the Prince of Wales had better not pay the impending birthday visit to Berlin for fear that he should be publicly insulted. But perhaps he did not mean that to be quite final, for as soon as the Emperor answered that the Prince would be suitably welcomed he consented to his going. The turmoil in the Press died down and the Prince's visit went off without any untoward incident. He had a long conversation with Bülow, and they smiled and agreed with each other and explained Mr. Chamberlain away most satisfactorily. Bülow gave the Prince a short summary of Anglo-German relations from the Crimean War onwards, and they both felt sure that these would develop into a closer co-operation in the future. It was pleasant to have such a frank talk.†

* Bülow, *Memoirs*, 1897–1903, pp. 546–547.
† Lee, *King Edward VII*, ii. pp. 138, 139.

This incident of Chamberlain's speech showed how impossible it was that the alliance which the Emperor had invited a year ago could ever materialise. A few indiscreet words had raised a tempest which could never have arisen if there had been an ounce of genuine goodwill between the nations, and that often repeated hope that they would soon be better friends than ever had now become a mere formula without significance. As the Emperor had once complained to his grandmother, England owned most of the desirable territory on the face of the earth, and her insular position combined with the immense strength of her fleet made her practically impregnable, unless some other fleet challenged her supremacy. Germany recognised that and was already working on a naval programme which had that end in view. England, on her side, was busy over a secret treaty with Japan. It was not quite so secret as was hoped, for the Emperor certainly knew something of what was going on, but the King insisted that as soon as it was ratified he should at once be officially informed of it, and not find it out for himself. William was pleased at this piece of tact, he also regarded the treaty as a guarantee for peace in the Far East, and the King followed up this pleasant impression by asking him to Sandringham for his birthday in November. He would be delighted to come, and by way of response asked Lord Roberts and the Secretary of State for War to attend the German Army manœuvres in the autumn.

A hitch occurred which showed on how unstable a balance these cordialities were perched, for the smallest touch threatened to upset it. The South African War had ended in the summer of 1902, and three Boer Generals, Botha, De Wet and Delarey, came to England in August : London gave them an enthusiastic welcome, and the King, then recovering from the operation which had caused the postponement of the Coronation, received them on his yacht. From England they went to Holland and were hailed as national heroes, and from there to Paris. Paris, officially, was polite and no more : M. Delcassé and the Prime Minister gave them a short interview, but only as 'distinguished visitors.' There was no mistaking the intention of that coolness. The Boer War, which had been the cause of such violent popular Anglophobism in France, was over, those ebullitions would now die down, and the French Government, looking ahead and knowing King Edward's constant desire to come to an understanding with France, was extremely anxious to do nothing that could give offence. The official French reception therefore of the Generals was in strong contrast to the welcome given to Kruger. From Paris the Boer Generals went to Berlin, where they again received an almost hysterical welcome, duly reported in the English Press. Then came the hitch : the Emperor wanted to receive them personally. There was no real logical reason why he should not. They were now British subjects, and as such the King had received them : they had been received officially in France, they had had a roaring welcome in England, and it was not to be supposed that the Emperor would do more than give them a few civil words. But the King, recognising the precarious balance, wrote very firmly to his Ambassador in Berlin, telling him that the Emperor ought to know that his reception of the Generals just before his visit to England would be very unpopular, and in his mother's manner, when she had made up her mind and spoke for her grandson's good, he added that he wished 'no further comment.' But the Emperor wanted to see them and made a further comment : could they not be presented to him by the British Ambassador as distinguished English subjects ? But the British Government was against the Emperor's receiving

them at all, and, as in the case of Kruger, he refused to do so.
A most magnanimous gesture, he thought. When would
the ungrateful country do him justice ? *

When indeed ? Considering what he had been doing
this last summer, perhaps it was kinder that it should not
do him justice. He had paid the Tsar a marine visit at Reval
and had indulged in what might be called a serious naval
flirtation. One morning, walking arm in arm with the Tsar
along the deck of his yacht, he had called out to Bülow : 'Do
you know what we have decided to style ourselves in the
future ? Tsar Nicholas is Admiral of the Pacific, and I am
Admiral of the Atlantic.' He repeated this humorous remark several times, to the great discomfort of the Tsar, and
on parting signalled to him : 'The Admiral of the Atlantic
bids farewell to the Admiral of the Pacific,' to which the
Tsar merely replied 'Good-bye.' † But there was something
solid below this airy jesting, and the Admiral of the Atlantic
wrote the Tsar a most interesting letter soon afterwards,
commenting on their fruitful talks. They had established
in naval matters a complete mutual confidence. The Tsar,
in return for a sight of the secret designs (shown to no 'for-
eigners') of the Emperor's newest ships, had convinced him
that his own navy was powerful, well fitted and well
equipped and was 'preparing for business.' They must look
(wrote the Emperor) on their developing fleets as 'one great
organisation.' They were the rulers of the two great combinations : namely, Russia and France, and the Triple Alliance : these five Powers had the peace of the world in their
keeping. Only eighteen months ago he had declared that
with Germany and England in alliance 'not a mouse could
stir in Europe' without their permission. Now that plan
was scrapped and here was a new one. It was England who

* Eckardstein, pp. 235–238 ; Lee, *King Edward VII,* ii. pp. 147–149.
† Bülow, *Memoirs,* 1897–1903, p. 573.

was being encircled by the continental combination, and the English mice who must be immobile. This idea soon developed further in the Admiral's mind.* Still fretting a little at the want of confidence shown him by the English, he went to Sandringham for his uncle's birthday. Mr. Chamberlain was among the guests : no doubt the King thought that a meeting under his roof would symbolise reconciliation. There was shooting by day and music and acting and conjuring tricks in the evening, and after a week of family life the Emperor stayed for five days more with his friend Lord Lonsdale, and embarked on the *Hohenzollern* at Queensferry on the Firth of Forth. Baron Eckardstein gives a curious story that 'as he disappeared on board his yacht, King Edward was heard to breathe "Thank God he's gone." ' † The King may have felt that, but he could scarcely have seen him disappear on board his yacht, for he was at Windsor entertaining the King of Portugal. Geography forbids.

* *Willy-Nicky Letters,* pp. 89, 90. † Eckardstein, p. 245.

CHAPTER XII

THE King had made an excellent recovery from his serious operation in the summer of 1902 ; by the end of the year he was ready to resume that exuberant restlessness which was so characteristic of him. He had also come to the conclusion that any German alliance, such as the Emperor had suggested, was impossible. The tone of the German and English Press sufficiently testified to a mutual national repugnance, which no array of pleasant official speeches could modify. By her treaty with Japan England had now abandoned the principle of isolation which she had maintained since the Crimean War, and the time was ripe for making a treaty with a nation nearer home. Since, at the age of thirteen, the King had accompanied his parents on their state visit to Napoleon III and the Empress Eugénie he had been a true *boulevardier ;* the urbanity of the French, their wit and their lightness of touch, their pleasant indulgence of individual liberty in private life attracted him personally, and he was much at home in Paris. After the end of the Boer War the savage rancour of the French Press, which had so infuriated him with its unspeakable cartoons of his mother and himself, died down, and, officially, M. Delcassé at the Quai d'Orsay and M. Paul Cambon at the French Embassy in London had been working hard at the reconcilement of the numerous points, especially in Egypt and Morocco, where French and English interests clashed. The King saw himself lending a helping hand here, and he made up his mind to go to Paris again, to see a play at the *Théâtre français,* to attend a race meeting with his large cigar, to demonstrate his enjoyment at being back in the most civilised town in Europe, and find out whether he could not, by sheer geniality and total obliviousness of the disagreeable past, make the man in the street look on him with kindlier eyes. There was no doubt that officially he would receive a cordial welcome, for the French Government was at one with his own in deploring the bad relations of the two countries, and he wanted that welcome to be as splendid as possible : 'the more honours that were paid to him,' ran his commands to the British Ambassador in Paris, 'the better it would be.' He was no diplomatist in any strict or technical sense of the word, for the professional diplomatist who really unravels knots and makes smooth places plain must be infinitely patient, suave of temper and incapable of taking offence. King Edward was impatient, he was quick to anger, especially when he suspected a personal slight, and he was lacking in intellectual subtlety and tactful persistence ; if opposed, he did not seek other methods of approach, but grew irritated. His geniality, however, was the most valuable asset on such an expedition, and he had good reason to feel confidence in it. He was out to make Paris like him again.

He himself arranged the first of those foreign tours which were to become so large a feature in his monarchical activities and which he so vastly enjoyed. A yachting tour in the Mediterranean in the spring of 1903 was the camouflaged title of it, for the chief point in the tour was the visit to Paris on his homeward journey, and that was not officially announced to the French Government till after he started. Lisbon was the first port of call, and here was a convenient opportunity for returning the visit King Carlos had paid him last November. There he spent the first five days of

April 1903 working at full horse-power. He assured the Chambers of Commerce that the history of the ancient alliance between the two countries furnished one of the most precious and glorious chapters in the annals of his Empire. The preservation in all their integrity of Portuguese colonies — the German Anglophobe Press had been saying that England had designs on Delagoa Bay — was one of his dearest aims and objects, and he predicted that the future history of their countries would outshine the past. These golden words, as the Portuguese Prime Minister so aptly termed them, were cheered to the echo, and whether, had there been matters of dispute current at the time, they would have smoothed difficulties away, is irrelevant. The King's mission here was to confirm existing cordiality, and he fulfilled it. A bloodless bull-fight, a pigeon-shooting match, a reception of English residents, a visit to an Irish convent, a state banquet, a gala performance at the opera, and picnics in the country filled the rest of the programme. The monarchs embraced and the *Victoria and Albert* steamed away to Gibraltar.*

An interesting occasion ; no English reigning monarch had ever set foot on the impregnable rock during the two hundred years in which it had been his possession. Indeed the associations of the rock with the Royal House were far from happy, for the King's grandfather, the Duke of Kent, had been sent out after a mutiny that had occurred there, just a hundred years ago, and had employed the cat and the gallows with such revolting severity that his father, King George III, dispensed with his further services in his army. Malta was the next port, again virgin soil to the foot of English kings, and so to Naples for an official visit to the King of Italy at Rome. There had been a great deal of telegraphy over this visit : should the King pay a call on the aged Pope

* Lee, *King Edward VII*, ii. pp. 224-227.

Leo XIII, and thus risk the disapproval of his Protestant subjects, or should he refrain and incur the censure of loyal
Catholics ? As a boy of seventeen he had had an audience
with Pope Pius IX, which had caused his mother some nervousness, and she had insisted that his Governor, General
Bruce, should be present and note down every word that
passed, for fear that the Holy Father might tell people that
'Bertie had said God knows what.' . . . But the King was all
for religious tolerance, and he had a most cordial interview
without rousing any acute ecclesiastical resentment in his
Protestants.

One important personage had been following the King's
progress with much chagrin. The Emperor of Germany,
who, since his accession fifteen years ago, had made a feature of state visits, considered them as his own patent and
strongly disapproved of his uncle's trespass — for that was
what it came to — on his Italian preserves. Evidently the
arch-meddler was tampering with his ally, with a view to
encirclement. William had been planning a trip to Rome
himself, to return King Victor Emmanuel's visit the year before, and he settled to pay it at once in order to obliterate the
very pleasant impression his uncle had made there. He
staged himself far more imperially. The King's suite had
consisted of only a couple of equerries and a representative
of the Foreign Office : the Emperor took his Chancellor with
him, and surrounded himself with a military staff of the
tallest men in his army, sons of Anak, led by Colonel Plüs-
kow, whom irreverent Paris had dubbed 'Colonel Plus que
haut' : these giants symbolised the mighty stature of twenty-
two army corps. The King had driven about Rome in a
landau from the British Embassy, often in mufti ; so the
Emperor brought with him his state gala carriage, and seldom appeared except in full uniform with a spiked silver
helmet. Two squadrons of his Gardes-du-Corps rode fore

and aft of his great coach. All the millinery and manne-
quins of majesty were magnificently displayed, but Rome
was not very much impressed. The man in the street was as
irreverent as Paris had been about Giant Plus que haut.
'Che prepotenza !' (What swank !) was the general verdict as the War Lord, with stern and constipated frown,
featured the traditional bearing of the All-Highest. At
times he really seemed to be caricaturing himself with withering fidelity.

Then there was the visit to the Pope, and the meeting of
the Vicar of Christ and the instrument of the Most High was
designed to complete the effacement of the encircling uncle.
It was conducted *in camera,* but the Emperor dictated a
verbatim report of it in the form of dialogue within an hour
or two of its conclusion, so that nothing be lost : 'Myself' and
'The Pope' were the characters. The Pontiff, it stated, saluted the Emperor (who, by the Canon of Holy Church, was
a heretic) as the spiritual successor of Charlemagne. Just as
Leo III had entrusted Charlemagne with the mission of
bringing the civilised world to the Cross of Christ, so today
Leo XIII saw himself, as in a dream, entrusting William II
with the mission of warring against atheists and Socialists
and bringing Europe back into Christianity. Other monarchs ought to take example by him, and though, politically,
Europe (so His Holiness acutely observed) consisted of
various nations, the Kaiser of the German Empire could influence and exhort them all to return to the Church : 'Je suis
devenu,' said he, 'presque un demi Allemand.' As such he
had the warmest admiration for William II's great ancestor
Friedrich II, but William was his superior in the firmness of
his religious convictions. In turn the Emperor told the Pope
that he regarded him as the heir of the Roman Caesars and
therefore the 'Imperator Imperii Romani.' Holy Father
looked at him with astonishment, and then, 'with gratitude

shining in his eyes, said "Eh bien, ce n'est pas mal cela, et peut-être vous avez raison." ' As a postscript to this report the Emperor added : 'The Pope also asked His Majesty how German naval construction stood ; how much he hoped that he would get a strong and powerful navy to safeguard peace and German cultural interests.' *

It is hardly possible to accept this flowery dialogue (from which the above is culled), exactly as it stands, as an accurate record of what passed : the Pope, for all his shrewd discern-ment, could not have told the Emperor so clairvoyantly and minutely how he regarded himself and wished to be re-garded by the world. But only a slight rearrangement in the assignment of the speeches is needful. If we suppose that 'Myself' said 'How about me and Charlemagne ? Has there ever been another sovereign who has thought and acted with the same spirituality as I ?' we can easily imagine that 'The Pope' replied very suitably : or if it was 'Myself' who said 'My strong and powerful navy is for the safeguarding of peace,' 'The Pope' would surely have replied 'Quite !' But, psychologically, the Emperor's account is more valuable than any independent shorthand report could be, for it gives a unique presentment of his own self-portrait.†

While the nephew, at the Quirinal and the Vatican alike, was thus erasing his uncle from the map of Italy, King Ed-ward was simultaneously engraving himself on the map of France, and it is pleasant to imagine the Emperor, attended by his giants, stepping into his special train at Rome on May 5 and picking up the Italian papers to see what they said about him. All very polite, but then the Imperial brow

---

* Bülow, *Memoirs,* 1897–1903, pp. 600–604.

† The Pope, however, was certainly much impressed with him. In private audience not long after with M. François Sabatier, His Holiness bewailed the irre-ligion of France, the degeneracy of the whole nation as indicated by the separation of the Church from the State. He thought that the only thing that could save France was that she should put herself under the direction 'of that great and good man the German Emperor.' . . . (Private information.)

clouded as he read what had been happening in Paris the
day before. It was without undue pain that he had already
seen in the Press that the King's reception there had been far
from enthusiastic. He had driven with President Loubet
to the British Embassy through streets lined with crowds
that did not seem pleased to see him, and there had been cries
of 'Vivent les Boers !' 'Vive Fashoda !' Then, according
to Imperial standards, how cheap the King had made himself ! He had spoken at the British Chamber of Commerce
— England was always a nation of shop-keepers — about the
pleasure he felt in finding himself in Paris again, about the
admiration and affection the English cherished for France
and her glorious traditions. He had gone to the theatre and
shaken hands with a French actress in the foyer, assuring
her that she was the embodiment of the grace and *esprit* of
France ; he had spoken at the *Hôtel de Ville,* and said Paris
always treated him as if he was at home ; he had attended a
review and a race-meeting and a state dinner ; the bonds of
friendship between the two countries, he said, were already
strong and sure. He had brought out all his old tricks again,
thought the Emperor, his *bonhomie,* his power of enjoyment, his deplorable lack of majesty, and they had taken
everybody in. For he now observed in this morning's paper
that, as the King drove through the streets again yesterday
on his departure, the yelling crowd swarmed round his carriage shouting 'Vive notre Roi !' It was sickening, and the
Emperor read no more. This visit to Paris was obviously
intended as an unfriendly act towards Germany, but a little
shouting in the streets had no political significance. Still, it
was annoying, and the King had now paid state visits to
three foreign countries, Portugal, Italy and France, and had
not even suggested paying one to his own nephew.

To hail the plucky and personal triumph of King Edward
in Paris as a unique political achievement which brought the

entente cordiale to birth would be a gross overrating of its importance, for statesmen and ambassadors, Lord Lansdowne, M. Delcassé and M. Cambon, were already making excellent progress with it, and the success of the King's visit did not contribute in the smallest degree to the reconciliation of conflicting points of view or the unravelling of knotty questions. But, in conjunction with the King's well-known dislike of Germany and of his nephew, the visit certainly produced an optimising effect on the French negotiators : they felt that, when they had come to agreement with their English colleagues, the treaty (or whatever was the result of their labours) would be unlikely to provoke popular opposition. Paris and the French Press had decided to forget Fashoda and the martyred Boers. The King had also made it possible that President Loubet and M. Delcassé should pay an official visit to England, which since the days of Fashoda had been out of the question : no invitation could have been sent, nor, if it had, would it have been accepted. They came in July, and, in addition to the usual forms of royal cordiality, there was a military review at Aldershot with most unusual musical honours. Twelve years ago, on the occasion of the visit of the French fleet to Portsmouth, the Queen, entertaining the officers at Osborne, had, with some reluctance, stood up while the *Marseillaise* was played ; today, by special order of the King, it was played three times through entire, their Britannic Majesties both standing, and it was followed on each occasion by only six bars of the English National Anthem. That was typical of King Edward's diplomacy, the object of which always was to produce a jolly and welcoming atmosphere, and the visitors, though slightly astonished at so much *Marseillaise,* could not fail to be gratified. In the intervals of such robust cordialities M. Delcassé had business conversations with the French Ambassador and the English Foreign Secretary.

These effusions made depressing reading for the Emperor, and he heartened himself up by a summer yachting tour in the Norwegian fjords with all the old boon companions of fifteen years ago, a comic singer, a musician, a caricaturist, and above all the devoted Troubadour Philip Eulenburg, now retired from diplomacy and created a Prince. There were many who had attained eminence, they had become Excellencies and Privy Councillors and Professors, and, though they had passed into middle age and obesity, there were still the gymnastics on deck, and the Emperor still played his juvenile jokes and made puns at breakfast : the whole atmosphere, 'Phili' wrote to the Chancellor, was that of 'a frivolous lieutenant's casino' : it was like living on a 'floating theatre.' The Emperor's restlessness and excitement were frightful, and between his bouts of high spirits and horse-play were moods of irritability and depression when reports of the unfavourable General Election came in, or when he seemed to realise that his diplomacies had brought him no nearer to Russia and had only forwarded that dreaded *rapprochement* between England and France, with Russia in the background ready to be presented to France's new friend. If any serious political disturbance occurred, it seemed likely that he would have a complete nervous breakdown. But the trip did him good, and, returning, he absorbed himself in his autumn military manœuvres. He himself commanded the Blue Army, and sent an aide-de-camp as a spy to the headquarters of the Red Army in order to overhear their plan of campaign for next day. With this foreknowledge of the enemy's movements he could thwart them and thus score a smashing victory.* That was a sedative to this ill-dreaming about the encirclement of Germany.

King Edward in his own manner was almost as restless,

* Haller, *Philip Eulenburg,* ii. pp. 156–161 ; Bülow, *Memoirs, 1897–1903,* pp. 606, 607, 612.

and as soon as the French guests left England he prepared for a visit to Ireland. During the war there had been the most violent pro-Boer demonstrations in Dublin, Nationalists in the House of Commons had cheered British defeats in South Africa, and even now when, in July 1903, the King and Queen entered Dublin, the Corporation refused to present an address of welcome. To deal with such hostility required neither diplomacy nor patient unravelling : indeed it only served to develop the King's sheer horse-power of geniality and his superb unconsciousness that anybody was other than delighted and honoured to see him, and, as at Paris and with precisely the same success, he set himself to captivate the crowds with his own jovial enjoyment. An orgy of popular enthusiasm greeted him. Off he went in August to Marienbad for his annual cure, where in mufti he met two more Sovereigns, his brother-in-law, King George of Greece, and his cousin, Prince Ferdinand of Bulgaria, and, as soon as his cure was over at the end of the month, he pushed on to Vienna for a state visit to the Emperor of Austria. He arranged to meet the mother of the young King of Spain *en route,* and explained to her why, when he had been to Portugal in the spring, he had not paid his respects to her at Madrid.

William was aghast at these indefatigable activities of his uncle. He knew that the Tsar was to pay a state visit to Vienna at the end of September, and he at once proposed to the Emperor of Austria that he should pay him a visit directly after King Edward had left, just as, in the spring, he had appeared in majesty at Rome as soon as the King had gone to Paris. This was the second time this year that the King had paid an official visit to a member of the Triple Alliance, and the Emperor of course suspected some sinister design. He would have to ferret that out, and, in any case, the genial impression his uncle was sure to have made must be erased before it had time to sink in. How meddlesome and interfering he was ! It was most necessary, as William had told his grandmother when first he came to the throne, that 'We Emperors must stick together,' and he promised himself some fruitful talks with the Tsar when, after his visit to Vienna, he went to stay with his brother-in-law, the Grand Duke of Hesse.

So Emperor Francis Joseph, now over seventy, had to entertain these three prodigious Sovereigns one after the other in the space of five weeks : their visits were accompanied with the ritual appropriate to his guests. The King led off : he drove from the station with his host through streets unguarded by soldiers, the police alone kept the way clear between the crowds of Viennese citizens. He and the Emperor made each other Field-Marshals of their respective armies, there were the usual banquets and gala performances, but between these public engagements the King went about as if he was at home, and read the papers in the Jockey Club and called on friends. . . His nephew came next : William was in a mood of dynastic severity, determined not to recognise Countess Sophie Chotek who had lately married the Archduke Francis Ferdinand, heir to the Austrian throne. Chancellor Bülow argued with him in the train : His Majesty, he told him, was not coming to Vienna in order to show his disapproval of royal personages marrying beneath them, but to confirm the cordial relations of the Hohenzollerns and the Hapsburgs. The Hapsburgs had recognised Countess Sophie as the wife of the heir, and they would be mortally offended if he did not. Not till the train slowed down in the station at Vienna could he be persuaded not to consider her invisible. Thereafter all was majesty and military pomp ; it was soldiers, soldiers all the way, as befitted the reception of the first War Lord of the Triple Alliance. . . The Tsar came next. For fear of Nihilist at-

tempts on his life he left his camouflaged saloon carriage at
a suburban station. Thousands of soldiers lined his route,
police and detectives swarmed round him like bees, and the
citizens of Vienna never saw him at all.*

But in tranquil Hesse the Autocrat felt himself safe ; he
and the Tsarina went there a few weeks later. They stayed
at the castle of Wolfsgarten outside Darmstadt, and walked
about the park unattended, and played lawn tennis and went
to the theatre. Here was an admirable opportunity for the
Emperor to have quiet talks with him, as Queen Victoria
had had in that domestic fortnight at Balmoral seven years
ago, which promised so well and performed so little. William visited the Tsar at Wolfsgarten and, pursuing the well-
trodden paths of his own diplomacy, tried to sow distrust
between Russia and France. This was more than ever desirable now, for the Anglo-French *entente* was approaching
ratification, and who knew what unwelcome combination
might develop out of that ? The Tsar was the most pious,
the most religious of men, and William renewed in personal
conversation the theme of one of his letters. He deplored,
just as his grandfather Albert had done, the utter godlessness
of the frivolous French. They were unthinkable allies for
a Christian monarch : moreover, they were an antimonarchical nation, prone to revolution and regicide : was it wise to
link the fortunes of Holy Russia with such atheistical cut-
throats ? Nor had the French Government any more sense
of honour than their new friend, perfidious Albion. But it
was impossible to get anything out of the Tsar ; he smiled,
he shook his head over the impious, regicidal tendencies of
the French, and slid gently away, repeating, like a child
that has learned its lesson, that there was no point of dispute
between Russia and Germany. They were good friends and
he hoped that they might become, in the future, even more

---

* Bülow, *Memoirs*, 1897–1903, pp. 613, 614 ; Lee, *King Edward VII*, ii. p. 263.

friendly than they were already, but let us not talk of alliances. . . Those noncommittal sentences had a familiar, a stale ring to the Emperor's sensitive ear. How was it that neither Russia nor England would fall into his welcoming arms ?

This track seemed to lead nowhere ; but there was another branching off from it, also well trodden. If Russia still stuck to France and (by inference) was tending towards France's new ally, the obvious course was to work for her weakening and for any chance of making friction between Russia and England. The Far East seemed to hold out hopes of trouble for her, which, failing alliance, was the best wish of the fairy godfather. Russia had two ports, Vladivostok and Port Arthur, on the eastern coast to the north of China, and for a year she had been occupying Manchuria, the hinterland across which she was building railways to those ports. Between them lay Korea, and Russia refused to recognise its independence or the independence of China, nor would she evacuate Manchuria. Japan was thus directly threatened. Here there was an opportunity of the sort that the Emperor never failed to find attractive.

If Russia — no longer regarded as a possible ally but a menace — went to war in the remote East, her military strength on the Eastern German frontier must be lessened. That had long been an uneasiness to him, though it had been pleasant occasionally to assure the Tsar that, if he was disposed to advance towards India, the German army was at his back to prevent 'another Power,' whom he unsuccessfully wooed, from stirring. In this fresh policy he had the support — perhaps the initiative — of Bülow, for the Chancellor had pronounced that 'Russia at war in the East removed the latent war-danger for us in Europe.' * So the Emperor wrote letter after letter to the Tsar, as 'his affectionate cousin

* Bülow, *Memoirs*, 1897–1903, pp. 617–621.

and friend,' *alias* 'the Admiral of the Atlantic *en vedette,*' urging him to stand no nonsense from Japan : 'Korea and Manchuria must and will be Russian.' The real mischief-maker, he told him, was England. England, now allied with Japan, was backing her up, 'blowing on the flame where she can,' and supplying funds for Japanese mobilisation.

Negotiations between Russia and Japan dragged on. It became perfectly clear that Russia was protracting them merely in order to consolidate her hold in Manchuria, and in February 1904, as the Emperor and Bülow had hoped, the Japanese declared war, having previously torpedoed two Russian battleships and a cruiser lying off Port Arthur. During the spring King Edward signified that the British Government was ready to act as mediator to bring the war to a close, but that did not suit the Emperor at all. He told the Tsar that he would beg Uncle Bertie not to worry him with any more proposals of the sort. If Nicky wanted a mediator, the request would come from him, and William would be at his disposal.*

King Edward had not yet returned his nephew's visit to England in the autumn of 1902, and in March 1904 he proposed to come to Berlin. He was told that this was impossible, for the Emperor had been ill and was ordered south for a cruise in the Mediterranean. The King was not pleased at this refusal ; William could surely have put off his departure for a few days. But it was quite true that the Emperor was not fit for the fatiguing splendours involved by a state visit. He had suffered from hoarseness in the autumn, and a medical examination showed some sort of growth on one of the vocal chords. He had an operation for its removal, and his pluck had been beyond all praise. He knew that his father had died of malignant disease, of which the

* *Willy-Nicky Letters,* pp. 101–119.

first symptoms had been identical with his own in precisely
the same region of his throat. Like his father, he was forbidden to speak, but he carried on his work exactly as usual,
writing questions and orders to his Ministers on slips of
paper, completely unperturbed, waiting for the microscopical examination of the detached fragment of the growth,
which proved not to be malignant. So, failing this meeting
in March, another was arranged for June at Kiel.

The Emperor was immensely excited about this visit. He
had given orders that the entire German fleet should be assembled at Kiel so that the King should see how lustily that
infant had thrived in the last few years, and the notion of
giving him a most disagreeable surprise was irresistible.
Japan had built up her fleet almost unobserved, and had
scored by reserving that surprise until she was ready to fight,
but it was in vain that Bülow urged a similar discretion.
This visit, though conducted at sea, was really a state visit :
the Emperor was attended by his Chancellor and the entire
Cabinet, King Edward by the First Lord of the Admiralty,
in addition to the usual suites, and the King had also brought
with him on the *Victoria and Albert* Baron d'Estournelles de
Constant and the Prince of Monaco, by way of signifying to
France that the meeting had no political intentions. The
upper deck of the *Hohenzollern* was embowered in banks of
flowers, among which fountains played ; as the King came
on board the Royal Standard was broken at her masthead
and floated beside the Black Eagle, and a state banquet for
a hundred and eight persons with speeches *en cliché* to follow was the opening ceremony. The King spoke of his
most earnest desire that this personal intercourse should knit
even closer yet the ties of intimate relationship between the
two Royal Houses, and concluded : 'May our two flags float
side by side to the most remote ages even as today, for the
maintenance of peace and the welfare not only of our own

countries, but also of all other nations.' Admirable sentiments, and most suitable to these decorative occasions, but
both host and guest and every German and English person
who heard them knew that there was not the faintest chance
of their fulfilment. The wish was not even father to the
thought, for, though the King was all for friendly relations
with Germany, nothing was further from his personal wishes
than to establish such relations with her as the juxtaposition
of the two flags implied. As for national feeling, any Government in either country that announced alliance with the
other must immediately have fallen, for the hatred and distrust between the two nations was irreconcilable. Then
uncle and nephew inspected the German ships and the new
dockyard at Kiel, and the municipality of Hamburg, the
chief port of Germany, gave so warm a welcome to the King
that he said that Liverpool itself could not have been more
pleased to see him. Once again after dinner on Prince
Henry's ship the Emperor proposed the King's health, and
was careful to explain that his new navy, which had impressed the King far more than his nephew had anticipated,
was designed solely for purposes of defence ; he thought
there might be some faint suspicion in the King's mind that
it was meant for more than that, and he added that all the
navies of the world ought to be bound together in trustful
comradeship. The King was not quite so rosily Utopian,
but he impressed on Bülow that the Anglo-French *entente*
was not directed against Germany for the purpose of her
isolation : that was as far as he could go. The Emperor's
surprise, however, had been a shock, and it was pleasant to
remember that Admiral Sir John Fisher, who had better
information about Germany's new fleet, was already engaged on a comprehensive scheme of naval reorganisation.
Unless the British Navy was immensely strengthened without any delay at all, his opinion was that England 'might as

well pack up and hand over to Germany.' Indeed the most practical result of these compliments at Kiel was that Fisher was appointed First Sea Lord of the Admiralty. Henceforth the King endorsed, whenever required, his view that the German naval programme could only be met by a proportionate increase in the English fleet and by its readiness to go to war at any moment. The Emperor's plea for comradeship between navies ? Put differently, the armament competition, which, after ten years' ruinous bidding, was to end in war, had definitely begun.*

On July 30, 1904, the Tsarina, now the mother of four daughters, gave birth to a son, and every town in Russia blazed with flags and was loud with saluting guns and bells of national rejoicing. Never had any event so moved the Tsar, for now the Crown of all the Russias would pass in the direct line to Alexis, and his father vowed to bequeath it to him as even he himself had received it, in all the absolutism of autocracy. Immediately after came disastrous news from the seat of war in the East. On August 10 the Japanese under Admiral Togo inflicted a crushing defeat on the Russian navy off Port Arthur. One battleship and a cruiser alone escaped to Tsin-Tao, where they were interned, and the ships that were not sunk put back, badly damaged, into Port Arthur again. Four days later the Russian squadron at Vladivostok was defeated, and the Japanese were in possession of the Pacific.

The Emperor, who with King Edward was godfather to Alexis, wrote to the Tsar in excellent spirits when he heard of these disasters, signing himself Admiral of the Atlantic, though the Admiral of the Pacific just now was Admiral Togo. He sent his godchild a goblet for his use when he came to crave for something other than milk, and quoted

* Ludwig, *Kaiser Wilhelm II*, pp. 248, 249 ; Lee, *King Edward VII*, ii. pp. 328–333 ; Bülow, *Memoirs*, 1903–1909, pp. 22–24.

pretty maxims in accordance with which he would like to
see his godchild educated. There was :

> 'Ein gut Glas Branntewein
> Soll Mitternachte nicht schädlich sein' ; *

and 'the classical word of our great Reformer, Dr. Martin
Luther' :

> 'Wer nicht lieb Wein, Weib und Gesang,
> Der bleibt ein Narr sein Leben lang.' †

Then followed elaborate notes about the conduct of the
Japanese war, and sympathy for these grave reverses. Strong
reinforcements, he told the Tsar, were needed on land, for
General Kuropatkin seemed to have only 180,000 troops
against the Japanese 250,000 or 280,000. He worked it out
for him and twenty divisions or ten army corps would be
wanted, of which the Siberian armies would supply four :
cavalry corps would, of course, accompany them. Then
Nicky's Baltic fleet must go out : it would force the Japanese
back into their ports, it would restore to him the command
of the sea, and deprive the enemy armies of support and re-
inforcement from their base, etc. etc. No doubt all would
end well, though the task would cost much money and thousands of men, but to put overwhelming numbers into the
field was essential, so also was time and patience. Victory
rested, as Napoleon said, with the big battalions.‡

The resemblance between these reflections and the Aphorisms which the Emperor sent to his uncle when the early
stages of the South African War had brought such disasters
to British arms is very remarkable, but in no way surprising,
for an identical policy dictated both. In the Aphorisms, with
a view of shepherding England into the German fold, the

---

* 'A good glass of brandy at midnight does not hurt anybody.'
† 'Who loves not wine, woman and song, remains a fool for all his life.'
‡ *Willy-Nicky Letters*, pp. 123–126.

Emperor warned his uncle that the Boer War would be a long and expensive affair, and that England must have some friend in Europe who would guarantee her safety from other Powers. Now, with the same object in view with regard to Russia, he pursued the same tack. He impersonated the wolf, ominously howling, by telling the Tsar that Japan was arming and drilling Chinese troops who would fall upon Russia's rear,* and then, when the early stages of the war went badly for Russia, he snatched up the shepherd's crook. An alliance with Russia was once more his objective, and within a few months he had, at the Tsar's invitation, drafted a treaty.

The Baltic fleet, as the Emperor had advised, was sent out in October 1904 on its ultimate journey. As it steamed through the North Sea on the night of October 21, it opened fire on the Gamecock Fishing Fleet from Hull, which was trawling on the Dogger Bank, sinking one boat and disabling others and killing two men. Though its searchlights must have revealed that these were English fishing vessels, it went on its way without rendering aid. Not till three days afterwards did the Tsar telegraph to King Edward saying that he had learned of this 'sad incident' from a foreign source (*i.e.* not from Admiral Rozhdestvensky, who was in command of the Baltic fleet). He explained that many warnings had been received that the Japanese were 'lurking about' in order to torpedo his ships, and that orders had been given that great precautions should be taken, especially by night, whenever any vessel or boat should be in sight. In fact he defended his admiral's action, and claimed the right for his Baltic fleet, bound for the Pacific, to fire on any ship it sighted, if his captains chose to consider that it was a Japanese ship camouflaged as a trawler. Every vessel must keep out of range of his fleet or risk being

* *Willy-Nicky Letters*, p. 101.

shelled. The Tsar sent his best love to his uncle, and hoped that no complications would arise.

For a few days it looked as if the Tsar's hopes were to be disappointed. The whole of the English Press blazed with fury, and the King, sharing it, expressed his views to the Foreign Minister with something of the impetuosity of his nephew. 'Some punishment,' he wrote, '*must* be meted out to the Russian officers, whoever may be the responsible ones,' and he repeated the same counsel two days later, having fixed on the culprit : 'The Russian Admiral *must* be punished for his conduct, and we have, I think, a *right* to demand it.' Then a report was received from the Russian Admiral affirming that a Japanese torpedo-boat had been seen steaming full speed for the Russian fleet. Nobody believed that, but the King began to consider what would be the effect of this demand on which he had insisted. If Russia refused there would be war, unless England suffered the humiliation of withdrawing it. He veered completely round, and wrote to his slightly bewildered Foreign Secretary asking if we were prepared to go to war 'for the sake of the heirs of two harmless fishermen.' The indignation of the Press, though no more violent than his own, thoroughly alarmed him, and he overtook his own letter to Lord Lansdowne by a telegram : 'Strongly deprecate pressing for punishment of Admiral. Russia could not accept such a humiliation,' and then left Lord Lansdowne in charge. No one was more relieved than he when, by the efforts of the Russian and British Ambassadors, it was decided to submit the case to the Hague Tribunal.*

* Lee, *King Edward VII*, ii. pp. 302–304.

CHAPTER XIII

WHILE Admiral Rozhdestvensky, after his victorious engagement on the Dogger Bank, continued his voyage without, for the present, encountering any more Japanese torpedo-boats, the Emperor got very busy again with letters and telegrams to the Tsar over a Russo-Germanic alliance. France, he now hoped, would by her treaty obligations be forced to join it, for the English Press had been strongly protesting against German coaling stations (Germany being neutral) supplying coal to the Russian fleet on its way East, and if Japan and England together took steps to stop this, it would be an unfriendly act against Russia on the part of two Powers in combination. The three strongest Continental Powers would thus be combined against England ; this would be a due retribution for her having refused to join Germany and the Triple Alliance. Such was the main purport of the Emperor's opening telegram in this section of his correspondence with the Tsar, and, in postscript, as commercial traveller for German industries, he told him that he 'ought not to forget to order new ships so as to be ready with some of them when the war is over. They will be excellent persuaders during the peace negotiations. Our private firms would be most glad to receive contracts.' He returned to this subject later : Stettin and Kiel could furnish handsome specimens of battleships, and Krupp would supply batteries of guns.* The Tsar responded eagerly : he thought it was high time to stop England dictating her own rules of neutrality about the question of the Russian fleet coaling at German stations.† 'The only way,' he continued, 'as you say, would be that Germany, Russia and France should at once unite upon arrangements to abolish English and Japanese arrogance and insolence. Would you like to lay down and frame the outlines of such a treaty ? As soon as it is accepted by us, France is bound to join her ally.'

Would he like to frame this treaty ? He could give a practical answer to that question, and on the very day on which he received this telegram the Emperor, in consultation with Bülow, drew up a draft and sent it to the Tsar. This draft was emended a few days later by suggestions from both sides, and its final form for the present contained the following provisions :

'1. If either Empire should be attacked by a European Power, its Ally will come to its aid with all its forces by land and sea. The Tsar will inform France of this understanding and ask her to associate herself with it as an Ally.

'2. Neither of the high contracting parties shall make a separate peace with a common adversary.

'3. This Treaty shall remain in force for a year after either party has renounced it.

'4. (Secret Article.) The high contracting parties shall make common cause if acts committed by either side in the present war, such as the delivery of coal to a belligerent, causes a third Power to complain that neutrality has been violated.'

Twice in his covering letter the Emperor was careful to

---

* *Willy-Nicky Letters*, pp. 138, 156.

† The Emperor regarded the acquisition of these coaling stations as his personal achievement. He had insisted that it was 'his will' to have them, and had got them in spite of the most determined opposition from England and Russia. (Diary of Mr. Frederick Whitridge.)

inform the Tsar that he and Chancellor Bülow had drawn up this treaty together. Bülow must surely have known that though both Sovereigns signed the treaty fifty times over it had no force of any kind until France had subscribed to it, for her approval of the admission of a third party into the Franco-Russian alliance was necessary, but he consented to the draft being sent to the Tsar, as the joint work of the Emperor and himself. Hardly was it despatched than the Emperor began to visualise lurking perils, and his heart failed him. The Tsar had suggested a clause concerning the localising of the Japanese war, but that was not to be thought of ; if by some indiscretion, wrote the Emperor, the treaty, at present to be kept secret, became known, this would be taken to refer to the possibility of England going to war on the side of Japan, and England would consider that provocative and directed against her. In reality, he allowed, it was so, but it would never do to say so : England must not be provoked, or, at any rate, Germany must have no hand in such provocation. But why should not Russia, on her own account, 'cool British insolence and overbearing' by making a military demonstration on the Afghan frontier ? That would make the British Jingoes moderate their swagger. . . A week or two later fresh qualms seized him. England had forbidden German vessels to supply coal to Russian ships of war, and so unless the Tsar would give positive guarantees that, if England went to war with Germany on this point, Russia would stand shoulder to shoulder with her, the Emperor regretted 'the necessity of immediately forbidding German steamers to continue to coal your fleet.' Finally, in answer to the Tsar's demand that France must be informed about the proposed treaty before definitely concluding it, the Emperor declared this to be quite impossible, for indeed there was no chance of France's throwing over the Anglo-French *entente* and joining Germany, since the whole direction of her policy was to bring Russia and England together and thus form a Triple Entente. But it would not do to admit that, and he wrote : 'Loubet and Delcassé are no doubt experienced statesmen. But they not being Princes or Emperors I am unable to place them — in a question of *confidence* like this one — on the same footing as you my equal, my cousin and friend.' So, for the present, this precious treaty was shelved, but the Emperor did not give up the notion of procuring a continental alliance against England. Some better opportunity might present itself.*

Russia was in a miserable plight. Port Arthur fell on New Year's Day, 1905, and internally the country was seething with revolutionary ferment. There was a general strike, and when a deputation of strikers marched, unarmed and peaceful, to the Winter Palace to present to the Tsar a petition setting forth their grievances under the tyranny of the bureaucracy, he refused to see them, and, as the crowd would not disperse, they were fired on by the Guards. As for the war, now that it was going so disastrously, the Emperor made a complete *volte-face*. Only a year ago he had insisted on the necessity of it : Russia must have iceless harbours for her commerce : Korea and Manchuria must and should be Russian. Moreover the war was a Crusade, a holy war against the Yellow Peril, and he had sent the Tsar at least three allegorical pictures to inspire him with the sense of religious duty. One represented Russia leaning on the shoulder of Germany, while St. Michael, wearing the Iron Cross (evidently bestowed on him by the successor of Charlemagne), encouraged them to advance against the Buddhist demons of Japan : a second showed the Emperor in armour holding up an immense crucifix before the adoring Tsar : in the third the Emperor himself figured as an archangel

* *Willy-Nicky Letters,* pp. 133–152.

with a fiery sword and exhorted the Great Powers to attack the writhing dragons of the Orient. He told the Tsar that these fine pieces were painted by himself, but in reality his favourite artist, Herr Knackfuss, executed them under his supervision. But Russia had gone out on that Crusade alone with disastrous results, and now the Emperor informed him that from the first the war had been very unpopular with all classes of his subjects, and was in fact a great mistake.*

Russia then might safely be left to stew in her own bitter broth, and the Emperor turned his attention to France. He had long regarded the Anglo-French *entente* as a formidable link in the dreaded encirclement of Germany, and some judicious filing might be done. Bülow had a suggestion as to this : Morocco was an admirable file. France had acquiesced in the English occupation of Egypt, in return for which England had given France a free hand in Morocco, and any interest Germany might have in Morocco had been brushed aside. An excellent opportunity, thought Bülow, for the Emperor to make a personal and paternal visit to his German subjects there and thus to trouble the waters in which he hoped subsequently to fish. Possibly some embroilment with France might lead to the fall of Delcassé, who had been an architect and was now a pillar of the Anglo-French *entente,* and this was Bülow's ultimate object. The Emperor did not like the scheme, for he thought that such interference would be a provocation to France that might end in war, and his deep-rooted timidity abhorred the thought. But he consented. His second son, Prince Eitel Friedrich, recovering from pneumonia, had been ordered a southern cruise, and the Emperor chartered an empty steamer, the *Hamburg,* which was going to

* Bülow, *Memoirs,* 1903–1909, pp. 125, 126.

Naples, instead of voyaging more conspicuously on the *Hohenzollern.**

He made a remarkable speech at Bremen before he sailed. He was frightened at the part that Bülow had cast for him, he thought it dangerous, and perhaps (though consenting to it) he desired to dissociate himself from it. His opening at any rate breathed a pacific idealism for his country. He said :

'When I came to the throne, after my grandfather's mighty reign, I swore in my military oath that I would put aside bayonets and cannons, yet keep them always burnished and in good repair, so that jealousy and rivalry from without should never call us away from the completion of our garden and our stately house within. My study of history led me to take counsel with myself, and inwardly to vow that never would I strive for a vain Empire of the world. . . The world-wide dominion of my dream consists above all in this, that the new-made German Empire should everywhere be regarded with the most absolute confidence, should enjoy the reputation of a tranquil, fair-dealing, pacific neighbour ; and that if ever, in the future, history should tell of German world-dominion or a Hohenzollern hegemony, neither of these things should have been founded on conquests by the sword, but on the mutual confidence of nations animated by a similar ambition. Her material frontiers round about her — and the frontiers of her spirit nowhere to be traced !'

Then his habitual mood, the bawling about shining armour and God-protected aggressiveness, swept like a squall over this serene prospect. He thought of his growing fleet, which was to drive the British cockle-boats from the seas, and he proclaimed that the naval spirit of Germany was that of the Prussian officers at Königgratz and Sedan. This

* William II, *My Memoirs*, pp. 104, 105.

might possibly be mistaken for that spirit of conquest by the sword which he had so emphatically repudiated ; so, in order to reconcile these opposing points of view, he concluded by telling his bewildered audience that every German warship launched upon the waters was a guarantee for peace on earth.*

He set off. The first port of call was Lisbon ; he visited the King of Portugal, and telegraphed to Bülow his keen misgivings about this descent on Morocco, but Bülow was firm. On the last day of March the *Hamburg*, after a fearfully rough passage from Lisbon, arrived off Tangier, and Herr von Kuhlmann, German chargé d'affaires, came on board drenched with spray in his passage from the shore. It was with great difficulty that the Emperor was persuaded to land, but the Sultan of Morocco's uncle was waiting for him on the quay, his German subjects expected him, and Bülow had ordered a steady horse for him to ride. So he pulled himself together, and there was the white horse, which proved to be a Barbary stallion of excitable and uncertain temper, and the Sultan's black uncle to escort him. He became very imperial again when this horrid ride was over, and told the German colony that Morocco was an independent country and that his visit was a recognition of its independence. That was the essential point, for he thus challenged the French protectorate, and claimed equal rights for Germany in its affairs. The streets appeared to him, in this very uncomfortable excursion, to be lined with French and Italian rogues and adventurers and Spanish anarchists who waved banners and uttered loud cries, but when it turned out to have served its purpose he revised his impression and recorded that he had been warmly received by British and Spanish residents, who welcomed him as their

* Ludwig, *Kaiser Wilhelm II*, pp. 252, 253.

deliverer from French oppression. Two hours sufficed, and the *Hamburg* proceeded to visit Gibraltar.*

The King was already annoyed with his nephew. The increase in the English fleet had caused war scare in the German Press, and he did not think that the Emperor appreciated the friendly intention of his visit to Kiel last summer. It had been settled that the Prince of Wales should represent him at the forthcoming marriage of Crown Prince William of Germany in June, but now in a fit of exasperation the King cancelled this visit on the grounds that the young King of Spain was coming to England on that date, and that the Prince must be at home. In vain the British Ambassador in Berlin pleaded the importance of the occasion and said that the Emperor would take it very ill if this engagement was broken ; it would be surely unwise to give him this cause for personal offence. The King refused to reconsider it.†

Then came the news of the Emperor's epiphany at Tangier. The King was just starting for his own spring cruise in the Mediterranean, and he stopped in Paris to talk it over with President Loubet. The President shrugged his shoulders : it was in execrable taste and no doubt intended as an insult to France, but it was better to take no notice of it. But the King went south, simmering with rage, and, learning more from Admiral Prince Louis of Battenberg, who had seen the Emperor at Gibraltar immediately after the Tangier visit, he fairly boiled over, and wrote with extreme vividness to his Foreign Secretary. It was the most mischievous and uncalled-for prank — worse than the Kruger telegram — that the Emperor had ever played since he came

---

* William II, *My Memoirs*, pp. 104, 105 ; Bülow, *Memoirs*, 1903–1909, pp. 102, 107.

† Lee, *King Edward VII*, ii. pp. 335–336.

to the throne : luckily it was a complete fiasco. He was a political *enfant terrible,* and it was impossible to believe a word he said. His delight was 'to set every country by the ears.' His annual cruises were most deplorable, and their only object was to make mischief. His guests were a 'motley crew,' and there were nine retired admirals among them. A relief to express one's mind.

All this annoyance was very natural, but it must be remembered that the King's own cruises (he was on one now) were just as deplorable and no less mischievous from the Emperor's point of view. Each of them claimed exclusive rights of political cruising, and regarded the other as invariably engaged, under the pretext of a recuperative holiday, with sinister designs. The King's methods on these excursions were very different from his nephew's : his visits to any country were intended to promote cordial relations by his jollity and geniality ; the Emperor's by a display of majesty and giants to typify the might of Germany and to sow suspicions in his host's mind as to the sincerity of some country with which he had friendly relations. But to both monarchs the security of their own countries was the end in view, though the King sought to procure it by friendly attachments, the Emperor by detaching the ties that bound foreign nations to each other.

Both the King and President Loubet missed the significance of the Emperor's descent on Tangier. Loubet thought it an insult, best to be disregarded, the King a malicious prank which had proved a fiasco. In reality, it was an extremely clever move on Bülow's part. The Emperor had been shot up, a reluctant and timorous Mephistopheles, through a trap-door in the stage of Bülow's theatre, to speak the prologue, vanishing through it again in a cloud of sea spray when he had said his lines, and now for the play. Under pressure from Bülow the Sultan refused to accept the administrative reforms proposed by the French, and asked for a Conference of the Powers to adjudicate. France was in a cleft stick : if she was represented at the Conference, she admitted the right of the Powers to have a voice in the affairs of her protectorate ; if she refused to join it, they would be settled without her. The French Cabinet, fearful of a rupture with Germany, eventually accepted this invitation, and Delcassé, who stuck to the principle that no assembly of Principalities and Powers could be allowed to interfere in the management of a French protectorate, resigned. So far Bülow's play was a rousing success : he had got rid of the main pillar of the Anglo-French *entente,* and the gratified Emperor made him a Prince and haloed himself as the deliverer of Morocco from French tyranny.

But the next act of Bülow's play was a sad disappointment. He had hoped that without Delcassé the *entente* would crumble. The effect was precisely the opposite. Both countries saw that, in the face of this German aggression, it was more vitally essential than ever, and they signified this in the usual manner by the exchange of naval visits. The British Atlantic fleet in full strength spent a week at Brest in July, and the French Channel fleet a week at Portsmouth in August. The welcome on both sides was enthusiastic, and here was a parable easily interpreted. The Emperor perceived but did not relish the meaning of it, and, after the visit of the British fleet to Brest, he wrote to the Tsar with pretty metaphors : 'Marianne [France] must remember that she is wedded to you and that she is obliged to lie in bed with you, and eventually to give a hug or a kiss now and then to me, but not to sneak into the bed of the bedroom of the ever-intriguing *touche-à-tout* on the Island.' The return visit of the French fleet to Portsmouth confirmed the disagreeable impression of Marianne's loose notions of concubinage, and again he wrote : 'The British have prostituted themselves before France and the French sailors in the hope of gaining them over from you and stopping any *rapprochement* between you, me and them. The French felt much flattered, but I hope the sensible people have kept their heads cool and clear, and see that all is "cousu de fil blanc" and that Britain only wants to make France her "catspaw" against us, as she used Japan against you.'*

Meantime the Russo-Japanese War had come to an end. Admiral Rozhdestvensky in charge of the Baltic fleet had at last met real Japanese torpedo-boats and other vessels of war, and on May 27, 1905, the Russian fleet was practically annihilated by Admiral Togo off the coast of Korea. The disaster was crushing, and both sides accepted the mediation of President Roosevelt. The Emperor wrote with deep and didactic sympathy to the Tsar, reminding him that even Napoleon and Frederick the Great had suffered defeat, with the advice that further resistance was useless. He suggested that they should meet, and a secret rendezvous on their yachts was arranged for July 23 in the Bay of Björkö, off the coast of Finland.

He had planned a tremendous piece of statecraft for this secret meeting. He copied out afresh the treaty between himself and the Tsar which had been pigeonholed last autumn, omitting the clause about the coaling of Russian ships by German colliers which had frightened him, for there was now no need for it, since there were no longer any Russian ships to be coaled. He added a clause that the present treaty should come into force as soon as peace was signed between Russia and Japan, and that its contents should then be communicated to France. He also inserted in the first clause the words 'en Europe.' It thus provided that the two allies, Russia and Germany, should give all aid to each other by land and sea if either was attacked by a

* *Willy-Nicky Letters*, pp. 193, 194, 197.

third Power in Europe. He told the Tsar that he was bringing no German Minister with him, for this was to be an
informal meeting, but actually he took Herr von Tschirschky, the Minister in Hamburg, to represent the Foreign
Office, in case his services were needed.* The two Sovereigns had a preliminary talk at which the Tsar agreed that
the war which had lost Russia her entire navy had been engineered by King Edward, who was the greatest mischief-
maker and the most dangerous intriguer in the world. He
gave the Emperor his word of honour that he would never
ally himself with England against Germany, and that he
would never support France over the question of Alsace and
Lorraine. A very promising beginning, and the two spent
a diverting evening on the *Hohenzollern*.

Next day came the great scene. The Emperor, as instrument of the Most High, prepared himself for it by prayer,
and, opening his Bible at random, his eye fell on the text in
the Psalms : 'He shall reward every man according to his
works.' This was very encouraging ; he augured that the
Divine approbation rested on the work before him, and he
was rowed across to the *Pole Star* for lunch, with the
emended treaty in his pocket. He produced it, and while
the Tsar, who well remembered the projected but unsigned
treaty of the year before, read it through, the Emperor prayed
that God would guide his young brother aright, and sweated
with suspense. He looked out of the cabin window and saw
the Imperial Standard floating on the *Hohenzollern,* and its
motto 'Gott mit Uns.' The Tsar finished his perusal, he
thought the proposed arrangement excellent, and the Emperor, overcoming his intense excitement, said quite casually
that, if he would like to sign it, it would be a nice souvenir
of this meeting, and he suggestively opened the lid of the
inkstand. They signed, they embraced, and Tschirschky

* Bülow, *Memoirs*, 1903–1909, pp. 131, 132.

and Admiral Birileff countersigned ; the Admiral was not even allowed to see the document to which he had appended his signature, as the Emperor placed his hand over it.*

The Emperor felt sure that the spirits of their ancestors, Frederick William III and Queen Louise, Emperor William I and Tsar Nicholas I, were looking down on them from realms above with joy in their hearts that at last their countries were friends and allies. Dazzling, not to say delirious visions unrolled themselves, and as soon as he reached German shores he wrote in highest ecstasy to the Tsar that July 24, 1905, the day on which the treaty was signed, was a corner-stone in European politics and a new leaf in the history of the world. France would join this Russo-Germanic alliance — Marianne would thus lie in bed with Nicky and give an occasional hug to William, and not sneak off to the *touche-à-tout* on the Island — and the other Powers of the Triple Alliance, Austria and Italy, would automatically come in. The smaller Powers, Holland, Belgium, Denmark, Sweden and Norway, would revolve in the orbit of this immense quintuple constellation ; even Japan might, in time, feel inclined to join it.†

There fell on this exaltation a sudden, grievous dismay, when Bülow studied the text of this treaty, of which in its original form he had been joint-author. It was worth nothing till France had approved the admission of Germany into her alliance with Russia, and he wanted to extricate himself from having had any part in it. With extraordinary ingenuity, he pounced upon that addition 'en Europe' to the first clause. He then wrote to the Emperor that these two words rendered the treaty entirely valueless to Germany. Russia could only be of use if she threatened India and was attacked by England, but this contingency was now ruled out, and in

---

* Ludwig, *Kaiser Wilhelm II*, pp. 228, 229 ; Bülow, *Memoirs*, 1903–1909, p. 132.
† *Willy-Nicky Letters*, pp. 191, 192.

Europe what help could Russia give Germany against a maritime nation ? In page after page of sound and solemn and involved argument Bülow demonstrated to his master how that fatal addition had ruined everything, and, in conclusion, he said he could no longer be responsible for the foreign policy of Germany. He begged to resign his post as Chancellor.

It was a brilliant stroke. He reasoned that the Emperor would not be able to face the thought of losing him, and he was superabundantly justified by the reply. William, as might have been expected, still maintained the transcendent value of the service he had rendered to Germany, for, whether Bülow was right or wrong in his view about the disastrous effect of those two words 'en Europe,' the Tsar had solemnly declared that Russia, though friends with France, would never take sides with her in her eternal enmity with Germany over the question of Alsace and Lorraine, for that was 'un incident clos' ; and he had with equal solemnity promised never to enter into an alliance with England against Germany. Why, if Bismarck had succeeded in getting but one of these pledges from the Tsar, he would have been beside himself with joy, and all the world would have acclaimed his master-stroke ! And he, William, unaided had secured both ! . . . Then followed an abject, a piteous appeal. He implored Bülow not to forsake him, for God had called them to work together for the Fatherland. He reminded Bülow how, at his wish, he with his crippled arm had ridden a horrible horse through the streets of Tangier, at the risk of his life, in a crowd of Spanish anarchists. He would see that the significance of 'en Europe' was 'weakened,' or he would get the Tsar to cancel it. But if Bülow deserted him life would be no longer endurable. His poor wife and children ! *

* Bülow, *Memoirs*, 1903–1909, pp. 134–141.

This extraordinary letter, threatening suicide, overwhelmed Bülow. He had a very genuine affection for the Emperor ; also he had dissociated himself from this absurd Björkö Treaty. He withdrew his resignation, and the Emperor telegraphed : 'Warmest thanks. I feel reborn.' With this complete recovery of his spirits there returned in full force the conviction that his achievement would bind Russia and Germany together in ties of permanent friendship. To this was added a sweetness of peculiar personal satisfaction — honey to the mouth — for, as he told the Tsar, the King of England, that 'Arch Intriguer and Mischief Maker,' knew that there had been this secret meeting at Björkö, but he could not find out what had happened there, and was tormented with the uneasiest curiosity. He had tried to pump Count Benckendorff, the Russian Ambassador in London, but he knew nothing about it ; he had inquired of his sister-in-law, the Tsar's mother, but learned nothing from her ; he had asked Lamsdorff, but Lamsdorff professed ignorance ; he had asked the Emperor's sisters, the Duchess of Sparta and Princess Frederick Charles of Hesse, who had been making a long stay in England, and they had laughed in his face. Never had the Emperor felt so ecstatically contemptuous of the wicked uncle, who would presently find England confronted by this European combination.*

The treaty was to be kept secret till peace was signed between Russia and Japan. This was done at Portsmouth (U.S.A.) on August 29, 1905, and next day the Tsar communicated the treaty to his Foreign Minister, Count Lamsdorff. One glance was sufficient : it was the most childish repudiation of the Franco-Russian alliance, and by its terms, if France went to war with Germany, Russia would be bound to fight on the side of Germany against the country

* *Willy-Nicky Letters*, pp. 198–200.

with whom she had been allied for fifteen years. 'These details,' said Lamsdorff very lucidly, 'no doubt escaped His Majesty in the flood of the Emperor William's eloquence,' and without a struggle or a sigh the Treaty of Björkö passed away.

But the Emperor could not believe that anything which he and the Tsar had signed had no inherent validity and was not binding on their nations. He still clung to the 'Continental Combine' for the encirclement of England as a project already realised, and a month after it was no more he wrote to the Tsar to tell him how it flourished. Indeed it had grown, for he now knew that America was joining it, and flanked by America it would effectively prevent the world becoming John Bull's private property, and no longer by his endless lies could he 'set the rest of the civilized nations by each others' ears (*sic*) for his own personal benefit.' . . . He followed this up by a telegram. France, he discovered, had behaved abominably to Russia in the Japanese war : therefore 'the obligations of Russia towards France can only go as far as France merits them through her behaviour.' But eventually she would come in with Germany and Russia. Besides (as a clinching argument) 'We joined hands,' he passionately wrote, 'and signed before God who heard our vows. I therefore think that our treaty can well come into existence. What is signed is signed. God is our testator.' *

But unfortunately the French and Russian and German Governments had to be testators as well as God, before the treaty was worth more than the paper it was written on. The disappointment was bitter indeed when at last the Emperor realised that, and he fixed the whole blame of his own fiasco on the Tsar. He was a 'Tsarlet,' 'a schoolboy idea-

* *Willy-Nicky Letters*, pp. 211, 212, 216, 217.

216 THE KAISER AND ENGLISH RELATIONS

logue . . . wearing a snivelling mask of eternal heartfelt
friendship.' * On the Tsar's country, so lately sought and
sued, which was to have formed with Germany the sure
foundation of a world-combine against England, he poured
the full measure of his scorn and hatred, and he told Mr.
Bellamy Storer, the American Ambassador at Vienna, that
'it was necessary that Russia should be and remain financially
helpless and crippled for a long time.' Those were her just
deserts.

King Edward, though knowing nothing of these Björkö
conversations beyond the fact that William had had a private meeting with the Tsar, was still fuming with rage at
the *enfant terrible* for his mischievous interference in Morocco, and he went for his annual cure at Marienbad with
the fixed intention of avoiding him. There was a ludicrous
side to this personal hostility, and it was fair game for the
German caricaturist who represented the King puzzling
over a map of Europe to find that route to Marienbad which
would involve the least risk of meeting his nephew. He
rejected Flushing, Lisbon, Madrid, Monaco, etc., in favour
of travelling straight to Berlin, for the Reise-Kaiser would
certainly not be there. But there was also a serious side to
their mutual antipathy, for though it had been often and
amply proved that cordial relations between Sovereigns had
no very markedly beneficial effect on the cordiality between
their nations, the lack of them could be harmful. The Emperor's dislike of his uncle accentuated his hostility to England, now that he had given up any hope of alliance, though
the King kept his genuine desire to be on good terms with
Germany unsoured by his detestation of his nephew. The
latter he really tried to keep apart, but he made no effort

* Ludwig, *Kaiser Wilhelm II*, p. 234.

to forget his numerous offences, his treatment of his mother, his conduct at Cowes, the moral exhortations he had sent him after the Tranby Croft scandal, and a thousand others. All were alive still and cherished, and they attested their vitality like crowing cockerels when another joined the brood. This year he absolutely refused to meet him, and when Count Seckendorff, who for years had been a devoted and loyal friend to the Empress Frederick, wrote to him that the Emperor would be at Homburg towards the end of the King's cure and suggested a meeting, the King considered this a great impertinence. It was a pity, perhaps, for Seckendorff's attempt must have been prompted by the Emperor ; yet no good ever came of their meetings. In any case the King would have none of it. He would not interrupt nor shorten his cure by a single day, and after that he had arranged to meet the Queen at Flushing, there were several people he wished to see in London, and then he was staying with Lord Savile for the Doncaster Races. Even if he had had no engagements at all, he said, he would not have consented to meet him. Perhaps next year. But he asked the Crown Prince of Germany and his newly married wife to pay him a visit at Windsor. No doubt the friendliest intention prompted that, but it was not tactful to invite the son of the man whom he had just refused to meet even for an hour's talk ; it only accentuated that refusal. The Emperor forbade the Crown Prince to go, and, remembering that the King had cancelled the Prince of Wales's visit to Berlin for the Crown Prince's marriage, because the King of Spain was to be at Windsor then, gave precisely the same excuse : the King of Spain was to be in Berlin on that very date. This did not happen to be true, for the King had ascertained from Madrid the date of King Alfonso's visit to Berlin and had asked the Crown Prince for the ensuing

week, but the Emperor could not resist this ingenious re-
tort.* A series of complaints at each other's conduct passed
between the monarchs through the distracted Sir Frank
Lascelles, British Ambassador at Berlin. He was like a
shuttlecock driven backwards and forwards between two
infuriated battledores, and he threatened to resign.

Such wranglings were farcical but they were also deplorable : the two were doing all that in them lay to identify
themselves with the ill-feeling which existed between their
countries, and that is not the most desirable function of
Sovereigns. For the rest of the year the royal rupture was
complete, the Emperor being in a very bad temper at the
complete fiasco of the Björkö meeting, and the King nursing
the sense of personal offence. But presently he thought that
his resentment against his nephew had been excessive, and
making a heroic effort he wrote him a letter for his birthday
on January 27, 1906, in which he swallowed all his grievances, gnat and camel alike, in one magnificent gulp. Tact
on such an occasion was a prior charge on truth, and he said :
'We are — my dear William — such old friends and near
relations that I feel sure that the affectionate feelings which
have always existed may invariably continue.' . . . 'Let byegones be byegones' was the handsome reply, and — let us
credit William with sincerity — he and his uncle should remember the hours of silent prayer and watching which they
spent by the death-bed of his grandmother. 'I feel sure,'
he wrote, 'that from the home of Eternal Light she is now
looking down upon us, and will rejoice when she sees our
hands clasped in loyal and cordial friendship.' The Emperor was fond of picturing the spirits of the departed watching him with loving appreciation. Quite a company of
them, it may be remembered, had joyfully witnessed the
signing of the Treaty of Björkö. Further expressions of

* Lee, *King Edward VII,* ii. pp. 346–354.

mutual esteem followed between uncle and nephew, and then both watched with the intensest mutual suspicions the stormy progress of the conference of the Powers at Algeciras convened for the settlement of the French protectorate of Morocco. Its findings did not allot to France the complete control she had aimed at, and Bülow, speaking in the Reichstag, claimed a diplomatic success for Germany in her having upheld her economic interests, and having secured a voice in Moroccan affairs. To that extent the Emperor's distressing ride on the white Barbary stallion had not been in vain : on the other hand, the bond of the *entente cordiale* had been undeniably strengthened by the consequent firmness of England's co-operation with France.*

After those birthday greetings of affectionate regard the King and his nephew had to meet again ; but neither desired it, and much circumspection was needed. Count Witte, the Russian Prime Minister, was very anxious that the King should pay a state visit to Petersburg this summer, or meet the Tsar somewhere in the Baltic, which in the present disturbed conditions in Russia was a less hazardous *rendezvous,* and he guaranteed that good results would follow ; the time was ripe, he thought, for bringing England into closer relations with the Franco-Russian alliance, by associating her with both members of it. As for the Tsar, though, under the hectoring eloquence of William, he had pronounced the King to be a mischief-maker and an arch-intriguer, the humiliating fiasco of the Björkö Treaty had disillusioned him about the All-Highest and his silly schemes for a world combination to encircle England. They had all turned out to be rubbish, and in his mild, inconclusive way he would be glad to see the King again. But the King was against it, for he intended to meet William on his way to Marienbad for his cure in August, in order to resume personal relations

* Bülow, *Memoirs,* 1903–1909, p. 203.

again, and there would be little promise of cordiality if he came red-handed, so to speak, from conversations with the Tsar. So the Russian visit was postponed, and the meeting with his nephew was arranged to take place at Friedrichshof, the palace built by the Empress Frederick for her widowhood and now lived in by her youngest daughter, Princess Margaret, wife of Prince Frederick Charles of Hesse. The German Empress disapproved ; her inveterate spite against the King, which certainly influenced the relations between him and her husband, spurted out, and she told Bülow that the King ought to come and see William at Berlin or, at any rate, at one of his own castles. 'Why can't the fat old gentleman manage to get as far as Wilhelmshöhe ?' But Friedrichshoff was settled, and by carefully avoiding all dangerous topics they got on very harmoniously. They saw the ruins of a Roman fort at Saarburg, and they talked of the status of the Archduke Francis Ferdinand's morganatic wife, and how nice it would be if English Ministers paid visits to Berlin. This was a sore subject with the Emperor : not a single English Minister, he said, since he came to the throne eighteen years ago, had ever been there. But the meeting was more an examination in self-control than anything else, and, though both passed it with high distinction, it did not prove to be very useful in after life.*

* Bülow, *Memoirs*, 1903–1909, pp. 237, 238 ; Lee, *King Edward VII*, ii. p. 529.

CHAPTER XIV

To the Emperor's eye his uncle began the year 1907
very injudiciously. He spent a week with the
Queen in Paris, and the fact that he was incognito
made his conduct more suspect. This was a very poor return for the Emperor's Christmas gift to England of a statue
of King William III, and soon after the King went on one
of those spring cruises which his nephew regarded as an
infringement of his own prerogative. He spent the most
of March innocently enough at Biarritz, but his subsequent
programme was truly diabolical, for it comprised a meeting
with the King of Spain at Cartagena, and with the King of
Italy at Gaeta. It was no excuse for the King that his niece
Princess Victoria Eugénie of Battenberg had married King
Alfonso the year before, nor was it a consolation that he
himself was meaning to pay a state visit to Madrid in a
month or two : simply any visit his uncle made was charged
with sinister motive. And then, after having laid his net
of intrigue in Spain, he was going to visit the King of Italy
and tamper with the Triple Alliance. He was bent on encircling Germany, thought the Emperor, as he bitterly remembered his own dithyrambic letters to the Tsar which
proved up to the hilt that their secret Treaty of Björkö
would cause not Europe alone, but the very ends of the
earth, Japan in the East and America in the West, to encircle
England in an impenetrable ring of foes. He lost all the
self-control which it was hoped he had gained at Fried-

richshof, and, talking to a party of friends after dinner, he worked himself up into a frenzy about his uncle. 'He is a fiend !' he exclaimed. 'Nobody knows what a fiend he is !' *

Yet, in spite of such moods, each of which, while it lasted, was to him logical and convincing, he was not in any degree mentally deranged. In one mood he would see his uncle's plump fingers writing the doom of Germany on the wall : 'Mene, mene, tekel, Upharsin' was inscribed before his eyes : in another the slip of waste-paper signed by him and the Tsar foreshadowed the collapse of the British Empire, and he was filled alternately with blind terror or the highest exultation. The cause of all the trouble was that inferiority complex, which now in his forty-ninth year was unsubdued. As a boy he had combated the sense of his physical disabilities with admirable pluck and may be said to have conquered it, but psychically that complex stood ever by him like Banquo's ghost. He had striven to lay it by noisy self-assertion, by assuring himself and others that his will was law to the world, and out of this engrained habit had sprung his colossal vanity. With one part of his mind he believed himself to be the instrument of the Most High, but co-existent with that comfortable conviction was the secret consciousness of an essential timidity which shuddered and wailed in the innermost of his soul. It was his incessant preoccupation, in ways small no less than great, to silence it. When English women were presented to him, he grasped their hands in so iron a grip that they winced with pain, and he exclaimed 'Ha ha ! The mailed fist ! What ?' † Or at a shooting party he rolled a colonel in the snow to remind himself that he was War Lord. Or when

---

* Lee, *King Edward VII*, ii. p. 544.
† Topham, *Chronicles of the Prussian Court*, p. 15.

he came back from a pleasure trip to Palestine he ordered that Berlin should be hung with flags, as when his grandfather returned from the Franco-German War. Anything for the psychical reassurance of those quakings.

Buttressing his convictions concerning his Divine mission, firm stood his belief in his own all-round genius. Ludicrous as this was, there was something disarmingly attractive about it, for, even in middle age, incessant failures brought him no disillusionment, and he retained all the eager self-confidence of a very clever boy, who, dreaming the bright dreams of youth, sees glorious achievement within his reach in any branch of art or science to which he may turn his swift mind. It mattered not that a naval architect told him that his super-*Dreadnought* would, when launched, sink like a stone to the bottom of the sea ; undeterred he designed allegorical cartoons which must surely bring home to European countries the deadly imminence of the Yellow Peril. He discussed counterpoint with Frau Cosima Wagner, and her considered verdict that she could not teach him the elements of music, even if she spent three years with him on a desert island, would not have damped the composer of the *Hymn to Aegir*. This sense of being able brilliantly to turn his hand to anything was no doubt an inherited trait from his Coburg ancestry. His mother had something of it ; so, too, had his grandfather the Prince Consort, who instructed trained artists on the technique of painting in fresco, and when fresco, executed on these principles, unaccountably faded from the decorated walls, he turned his attention to sewage and soon discovered a cheap and simple scheme for its utilisation as manure. This was found to be quite impracticable owing to laws of gravity and other unforeseen obstacles, and, quite undismayed, he took to etching on copper, composed a *Te Deum,* studied cattle-breeding, made architectural plans for Osborne and Balmoral, and designed tartans.* William inherited all his grandfather's versatility, and dispensed with any previous knowledge of his subject. He planned, on his farm at Cadinen, to mate his cows with Indian buffaloes and thus produce a breed of unique and magnificent cattle. Such beef, such oceans of milk ! Already his meadows seemed to him peopled with those mammoths of fertility. Pending that, he started an Imperial porcelain factory which would revolutionise the history of ceramics. He knew no more about porcelain than about the sex-appeal of buffaloes, but the word went forth that from the beds of clayey soil at Cadinen should be fashioned porcelain reproductions of Della Robbia ware and busts of the Empress and himself. The clay was coarse in texture and full of iron, admirable for the manufacture of tiles and bricks but quite incapable of transmutation into porcelain. In vain his master-potters from Berlin and Dresden told him that the thing could not be done : he merely bade them persevere.†

The King made up his mind to ask the Emperor and Empress to pay him their first state visit in the autumn. The invitation had been rather long in coming, for he had been on the throne for nearly seven years, but he had sworn that while there was any likelihood of William's 'springing surprises' on the world, as he had done at Morocco, he should not be bidden. The Emperor overlooked his uncle's fiendishness and accepted at once, with the hope that they would meet before that, when the King went out to Marienbad in August. This meeting took place, and, though it was a private one, the Emperor had the streets of Cassel lined with 50,000 troops — was this a compliment or a warn-

* Strachey, *Queen Victoria*, pp. 131, 187, 193.
† Topham, *Chronicles of the Prussian Court*, pp. 94, 95.

ing gesture ? — and by a continued avoidance of controversial topics all went well.

A month later, on September 23, 1907, the Anglo-Russian
Convention was ratified and made public. It was only concerned with the adjustment of Russian and English interests
in Persia, Thibet and Afghanistan, and did not in any way
affect Germany, but it was very disagreeable to the Emperor to find that the traditional hostility between England
and Russia, which he had so long and so conscientiously
done his best to foment, was fading like the Prince Consort's
frescoes. It was also deeply wounding to his vanity to contrast the validity of this document with the fate of his own
master-stroke of diplomacy witnessed by God, but not accepted by France, at Björkö. This new treaty was less sub-
lime but more businesslike. It bore the signatures of the
Tsarlet and the Arch-intriguer, and the Russian Foreign
Minister and the British Ambassador at St. Petersburg, and
an Anglo-Russian agreement which, from the days of Bismarck, it had been a cardinal point in German policy to
frustrate as a knavish trick, had been signed and sealed.

How was he to express his just chagrin ? He thought of
an ingenious device. Less than a fortnight before he was
due to pay his state visit to Windsor he telegraphed to the
King that he had an acute cough following on an attack
of influenza, and did not feel up to it. He suggested that
the Crown Prince, whose visit to England he had vetoed
the year before, should take his place, or that the visit should
be postponed. Having despatched that, he telephoned to
Bülow that he had rolled off his sofa in a fainting fit and
had hit his head a stunning blow on the floor. This fall
from the sofa was quite imaginary : he went out riding a
few hours later, had a good dinner and went to the theatre.
Meantime his telegram had been received by the King, who
was furious. All arrangements had been made, the King

had asked a galaxy of royal personages to meet him, a menu of suitable subjects for conversation was being drawn up, and he did not believe that the Emperor's health was the real reason of his throwing over the engagement, but his fear of getting a bad reception in England. This fear, so Bülow believed, was the effect of the colossal scandal that was raging in the Press about the sexual abnormalities of Philip Eulenburg and others of his most intimate friends. The King refused to accept the Crown Prince as substitute, or to postpone the visit, and sent him a remarkably firm telegram that he hoped his cough would soon be better, and that the official programme should be cut down to suit him. This had its effect, and ambassadors and Foreign Office experts cured the Emperor's cough.

There was the usual state banquet at which the usual affirmations of imperishable family affection were made, and the Sovereigns hoped and trusted that these would be brightly reflected in the relations between their two countries. Except for a genially double-edged remark by the King that his nephew seemed in excellent health and to have completely recovered from his cough, these speeches might have been reported before they were delivered. The Emperor had talks with certain Ministers ; he had mysterious midnight interviews with Mr. Haldane about the Baghdad Railway, of which he did not appear to know much, and it is interesting, in view of later events, to find that he was vehement against the Jews in Germany : 'There are too many of them,' he said to Sir Edward Grey. 'They want stamping out. If I did not restrain my people there would be a Jew-baiting.' * He was the guest of the City of London at a lunch in the Guildhall, and in his speech expressed the hope that history would do him the justice of

---

* He had expressed the same sentiments a year before, declaring that Russian Jews must not be allowed to remain in Germany. (Private information.)

acknowledging that since he came to the throne he had unswervingly sought and ensued peace. Considering the endless embroilments he had so unswervingly sought to stir up and the mischief which had so often ensued therefrom, this claim might seem grotesque. But was there not a certain truth in it? Certainly he had not been a peace-promoter as between other countries, since to egg them on to quarrel with each other for the proportionate strengthening of Germany by their attrition had always been the keystone of his diplomacies, but never had he himself deliberately provoked a quarrel which might end in war for Germany. Bülow had dragged him reluctant into the dangerous Morocco escapade, and how strenuously, when out of sheer conceit and impetuosity he had sent his telegram to Kruger, he had tried to convince his formidable grandmother that he meant exactly the opposite of what he said ! *

The state visit lasted a week. Harmony reigned, and the Press both in England and Germany automatically hailed it as an outward and visible sign of the renewal of friendlier sentiments. It was therefore rather unfortunate that the day after the Emperor left Windsor the German Government announced that the naval programme for 1908 would provide for a twenty per cent. increase in expenditure. For Admiral Tirpitz, the inspirer and creator of German naval construction, was counting the months and the years, six perhaps, which must elapse before, at this accelerated speed, Germany might count herself safe on the seas, while the Emperor, in this perilous interval, was envisaging the British fleet roaring out from its harbours and annihilating his own. And the thought of his vast navy, now coming to birth, did not only minister to his craving for the security of

---

* Bülow, *Memoirs*, 1903-1909, pp. 296, 297 ; Lee, *King Edward VII*, ii. pp. 554-559 ; *Journals and Letters of Lord Esher*, ii. p. 255.

his country, but to the personal comfort of his inferiority complex. This spring he met his ally, the King of Italy, at Venice, and after various conversational snubs from his guest, the King, trying a more hopeful subject, spoke of the splendour of the growing German fleet. That touched the secret spring. 'All the long years of my reign,' cried the Emperor, 'my colleagues, the Monarchs of Europe, have paid no attention to what I have had to say. Soon, with my great Navy to endorse my words, they will be more respectful.' *

The Emperor went from Windsor to stay with Colonel Stuart-Wortley at Highcliffe Castle on the coast of Dorset for holiday and recuperation. The new German estimates had caused some anxiety in England, and he was hurt by this want of confidence ; it was disappointing to find that the English were still suspicious of his friendship, and in private conversations with his host he assured him of his sincerity. Then after a month in England he returned home, delighted with his visit, congratulating himself that he had done much to promote friendliness between the nations and abate the mischievous virulence of the Press. 'I have mended,' he said, 'the windows my people have broken,' and he proceeded to throw stones at some more on his own account by writing a truly amazing letter to the Tsar. He had removed, he told him, many causes of misunderstanding and had some secret and confidential information for the Tsar personally. The fact was that England was very angry about the voyage on which the American fleet had just started. It was to visit Australia and Japan, and the English were afraid of some 'encounter' between it and Japan, for then they would be forced to take one side or the other. He had talked with officers in the Army and Navy and they were disgusted with the English alliance with a Yellow

* Bülow, *Memoirs*, 1903–1909, p. 310.

KING EDWARD VII, THE DUKE OF CONNAUGHT AND THE KAISER
AT A SHOOTING PARTY AT WINDSOR (1907).

race. But if England dropped the Japanese alliance they would instantly lose India, for Japan, foreseeing this possibility, was busy fomenting revolution there. Or perhaps she would first pick a quarrel with America by seizing the Philippines. They were busy in Mexico ; there were already 10,000 Japanese working in the plantations there in military jackets with brass buttons, who, disguised as labourers, drilled on the sly and meant to occupy the Panama Canal and cut off all land communication with the United States. (Apparently the Emperor thought Mexico was in South America.) England would have to send a squadron to the Pacific, while if France went to her aid in India she would lose Saigon and Annam, for the Japanese intended to annex the whole of Asia. With London in this state of extreme nervousness, Count Okuma's speech about India a few days ago had had the effect of a Shimose shell. This letter was most private, but, like all the information which the Emperor had ever sent the Tsar, absolutely reliable.*

The Emperor never wrote a more characteristic letter. He had just come back from England, with whom, both in private and public, he had reaffirmed his goodwill and affection, and his unswerving pursuit of peace for all the world. But with what gusto does he look forward to trouble between his beloved England and Japan ! Japan was out to cause revolution in India and lay hands on it herself, and this charming prospect so dazzled him that he failed to observe that Count Okuma, whose speech had produced so devastating an effect in England, was only talking about commercial rivalry and the capture of Indian markets. And America was likely to come to blows with Japan, and France, Russia's ally, would lose her Eastern possessions ! As always, the hope of trouble between other nations, even those with whom he desired to be friendly, was the dearest

* *Willy-Nicky Letters,* pp. 235–239.

aspiration of his heart. Dr. Johnson once cynically observed that the misfortunes of our friends do not cause us unmitigated pain ; to the Emperor they afforded infinite refreshment.

Such was the man with whose country and whose person King Edward truly desired to be on good terms. He realised that, personally, the more he saw of him the less he liked him, and much though he enjoyed state visits, and valuable though he believed them to be in promoting national cordiality, he explicitly stated that the Emperor's late visit to Windsor was to be regarded as the response to his own visit to Kiel over three years ago, and did not entail on him any further visit to his nephew for a considerable time. But so great an adept in exasperation as the Emperor could never be at a loss for long, and he soon found an opportunity. Lord Esher, Governor of Windsor Castle, refused to join the Imperial Maritime League, which, in view of the German naval programme, wanted to make inquiries into the measures taken by the Admiralty to meet it. His grounds were that Sir John Fisher and the Sea Lords could not have accepted a reduction in Naval Estimates which they considered dangerous, and that the proposed inquiry was directed against them. His letter, which was published in *The Times,* contained this sentence : 'There is not a man in Germany from the Emperor downwards who would not welcome the fall of Sir John Fisher.' That was enough, and the Emperor instantly wrote an autograph letter of nine pages to Lord Tweedmouth who, as First Lord of the Admiralty, was in the Cabinet, saying that Lord Esher had better confine his energies to looking after the drains of the royal palaces, and that the idea that any German desired the fall of Sir John Fisher was unmitigated balderdash, and had created vast merriment in German naval circles. The increase in the German fleet, he must repeat

once more, was in no way a challenge to British supremacy.
The notion was ludicrous, etc. etc.

That a foreign Sovereign should personally write on such
a topic to the First Lord of the Admiralty was unheard of.
The Emperor had once before written to his grandmother
abusing Lord Salisbury and had got one of her firm replies,
but this was going a step further. 'What would *he* say,'
asked the Prince of Wales, 'if the King wrote to von Tirpitz
a letter of this kind ?' A pertinent question, for the clear
purpose of the Emperor's letter was to impress on the First
Lord that England need have no anxiety about the increase
in the German naval programme. This gratifying assurance caused the wildest exasperation in the English Press,
and hardly less in the King. All the trouble he had taken
to make the Emperor's visit agreeable had been wasted and
monarchs and nations alike were at loggerheads again. Sir
John Fisher made the attractive suggestion that the British
fleet should put to sea and sink the German fleet without
any declaration of war, and there would be no more bother
with it. Nelson had done the same to the Danish fleet at
Copenhagen ; but, alas, Sir Henry Campbell-Bannerman,
Prime Minister in 1908, was not up to Pitt in 1801.*

Having rejected the healing power of the Nelson touch,
the King went off to Biarritz in March 1908, where, owing
to a recurrence of the bronchial trouble from which he always suffered in the spring, he stopped for six weeks. His
absence caused great inconvenience to his Government, for
the Prime Minister was forced to resign owing to ill-health,
and the Licensing Bill had to be hung up while Mr. Asquith
was summoned to Biarritz and, in a hotel in the South of
France, appointed Prime Minister.

The King got back to England in the middle of April,

* Lee, *King Edward VII,* ii. pp. 603–609 ; *Journals and Letters of Lord Esher,*
ii. pp. 285–288.

and within a week started on a tour of those state visits which he regarded as among the best services he could render his country, but which the Emperor believed to be so deliberately Satanic. The first batch of these gave rise to no suspicions ; the King only visited Denmark, Sweden and Norway by way of shaking hands with their Sovereigns over the Baltic and the North Sea Conventions of which Germany approved. There followed a state visit of M. Fallières, President of the French Republic, to England, on the occasion of the Franco-British Exhibition, and no objection could be made to that. Then came Russia's turn. Two years ago Count Witte had suggested a visit, believing that it would result in some agreement between England and Russia, but that had been abandoned because the country was in a very unsettled state, and because the King did not want unduly and unnecessarily to irritate his nephew. But now this Anglo-Russian Convention had been signed and sealed, an exchange of royal cordialities was called for, and a meeting of yachts was arranged off Reval for June. But trouble arose over this in England : Radicals and the Labour Party in the House of Commons made a strong protest against the King paying a state visit to a Sovereign whose Government had imprisoned, exiled and executed political prisoners without a trial. They held the Tsar to be responsible for these atrocities, and that the King should pay him an official visit implied that he and therefore his country condoned them. The Tsar was a 'bloodstained murderer,' wrote a future Prime Minister of England in the *Labour Leader,* and the King must not hobnob with him. But the Government agreed with the King that such a visit promoted national friendliness, and that the internal affairs of Russia were not Britain's concern any more than the British naval programme was the concern of Germany. So, early in June, the King and Queen sailed on the *Victoria and Albert* and, after passing through the Kiel Canal, had the pleasure of seeing an impressive display of German sea-power. The whole fleet was assembled in the harbour and destroyers escorted them into the Baltic, while torpedo-boats practised their manœuvres in a very masterly manner. This fine sight served a double purpose of doing honour to the distinguished visitors and of exhibiting once more the strength and vast increase of the German navy. The two royal yachts met off Reval, and the National Anthems and the speeches of the Sovereigns on mutual friendliness and affection meant more than usual, for a definite step had been taken towards the *rapprochement* of their countries.

The King was not accompanied by any of his Ministers, but he had conversations with M. Stolypin, the Russian Prime Minister, and with M. Isvolsky, the Russian Foreign Secretary, who had played much the same part in procuring the Anglo-Russian Convention as M. Delcassé in the Anglo-French *entente*. There was certainly a constitutional im-propriety in such a proceeding, and the British Government thought it a dangerous innovation. But where was the use of discussing international politics with the Tsar ? He had no effective will, but was timid, obstinate and evasive, and it was wiser only to talk about his children, his visit to Bal-moral to see his grandmother, and other domestic topics. The Emperor always confused and frightened the Tsar with his harangues and his bogus treaties suddenly whisked out for signature : it was far better to make him feel comfortable with the realisation of a friendly presence who was not go-ing to open a jack-in-the-box under his nose. The King made him an Admiral of the British Fleet, which he had no right to do without the consent of his Admiralty, and the Tsar made the King an Admiral of the Russian Fleet.

Though ships were on the stocks, the Russian fleet at present lay at the bottom of the Pacific, with the exception of one battleship, which thereupon saluted its new Admiral.*

Whatever good results there may have been from this visit, it was soon clear that there were bad ones. It vastly increased in the minds of the Emperor and of Germany generally the belief that King Edward, in his European tours, invariably sowed dragons' teeth from which sprang up hosts of armed men, while he tried to hoodwink his nephew by welcoming him to Windsor and assuring him of his friendly sentiments. There can be no doubt that the maintenance of peace and the cultivation of good relations with Germany were the King's sincere and constant aim, but it may be questioned whether his methods promoted it. Knowing his nephew, he knew also the effect these visits produced on him, and Bülow, who usually had more sense, told the Emperor that nothing amused the King more than to irritate him. Where the King prided himself on obliterating, by means of these magnificent junketings, old dissensions between his country and another, it was inevitable that his nephew should interpret such obliterations as the forging by England of another link in the ring of Germany's enemies. He judged his uncle's motives by his own, and read into this meeting at Reval, coming on the top of the Anglo-Russian Convention, what he himself would have meant by it. He had long tried to make bad blood between the two countries by assuring the Tsar of the perfidy of England, and of her having instigated the Japanese war ; and now that England had established friendly relations with Russia, in spite of all his efforts, his mentality forced him to believe that the direct object of this visit was to get Russia at loggerheads with Germany.

* *Journals and Letters of Lord Esher,* ii. pp. 319–322.

A second consequence was that the Emperor now convinced himself that the British Government's proposals for
a reduction in British and German naval programmes, on
the grounds that this piling up of armaments produced a
general sense of insecurity and apprehension throughout
Europe, were not made in good faith. Any proposal therefore to limit German naval expenditure, though British expenditure would be correspondingly reduced, he took to be
a most impertinent interference in Germany's internal affairs. Whatever England chose to do, Germany should go
on building at the accelerated rate laid down in her last
naval estimates.

The King was going for his annual cure to Marienbad
in August, and, as he intended first to visit the Emperor of
Austria at Ischl to congratulate him on his Diamond Jubilee, it was wiser to spend a few hours with his nephew at
Friedrichshof on the way ; he arrived in the morning and
resumed his journey after dinner. He hoped to have an
amicable discussion on naval expenditure, and took with
him two memoranda which Sir Edward Grey had prepared.
But when the King introduced the subject the Emperor only
said that the German programme was fixed by law and had
to take its course, and he did not show the slightest interest
in Grey's memoranda. The King tried another topic : he
had heard that his cousin Prince Ferdinand of Bulgaria was
thinking of throwing off Turkish suzerainty and establish-
ing himself as King of an independent nation : what had
William to say about that ? William said that he was a
vassal of the Sultan, and in turn asked what the Emperor
of Austria would think of it. The second topic was therefore abandoned, but Sir Charles Hardinge, who was with
the King, made a highly unsuccessful attempt to renew the
first. He suggested to the Emperor that Germany and Eng-

land might abandon any further shipbuilding, or slow the programmes down, but the Emperor, showing temper, replied : 'That's a question affecting national honour and dignity. We should prefer to fight.' Then he recovered his temper, and conferred on him the Grand Cross of the Red Eagle. As soon as the King had left, travelling through the night to Ischl, he telegraphed to the Emperor of Austria to warn him against permitting any naval discussions, as the King was bent on isolating Germany. He was much pleased with himself for having snubbed Hardinge so successfully, and sent a prodigious telegram to Bülow saying how clever he had been. As for the impression the monarchs produced on each other, there was a great divergence of opinion : the Emperor told the Tsar that his uncle had been 'all sunshine,' while the King briefly recorded that his nephew had been 'impossible.' *

The King's visit to Ischl was not solely to felicitate 'that dear old man' the Emperor of Austria on the sixtieth anniversary of his accession : he hoped, especially since he had made no way with his nephew over naval programmes, that the second partner in the Triple Alliance might use his influence with him. But the Emperor had already received that warning telegram from Friedrichshof, and he refused with all possible courtesy to intervene or to discuss. Otherwise he was most frank and friendly. He saw no sign of trouble even in the Balkan States, which were the source of most European disturbances, and assured the King that he and his Government were determined to do nothing that could possibly disturb peace. Sir Charles Hardinge had a satisfactory talk with Baron von Aehrenthal, the Austrian Foreign Minister, and, though the King had not been able

---

* Lee, *King Edward VII*, ii. p. 618 ; Ludwig, p. 258 ; Bülow, *Memoirs*, 1903–1909, pp. 312–314 ; *Willy-Nicky Letters*, p. 239 ; *Journals and Letters of Lord Esher*, ii. p. 343.

to say a single effective word about the business on which he had intended to talk to the Emperor, he was fondly delighted with the meeting. It was a comfort to think that this dear old man, wise through long experience and bent on prudent and pacific courses, was so solid a counterweight to William's fickleness and impetuosity. The Sovereigns embraced, they looked forward to a 'baldiges Wiedersehen,' and the King betook himself to his cure at Marienbad, and the Emperor Francis Joseph to important talks with Baron Aehrenthal.

The King's programme of royal travel for 1908 was now complete. For a man who, in the spring, had been so incapacitated by bronchitis that he could not return to his own country for a political crisis, he had borne the fatigue of journeys and functions without hurt, and rejoiced in his good services. He had paid state visits to Copenhagen, Stockholm, Christiania and Reval, he had twice been to Paris, he had seen his nephew at Friedrichshof and had promised him a state visit in the spring of 1909, but the most fruitful surely in peacemaking of all these excursions was this last visit to Ischl. Consequently, when, immediately after his arrival at Marienbad, Mr. Wickham Steed, *The Times* correspondent at Vienna, told him that Austria was intending to annex the provinces of Bosnia and Herzegovina — there was nothing definite yet, but it was in the air — the King simply did not believe it. Such a step would be the gravest menace to the peace of Europe, and the Austrian Emperor in those frank talks at Ischl must have mentioned it to him if there was any truth in such a rumour. Having dismissed this, the King had an interview with M. Clemenceau, Prime Minister of France, who came over to see him from Carlsbad. Clemenceau's marvellously correct view of current international relations gave him an uncanny insight into their development. Should there be war, he prophesied, Germany would instantly invade France by way of Belgium. That would make a great stir in England, but what France would need was 'not only a stir but help.' As long as England had not an army of a quarter to half a million men to throw across the Channel France would be in extreme danger. Such an army could not be improvised. England's fleet was not enough : it would enable France to transport colonial troops from Algiers and Tunis, but, for effective aid, she must have an adequate national army for foreign service, in addition to her fleet, or all Europe, as in the days of Napoleon, would be dominated by one Power. It was not at Trafalgar but at Waterloo that he was broken. . . In this forecast M. Clemenceau did not appreciate what the Territorial Army, which he considered a plaything, would grow into in the next six years, but otherwise he ranks with the most major of prophets.*

The King returned to England in the middle of September, full of confidence in the assurances of the dear old man. In Austria meantime the details of the coming *coup* had been settled, and on September 29 the Austrian Emperor wrote autograph letters to his Royal Brothers of Europe announcing that he had decided to annex Bosnia and Herzegovina. These letters were sent to his ambassadors with orders to deliver them to the Sovereigns on October 5. Two days before, Sir Edward Goschen, British Ambassador in Vienna, and about to be transferred to Berlin, asked Baron Aehrenthal, on instructions from England, whether he knew anything of the proclamation of Bulgarian independence, which was rumoured to be imminent. Aehrenthal said he had no knowledge of it. This, of course, was a lie, for it was proclaimed on October 5, and on the same day Count Mensdorff, Austrian Ambassador in England, delivered to the

* Wickham Steed, *Through Thirty Years,* i. pp. 282-288.

King at Balmoral his dear old friend's letter announcing the annexation of Bosnia and Herzegovina, which followed on October 7. The King was completely knocked over by it. He had been absolutely convinced of the Emperor's sincerity and frankness in assuring him that Austria was bent on preserving the peace of Europe, and this annexation, which violated the Treaty of Berlin, was an act that might have been expressly designed to provoke a European war. Those assurances had been meant to deceive him and had brilliantly succeeded. It was as well that there were no *Wiedersehens.*

The German Emperor's first reactions to the proclamation of the independence of Bulgaria were what might have been expected. He unhesitatingly put it down to King Edward's influence over his cousin, the new Tsar Ferdinand. The King had arranged it all, and in some obscure way — he had not time to work it out — it was directed against German capital invested in the Baghdad Railway. As to the annexation, both he and Bülow had known a month before that it was coming, but it was wiser to protest that he was in entire ignorance of it, so that none of the signatories to the Berlin Treaty could say that Germany had pushed Austria into it. It was particularly important that Russia should believe that, for she had very strong pro-Slav sympathies with Servia, whose dreams of a Greater Servia, that should include these provinces, were dissolved by this annexation. It really suited William very well, for any weakening of Servia implied a decline in Russian influence in the Balkans, but he feigned an intense indignation with Austria for doing such a thing without consulting her ally. 'I am the last person in Europe,' he scribbled on a despatch from Bülow, 'to hear anything whatever about it. . . Such are my thanks from the House of Hapsburg.' But he made up his mind at once that Germany must support Austria ; loyalty to her ally dictated that, and in no case must there be a rift in the Triple Alliance. Then there was Turkey to consider. For twenty years he had been her friendly counsellor and supporter, but it was impossible to subscribe to Turkey's protest to the Powers at Austria's having annexed two of the provinces under her suzerainty and having approved the independence of a third, while for the sake of the solidarity of the Triple Alliance he was bound to range himself with Austria. But England had supported that protest, and to his inveterately jealous mind there was his uncle filching his own policy of friendliness towards Turkey. 'A great score over us for Edward VII !' he bitterly commented. Moreover, since he himself was now condoning the flat violation of the Treaty of Berlin, once more his uncle scored, 'and henceforth could inscribe "Protector of Treaties" on his banner.' In whatever dilemma he found himself placed, he attributed the devising of it to the same sinister influence. This obsession was irrepressible and must find expression everywhere : the margins of state papers, submitted to him for perusal and signature, were a fine outlet, for so his Ministers would read the eloquence of his contempt, and he scribbled on them : 'England !' 'Uncle !' 'A most charming fellow this King E. VII !' 'Ineffable cheek !' 'Pharisee !' 'Rot !' 'Twaddle !' 'Bunkum !' 'Hurrah, we've caught the British scoundrels out this time !' *

Partly he heartened up his secret terrors by these withering ejaculations, partly he vented his spite against the man and the nation who would not trust him nor believe his sacred word of honour that all those German shipyards and foundries, incessantly pouring out of their furnaces the molten

---

* Ludwig, *Kaiser Wilhelm II*, pp. 366, 372 ; Bülow, *Memoirs*, 1903–1909, p. 327 ; Lee, *King Edward VII*, ii. pp. 635, 638.

steel to be fashioned into the raiment of his ships and their swift engines and the guns of their armament, were only engaged on protecting the commerce of his beloved and peace-loving Deutschland.

CHAPTER XV

HE was very uneasy. Russia was certainly moving in the direction of Powers who, he was convinced, were forging the chain of encirclement, and the Emperor turned his thoughts again to the land he hated and loved and feared. England had never understood Germany, he had complained to Mr. Frederick Whitridge, in spite of the thousands of German governesses who were employed there, and he planned yet one more approach. Perhaps he could yet make friends with her if he could somehow touch the very sentimental heart of the people who in his visits there — so many of them now since Grandpapa Albert swung the little brat in a napkin — had always given him a warm personal welcome. Had not London wept tears of emotion and gratitude when he cancelled his Prussian festivities to be present by the death-bed of his grandmother ? Less than a year ago he had stayed at Windsor, he had lime-lit himself at the Guildhall — history would do him justice — as the steadfast upholder of peace, and after that he had spent three weeks of holiday at Highcliffe, and had assured his host of the sincerity of his friendship with England. Colonel Stuart-Wortley was his guest in September this year at the annual German Army Manœuvres in Alsace, shortly after King Edward's visit to Friedrichshof and Ischl, and the Emperor expressed to him 'his personal desire that the utmost possible publicity should be given in England to the Anglophile views of himself and his House.' He enlarged further on this topic, and, at his request, Colonel Stuart-Wortley, combining what was said then with the notes he had taken of conversations with him at Highcliffe, compiled an article taking the form of a talk between the Emperor and an anonymous interviewer. A typed copy was submitted to him which he pronounced to be a faithful rendering of what he had said.

Then arose a disastrous muddle for which Bülow was entirely to blame. In his *Memoirs* he gives an utterly misleading version of it as follows. He received, he says, from Rominten, where the Emperor was shooting, 'a bulky and almost illegible manuscript on bad typing paper.' With it was a covering letter from his cousin Freiherr von Jenisch, who was attached to the Emperor as representative of the Foreign Office, asking him, on the Emperor's behalf, whether he saw any objection to its publication in an English paper. Bülow had not time to read it, and sent it to the Foreign Office with instructions that it should be carefully read and copied, and that all desirable corrections and deletions (underlined) should be marginally inserted. It came back with a few trifling corrections. Again he could not find time to read it, and gave it to his confidential secretary, Freiherr von Müller, instructing him to examine it critically (*prüfen*). Müller returned it to him with the definite assurance that there was no objection to the proposed publication. Accordingly it was sent back to Jenisch, in Bülow's name, as officially approved.*

The facts as proved by existing documents are otherwise. The covering letter from Jenisch which accompanied the typed interview contained definite instructions from the Emperor. These were that Bülow should read it himself, and that he should not let it be seen by any official of the Foreign Office : it was purely for Bülow's private eye and his personal

* Bülow, *Memoirs,* 1903–1909, pp. 328, 329.

verdict. Instead, without looking at it himself, he told Müller to send it to the Foreign Office. When it was returned, Bülow, still without reading it, directed Müller to send it back to Jenisch and dictated a covering letter conveying his approval. Bülow's assertion therefore, that Müller had read it and assured him that it was harmless, is unfounded : Müller never read it, nor did Bülow ask him to do so. As regards the typed document, which is still in existence, it is neither bulky nor illegible nor written on flimsy paper. It is of quite moderate length, as the published manuscript proves, and it is clearly typed on substantial paper. The entire responsibility for the publication is Bülow's, who had not followed the Emperor's instructions. But after Freiherr von Müller's death Bülow gave this erroneous account of the incident in his *Memoirs,* putting the deplorable consequences of his own neglect on him.*

The interview was published in the *Daily Telegraph* of October 27, 1908.

The Emperor began by scolding England for not trusting him : 'You English are like mad bulls — you see red everywhere. What on earth has come over you that you should heap on us such suspicion as is unworthy of a great nation ? What *can* I do more ? I have always stood forth as the friend of England. . . I regard this misapprehension as a personal insult. . . You make it uncommonly difficult for a man to remain friendly to England.' . . . After this striking prelude he once more enumerated some of the benefits he had showered on the nation. In the Boer War, after the Black Week he had written most sympathetically to his revered grandmother. He had worked out a plan of campaign which should bring victory to England, and after submitting it to the criticism of his General Staff had sent it (in the form of Aphorisms) to his uncle. This was the identical

* Private information.

plan which Lord Roberts had so successfully adopted. Then Russia and France invited him to join them in compelling England to make peace : 'What was my answer ? That Germany would draw the Sword to prevent so base an action.' Boer delegates had been enthusiastically welcomed in France : he refused to receive them, and he had told Kruger that it was idle for him to come to Berlin on such an errand. Again he protested that the German fleet was not designed for hostilities against England, but against the Yellow Peril of Japan and China. He had already warned the Tsar of that.*

The effect of this publication on Germany was quite frightful. Count Metternich, German Ambassador in London, read his morning paper and, limp with consternation, said : 'Now we may shut up shop.' Prince Bülow at once sent in his resignation, which the Emperor refused to accept, but he promised the Reichstag, on the Emperor's behalf, that for the future, even in private conversations, he would 'maintain that reserve indispensable to the interests of any consistent Foreign Policy.' As for the Press, it pronounced such advances to the country which it regarded as its national foe as amounting to treason, and with unconscious humour put them down to an unbridled family affection for his uncle. The unfortunate man scarce dared look at the serious journals, for fear that his aghast Imperial eye should meet such sentences as : 'The Sovereign's rights are counterbalanced by duties which to neglect is to undermine the very foundations of the monarchy.' The comic papers flouted with impunity the penalties for *lèse-majesté,* and the Emperor appeared cartooned as a small boy scribbling and smeared with ink, while Mother Germania and Father Bülow scolded him for making such a mess. 'Didn't we tell you that you weren't to

---

* Ludwig, *Kaiser Wilhelm II,* pp. 338-341 ; Bülow, *Memoirs,* 1903-1909, pp. 341-343 ; *Willy-Nicky Letters,* p. 239.

play at writing letters any more ?' was the intolerable caption. Our Emperor William I in the courts of Heaven pleaded with the Almighty to forgive his grandson, for he was Emperor 'by the Grace of God.' To which the Almighty replied : 'Now you want to put all the blame on Me !'

It was little wonder that William could not stand Berlin in such a tempest of ridicule and abuse. He fled from it for a week's stag-shooting with Archduke Francis Ferdinand in Austria, and telegraphed to Bülow that he had splendid sport and that he prayed for him morning and evening. From there he went to stay with Prince Max Fürstenberg, where a revelry of fox-shoots, bawdy stories, music-hall performances and practical jokes assuaged the horrid smart of censure and contempt. He had cried a little when he read the report of the unkind speeches made about him in the Reichstag — how cruelly they misunderstood him — but here was the same kind of diverting company as Eulenburg, whom the Emperor had instantly thrown over when the storm of scandal about his abnormal tastes broke out, had so often assembled for his entertainment. The Chief of the Emperor's Military Cabinet, General Count Hulsen-Haeseler, was there, who as a young man had so often amused him with his deft conjuring tricks on board the yacht, and on the last evening he glided on toe-points on to the stage in the hall, dressed as a ballerina, and danced before his Emperor. Alas, he was too old now for such dainty exertions, and, after he had earned and acknowledged the tumultuous applause, he collapsed and instantly died. They dressed him in his General's uniform again, and the Emperor cancelled a naval function at Kiel, and telegraphed to his wife that he had lost his best friend.*

Then the reception of this interview in England caused him bitter pangs. He had enumerated the tale of benefits

* Ludwig, *Kaiser Wilhelm II*, pp. 347-349 ; Bülow, *Memoirs*, 1903-1909, p. 357.

The Kaiser with Prince Max Fürstenberg

he had conferred on the nation : how he had brought them victory in South Africa, and kept Russia and France at bay ; but the lack of gratitude was deplorable.   A ribald Press was merely astounded at this rubbish, and sarcastically remarked that it had always been supposed that Lord Roberts had won the war.   The Emperor could hardly believe such baseness, and a few days after the interview had appeared he burst into the box of Mrs. Cornwallis West at the Berlin Opera-house, and with wild gesticulations shouted out : 'Well, this is the way I am treated in England when I try to show that I am her friend. ' Just wait a little while and we shall see how the English live to repent !' *   He could not have testi-fied more explicitly to the sincerity of his friendship.   Even remote and barbarous Japan resented his calling England's ally the Yellow Peril.   This world-wide ingratitude was quite inexplicable.   It was not till many years later, when he was an exile at Doorn, that he recollected that he had cut out from the typescript of the interview, as submitted to him, those sentences that gave such offence in Germany, but that the printers had taken no notice of his omissions.

So this remarkable olive branch was waved in vain : the ungrateful islanders stripped the leaves off it and sent it back to Germany, and his own people switched him smartly with the twigs.   He had no real influence over national sentiment, for who can follow the policy of a weather-cock that disre-gards the true wind, and only veers to its own internal im-pulses ?   His suspicions of England and of his uncle neither confirmed nor deepened those of his country, while his protestations of friendship only aroused suspicion against himself.   He whisked round to Russia again : perhaps she would be more susceptible to blandishment than the brutal English, and though it was now five months since he had had any correspondence with the Tsar, he sent him in

* *Journals and Letters of Lord Esher,* ii. p. 356.

January a long letter wishing him all prosperity for the new year 1909. Russia, ever ready to protect the Slav population of the Balkans, and ready also to snatch any advantage, such as the opening of the Dardanelles, from disturbances there, had been and was extremely indignant at the Austrian annexations, and William hastened to assure Nicky that he had known nothing whatever about them till the thing was done, and then of course he had to support his ally : Nicky would be the first to appreciate his loyalty. He assured him also that the Austrian Emperor, who was 'wise and judicious and such a Venerable Gentleman,' had no idea of attacking Servia. He had cause for uneasiness about Isvolsky's late visit to England and the growing friendship between her and Russia, which during this year resulted in the Triple Entente, and, following the pattern of his late advances to England, expressed the parallel conviction that the union of Germany and Russia 'would form a powerful stronghold for the maintenance of peace.' He reminded the Tsar of past benefits received : he quite understood that he was anxious to be on good terms with England, and had not felt a moment's uneasiness about his meeting with King Edward at Reval, but he regretted 'the patent fact' that Russia was drawing away from Germany and knitting herself up with nations unfriendly to her. Why this drift ? Why this unwarranted mistrust ? He, too, wanted to be friends with England, and he was rejoiced to think that Uncle Bertie and Aunt Alix were to pay a state visit to Berlin next month. That also ought to have great results for the peace of the world. Anything for peace. . .*

This visit had been promised when uncle and nephew had met last August at Friedrichshof. The King did not want to go ; he had stipulated that the Emperor's last visit to Windsor should not render him liable to returning it at Ber-

* *Willy-Nicky Letters,* pp. 240–246.

lin, but he had now been on the throne for eight years, he had paid state visits to Portugal, Italy, France, Greece, Spain, Norway, Sweden and Denmark, as well as meeting the Tsar at Reval, and never yet had he entered his nephew's capital : it was well that he and the Queen should remedy an omission which was becoming marked. February was not the ideal month for pageants, and the King was far from well, for in the months of early spring he was especially subject to bronchial attacks which were very exhausting and had begun to cause much anxiety.

The opening scene of the state entry did not promise very brilliantly. The *Victoria and Albert* had been delayed by fog in the North Sea, and showers of February sleet had damped and chilled the crowds who had waited long to see the Sovereigns, after many embraces on the platform, drive through the streets from the station. It was no wonder that they were not moved to enthusiasm ; but the Emperor made up for that, and throughout the visit he was in that loud, boisterous humour which Queen Alexandra particularly disliked. There was the usual state banquet, the usual speeches were formally read, as if they had been the minutes of the last meeting at Windsor, and duly confirmed. There was a lunch at the British Embassy, at which the King had the most alarming fit of coughing. There was a civic reception at the Rathaus, where the geniality and tact of the King's speech was more popular with the general audience than with his nephew. There was a gala performance at the opera, a visit to the Royal Mausoleum, a lunch with the 1st Dragoon Guards, of which the King was Honorary Colonel, a Court ball, and a family dinner with the Crown Prince. But to what purpose, it might be asked, was this waste ? These magnificent hospitalities were sown in stony ground, and were no sooner sprung up than they withered. There was no affection between the entertainers and the entertained ; the whole was no more than a splendid charade symbolising a cordiality which did not exist. The Sovereigns were careful to avoid all controversial topics, and not till the moment of departure on the station platform was the most crucial of all alluded to. The German Naval Estimates, said the Emperor, could not be altered. 'They will be adhered to and exactly carried out without any restrictions.' Again the Sovereigns embraced, the King climbed up the difficult steps of his saloon carriage, and the train moved out.

The two never saw each other again : all their meetings, for good or ill, were over. Never had any good come out of them, though again and again responsible statesmen both in England and Germany had hoped that friendly interviews and entertainments might inaugurate a better feeling between the nations ; on the other hand, they had not done any harm, and perhaps the omission of them would have minutely accentuated the national antagonism. But whenever they met King Edward had to suppress, not always with complete success, the irritation which his nephew's demeanour aroused in him, while the Emperor was alert in noting all that could be fashioned into causes of complaint. Even if ties of personal affection had united them, the King could never have run in harness with so incalculable a yoke-fellow, nor could the harness have failed to snap under William's jibbing antics. From the earliest days of the Emperor's reign his uncle had disliked him. Sometimes he had tried, in these private relations, to propitiate him by appeals to his vanity ; he had induced Queen Victoria, for instance, much against her will, to give him rank in the British Army, and after her death had made him a Field-Marshal. But it is ludicrous to suppose that the Emperor's childish pleasure in such additions to his collection of uniforms could conceivably affect national relations, though King Edward thought it worth trying. Moreover, William's was one of those un-

The Kaiser and King Edward VII

happy natures which detect a bribe in every token of friendliness to himself, and a design against himself in every friendliness to others. Often during the earlier years of his reign
he had made genuine attempts to secure a good understanding or even an alliance with England, but invariably he
defeated his own ends by the crookedness of his methods,
or, when things promised fairly well, by starting some new,
abortive, secret intrigue with another country. The keynote
of his policy was to make mischief between those whom he
feared, and the result was generally the opposite of what he
aimed at. His pantomime appearance on his white horse at
Tangier (though, it is true, he was reluctant) was an instance of this. The object was to make trouble between
France and England, but the ultimate effect was to render
the *entente* more solid than before. He had tried the same
game with regard to Russia and England, and by his efforts
he had been instrumental, owing to the deep distrust he had
inspired in Russia, in forging the Triple Entente. Such
methods made his policy as distasteful to his uncle as was his
person.

Again, how dangerous was any dependence on a man
whose lack of wisdom, in spite of his brilliant cleverness,
blinded him to the effect of his displays. In order to impress
upon Germany the might of German arms and the majesty
of himself and his Empire, he held yearly military manœuvres in Alsace, a parade of troops at Metz, a review at Stras-
burg, and, on the anniversary of Sedan, every school-child in
the province had a holiday. Up and down the streets of
Alsatian towns the children were massed and marched with
flags and banners, and, as the War Lord went by, they waved
and huzzaed with their shrill voices, 'Der Kaiser hoch !' to
testify their joy in being his subjects. So he had ordered,
and that was all he saw. But their mothers, while dressing
them in their best, had crowned them with wreaths of mauve

flowers, and tied mauve ribands in their hair, and whispered to them that mauve was the colour of mourning which France wore to commemorate the loss of her provinces. The civic authorities laid a wreath at the foot of the statue of the victor of Sedan, and while *Deutschland über Alles* was blared out by the military bands, they sang below their breath *Nous n'avons plus de Rhin,* and kept the bitter memory alive. The War Lord heard only the glory and honour of Germany in those fifes and drums, and never guessed how potent a whet they were to the undying hatred of France.*

The King opened Parliament a few days after he arrived back in England, and in his speech from the throne spoke of the success of his visit to Berlin, from which, yet once more, he augured the happiest prospects of cordial international relations. Early in March he went to Biarritz and had a yachting tour in the Mediterranean, hearing of which the Emperor proposed a meeting at the Achilleion, his house on Corfu, or at Malta. But they had met very lately at Berlin and the King made other arrangements. He paid a call on the King of Italy at Baiae, and, as in 1903, the same absurd pursuit took place : the Emperor followed on his tracks to Malta and then went to Brindisi to see the King of Italy and obliterate his uncle. Meantime the English Naval Estimates had been introduced, and the Houses of Parliament did not assess the probable value of the King's visit to Berlin as highly as he, for to meet the menace, or so they regarded it, of the German programme they passed the increase of £3,-000,000 which the Government asked for. He himself was desperately anxious about the swiftness with which the German navy was overhauling the British : with the querulousness born of failing health he declared he had been kept in the dark about it, that he ought to have been more fully instructed before he went to Berlin. But what could he have

---

* Topham, *Chronicles of the Prussian Court,* pp. 141–146.

done ? The Emperor in his parting words on the platform
had made it clear that Germany was not meaning to slow
down, and the only effective answer was to accelerate the
British programme. It was too late for anything else ; the
race between the two had started ; it was as if two competi-
tors tried to agree, as they sped down the track, not to run
too fast, or as if two boxers, in a fight for the world cham-
pionship, settled not to hit each other very hard.

It was important to knit more closely the bonds of the
Triple Entente, and once again royal visits were planned.
The mode was surely now outworn, but in spite of its tatters
it had still the prestige of national flags. This summer the
Tsar was to be flown as the emblem of solidarity : he was to
pay marine visits to Russia's friends, first to France, meeting
the President with the French fleet off Cherbourg. He
would not set foot on the soil of France — for who knew
what spectre of assassination might not disclose itself ? — but
the presence of his yacht with the Imperial Ensign in French
territorial waters would supply the needful symbolism. The
sea was rough, but from the shore could be discerned on the
bridge of the *Standart* two figures holding on to the rail ;
one the familiar M. Fallières, and the other without doubt,
small and remote and incessantly saluting, was the Autocrat
of all the Russias. Then came the second visit : three of the
new British Dreadnoughts hove in sight, and under their
protection the *Standart* steamed into the Anglo-French
Channel making for the Solent.

This visit was a return for the state visit paid by the King
to the Tsar at Reval a year ago, and provoked the same criticism from Labour and Radical Members of Parliament as
the other had done, and the same protest against any official
welcome being offered to that timid, kindly 'blood-stained
murderer.' On the very day of the Tsar's arrival a remon-
strance, addressed to the Foreign Secretary, appeared in the

Press, but it aroused no sympathy except in the mind of the German Emperor, who observed with satisfaction that seventy members of the House of Commons and two bishops subscribed to his own disapproval of the Tsar's visit. But that glow must have cooled when he read of the vast avenue of saluting British ships through which the *Victoria and Albert* and the *Standart* moved to their moorings at Cowes. Last year when the King visited the Tsar at Reval, his host's naval display was limited to exactly one ship, but now in the Solent there were certainly more. It was many years since, at this season, the Emperor, as Admiral of the British Fleet, had inspected that austere and menacing assembly, but never had he seen so formidable an array as that which welcomed its most newly appointed Admiral.

The Tsar was accompanied by his wife, and family of five children, four daughters who inherited the noble beauty of their mother, and the one boy, Alexis, youngest of all. Only once since his accession had the Tsar and the Tsarina set foot on British soil, when they spent that quiet domestic fortnight with Queen Victoria at Balmoral. He was practically unknown to the English, a symbol to some of that vast realm, gorgeous and barbaric, that reached from Germany eastwards to the Pacific, to others he was a blood-stained murderer, and to the very few who knew him a strange mixture of kindliness and indecision and obstinacy, a dreamer and an idealist, intensely religious, profoundly superstitious and shadowed by the dread of assassination. He had none of a ruler's gifts, he was himself entirely ruled by his adored wife, 'sweet simple Alicky,' and was happiest when, in the protection of his Guards — yet were they loyal ? — or of a friendly fleet, he could play with his children and almost forget the perils of the autocracy which was his by divine right and to which his wife encouraged him to cling with limpet-like tenacity. He was happy here, for he was safe, and, as at Reval, his uncle did not worry him with waste-paper treaties to sign, and hints that he should remember English firms in the rebuilding of his navy. There were no agitating splendours, no gala night at the opera, no lunch at the Guildhall, no review of troops, no perilous traverse of crowded streets, and the Tsar only went ashore once, privately and briefly, to see the house at Osborne, now a Naval College, where the German Emperor had so often goaded his uncle by his ill-manners. But dinner on board the *Victoria and Albert* had all the qualities of a state banquet ; Ministers were in attendance on the Sovereigns, and the King, in welcoming his guests, assured them that those miles of battleships through which the royal yachts had steamed were arrayed solely for the protection of British commerce and for the maintenance of peace. The Emperor had often used just those expressions about the German fleet, so peace should be tolerably secure. But how distrustful were the English ! They ought to have taken his word for that, instead of increasing their Naval Estimates.

A fortnight later, in the middle of August, the King went for the last time to Marienbad. No suggestion was made from either side that he should meet his nephew *en route* or visit the Austrian Emperor at Ischl. He still bitterly resented the Emperor's conduct to him last year. It had been a cruel shock that the dear old man with the kindly eye, the courteous manners and that serene frankness of speech should have so deceived him with candid promises of doing all that lay in his power to preserve the peace of Europe, and to that shock was added the personal humiliation of having been duped. Since then the semi-official Austrian Press, under Aehrenthal's inspiration, had launched a series of violent attacks on England, naming King Edward as the instigator of British unfriendliness in denouncing the breach of the Treaty of Berlin, and the King had hesitated whether he should go to Marienbad at all. But the omission of so regular an item in his annual routine would probably have been given a political interpretation of further unfriendliness, and he went. Those attacks still rankled, and, talking to Mr. Wickham Steed about them, his indignation exploded, and again and again he called out 'They lied about me !' to the consternation of the water-drinkers. Then the British Ambassador at Vienna thought of a quaint device. Baron Aehrenthal, he believed, was sorry for having inspired those offensive attacks in the Press, and he had been created a Count by the Austrian Emperor for his brilliant success in procuring the annexation of Bosnia and Herzegovina, which had brought Europe to the brink of war. Could not King Edward therefore send him a telegram of congratulation on his rise in rank, just a gracious word which would be highly prized ? Certainly not, said King Edward. A gracious word would imply that he withdrew those extremely forcible words he had spoken about the *coup* which had earned Aehrenthal this superior coronet. The Count shall not be congratulated.*

Balmoral and Sandringham again, and shooting parties, and his horses — Minoru had won him his third Derby this year — and his birthday in November, but no more royal visits were planned. What good had come, for instance, of that last visit to Berlin ? There had been great fatigue and exertion for himself, but no slackening of naval programmes, nor the gain of one ounce of confidence between the nations. How well he knew the routine of those glittering occasions which he had once valued so highly, and had himself so intensely enjoyed and so admirably conducted : the royal embrace on the platform of arrival, the drive through the troop-lined streets, the gala performance at the opera, the

* Wickham Steed, *Through Thirty Years*, pp. 317–318.

civic lunch, the state ball, and in particular the banquet with speeches expressing the conviction of close and permanent friendship ! Had the effect of such words lasted longer than the polite applause which followed them ? For himself his pleasure in those pageants had faded, and that inimitable jollity, once so spontaneous, had become an effort. What stimulated him before now only wearied him, and the failing of his physical powers produced fits of deep depression : sometimes he thought of abdicating. At home, as abroad, there were troublous times ahead ; there would be a General Election in January 1910, and the question of the relations between the Lords and Commons and of the power of the Lords indefinitely to veto any Bill sent up from the Commons would come up again. He looked with dismay on the prospect of a Radical Government handling that.* Political problems weighed on him unduly, the growth of the German fleet was like thunder in the air, and his bronchial attacks were draining his strength.

For many years the King, and his mother before him, had written birthday letters to the Emperor for the anniversary on January 27. This year he repeated with unusual emphasis the leading *cliché* in those numerous speeches at state banquets : 'It is essential for the peace of the world that we should walk shoulder to shoulder for the good of civilisation and the prosperity of the world.' In spite of his sincerity he must have known how impossible was the realisation of such hopes. Those new ships from the yards of Vulcan and Vickers would never go forth against a common foe, nor in conjunction with German armies by land keep a mouse from stirring. Yet what else was there to say, and what answer could his nephew give except to affirm once more that if the Anglo-Saxon and Teutonic races worked together, as had

* *Journals and Letters of Lord Esher*, ii. p. 419.

always been the aim of his political creed, 'the future of the world would be assured and safeguarded' ? Providence had imposed this task upon them, and there must be no more squabbling. He warmly thanked his uncle for his birthday gift of a walking-stick. The taste and style of it were most 'refined,' and it reminded him of the sticks which Frederick the Great used. One seems to see him brandishing the walking-stick, solely as a weapon of defence.*

King Edward died in the following May : the Emperor, with seven other kings, came to England for the funeral. He described in his *Memoirs* how, with deep emotion, he laid a wreath on the coffin, how he knelt in silent prayer, and then, rising, grasped the hand of the new King. This gesture, he wrote, made the most profound impression on all those who saw it. It signified that England and Germany had established firm friendship at last, and he recalled, when he had been in exile for over ten years, how one of his English cousins had said to him : 'That handshake of yours with our King is all over London : people deeply grateful and impressed.' † As at the funeral of Queen Victoria, what filled his mind was that the consciousness of all beholders was directed on him with the same eager intensity as was his own.

He neither felt nor pretended to feel any regret or sense of personal loss at his uncle's death, and we may wonder what thoughts chiefly occupied his mind as he knelt in silent prayer. A marginal note which he made on Bülow's letter of condolence possibly supplies the answer : 'The system of intrigue which kept Europe on tenterhooks will come to an end. . . I believe that European policy as a whole will be more quiescent : even if that were all it would be something.' His death therefore, personally unlamented, was on political

---

* Lee, *King Edward VII,* ii. pp. 693, 694.
† Waters, *Potsdam and Doorn,* p. 96.

grounds an immense relief, for the Emperor genuinely believed that the main aim of King Edward throughout his reign was the encirclement and ruin of Germany, and for that he feared and detested him. But there was more than that : memories of old days at Windsor with his grandmother flowed back upon him, bringing with them the sense of home, of his belonging here, and now that his uncle was gone they were purged of those painful quarrels, and he was happy to be among his English relations. A mood perhaps — was he not all moods ? — but it sprang from a source deep in that impetuous, unbalanced mind. Often he had poisoned it by his jealousy of England, his fear of her power, his conviction that she sought the undoing of Germany with relentless persistence, but it flowed clean, though now a trickle, till once again he shovelled into it fresh venom of his terrors and suspicions.*

* Ludwig, *Kaiser Wilhelm II*, p. 376.

CHAPTER XVI

WITH the accession of King George V the Emperor's long series of visits to England came practically to an end, and he only set foot in England once more, when in May 1911 he came to London for the unveiling of the memorial to Queen Victoria in front of Buckingham Palace. He had been spending Easter at his palatial villa in Corfu, excitedly excavating early Greek remains in the neighbourhood. Some interesting archaic sculpture had been unearthed and he proclaimed it 'one of the greatest antiquities of all time.' He wrote a characteristic letter from here to the Tsar. What was now causing the Emperor himself the greatest anxiety in international relations was the *entente* between Russia, England and France : he therefore sent the Tsar an article in the German Press written 'by an intimate friend of Uncle Bertie, an English politician,' which stated that King Edward had always feared a closer friendship between Russia, Germany and Austria, and that all his efforts had been directed to preventing that ; it was comforting to find that his uncle had been obsessed with fears so strictly analogous to his own. But how fruitless those efforts had been ! William was convinced — his Easter Communion had confirmed this conviction — that he and the Tsar would always be the firmest friends. In other words, he sought to hearten up his own misgivings by asserting as a fact that of which he was afraid the opposite was true.*

* *Willy-Nicky Letters,* pp. 264, 265.

In the summer of this year occurred the Agadir incident which for a moment endangered the peace of Europe. It was a variation on the theme of the Emperor's visit to Tangier in 1905, and, like that, directed against France and the Anglo-French *entente*. There had been an insurrection at Fez, and French troops, as was perfectly proper, were sent to restore order. Instead of the Emperor appearing in person to remind the world that Germany had rights there of which she was watchful, a gunboat, the *Panther,* with a crew of 150 men appeared off Agadir, a 'closed' port in South Morocco, symbolising Germany. While she remained there the situation was dangerous, for England was fully determined to give France her full support, in accordance with the *entente,* over the French rights in Morocco. The vigorous remarks of Mr. Lloyd George, Chancellor of the Exchequer, enabled German politicians to perceive that, and the appearance of a British ship of war, which saluted the *Panther* very politely and took up her moorings near her, threw a further light on the matter. Germany explained that she had no sinister designs of any sort ; the *Panther* had only been sent to Agadir because some German firms in South Morocco had asked for protection against raids by local tribesmen, and she was recalled.*

The Emperor had seen on this occasion how senselessly provocative the despatch of his little cruiser had been. It was an empty gesture, the shaking of a fist with no intention to strike. Just as in 1905 he had been most reluctant to ride through Tangier at Bülow's urging, so now he had opposed this threat. But in both cases he had yielded, though believing that such action was dangerous. For years his impetuousness and flamboyant utterances had encouraged the war spirit, and now he, the War Lord, fearful at heart

* Wickham Steed, *Through Thirty Years,* i. pp. 343, 344 ; Sir G. Arthur, *King George V,* p. 256.

though arrayed in shining armour, was no more than a shadow cast on to the gathering storm clouds, or a mascot, the Black Eagle, that decorated but did not drive the war chariot. But this fiasco at Agadir was none of his making, and the ridicule that followed, though directed at him, was undeserved except in so far as he had consented, against his better judgment, to so futile a piece of interference.

The ruinous race between Germany and England over their navies went on full speed ahead. This was one of the few policies to which, since its inception, the Emperor had been faithful. No more was heard, on either side, of those quaint theories that the two fleets were destined for the sole purpose of the defence of their trade routes and colonies, and to the Emperor's mind it was only by bringing his fleet up to or superior to the strength of the British that this night-mare of encirclement could be dispelled. Naval opinion in Germany was that, when once an equality was established, England would recognise that further competition was use-less and would accept the inevitable, with the result that the two countries might become friends. It was in vain that Count Metternich, now German Ambassador in London, pointed out that this was a lunatic theory. England had no choice about continuing to maintain her naval supremacy, for on it alone was based the security of her Empire and without it the Triple Entente was powerless either for ag-gression or defence. But the Emperor derided Metternich's counsel with his most withering marginalia. England could yet be brought to her senses (*i.e.* the surrender of naval supremacy) by 'sheer fright'; for that was the only way to get rid of his own. But to call a truce in naval construction was to leave England still superior at sea, and the bidding for supremacy continued to soar. It ceased to be possible and became probable that, unless something unconjectur-able happened, war, on some pretext or other (and of pretexts there would be no lack), would break out within the space of a few years. That was what the Emperor dreaded beyond everything, and the demon of perversity which moulded his destiny drove him into supporting the very policy which would render war inevitable.

King George did not pursue his father's practice of encouraging international amity by state visits to the Sovereigns of Europe, and there was no need for the Emperor to follow on his heels in order to overscore his visits by displays of superior majesty. The claims of Empire seemed to him more worth a journey in comparison with which his father's travels were suburban. Never yet, save for King Edward's landings at Gibraltar and Malta, had any British Sovereign set foot in his dominions oversea, but in the autumn of 1911 King George and the Queen went out to India to hold the Coronation Durbar at Delhi. They sailed in the *Medina* of the Peninsular and Oriental Line, and the Channel Fleet accompanied them out into the Atlantic. A member of his staff asked him if the fleet was escorting him to Bombay : he replied that with Germany behaving as she had done at Agadir it might well be needed at home.* In Europe he paid no state visit at all till, three years after his accession, in May 1913, he and the Queen went to Berlin for a remarkable family party of wedding-bells and reconciliation. Ever since the seizure of the Kingdom of Hanover by Prussia there had been feud between the Hohenzollerns and the descendants of Queen Victoria's Uncle Ernest, Duke of Cumberland and King of Hanover, and his grandson, the present Duke, was known in Germany as the 'Vanishing Duke,' by reason of the skill, as of a conjurer, with which he inexplicably disappeared if the Emperor was in the neighbourhood and there was risk of meeting him. But now his

---

* Private information.

only surviving son and the Emperor's only daughter, Victoria Louise, had fallen in love with each other, and the parents on both sides consented to the marriage which would make an end of that long quarrel. The Duke himself had married Princess Thyra of Denmark, youngest sister of Queen Alexandra and the Tsar's mother, and the Tsar came from Russia for the wedding and from England came King George and Queen Mary.

This was the last of those great royal gatherings, the final performance of those dynastic madrigals once thought to breathe harmony over discordant Europe. The railway line from the Russian frontier to Berlin was guarded throughout its length by troops for the safety of the Tsar : soldiers with loaded rifles were more numerous than the telegraph poles, and every road leading to the station at Berlin was stopped. There was a state banquet, and a banquet after the wedding, followed by the Torch Dance traditional at nuptials of the Hohenzollerns. Troops lined the walls of the White Hall and passed torches from hand to hand while the bride and bridegroom made the circuit of the room to ancient wedding music. Then their august relations joined them, forming groups of three. The bride led off, dancing with her father and her father-in-law, the bridegroom followed with his mother and his mother-in-law. Then the Tsar and King George danced with the bride, and Queen Mary and the Crown Princess of Germany with the bridegroom : never before, even in the dancing days of their grandmother, Queen Victoria, had kings and queens been woven into so many family permutations, symbolical of regal accord. There was a gala performance at the opera ; King George lunched with the 1st Dragoon Guards, of which his grandmother had been Honorary Colonel, and the Emperor led a march past. All went brilliantly save for one very suspect moment when the Emperor found the Tsar

and King George quietly chatting together in King George's
suite of rooms, and divined that they were putting the fin-
ishing touches on a plot whereby Russia and England should
suddenly attack Germany, but this unpleasant impression
was only momentary. Then came the parting : the Tsar
retraced his guarded route to his own dominions, which
were soon to become more perilous to him than any alien
soil, and the King and Queen returned to England. Never
did any of those three Sovereigns meet again, and before
the coming storm had passed, one with his wife and family
had been brutally murdered, and another had fled from his
kingdom to the safety of a foreign country.*

The French President, M. Poincaré, paid a state visit to
London next month, June 1913, and in April 1914 the King
and Queen paid the return visit to Paris. Both the King
and the President spoke confidently of the value of the
Triple Entente as a guarantee for the peace of Europe. At
the moment the disturbed state of Ireland was the King's
greatest anxiety. Asquith's Home Rule Bill was coming before Parliament, and Ulster was arming to resist inclusion
in it by force. Civil war in his own country seemed much
more likely than war anywhere else. The last three years,
it is true, had seen continuous trouble in the Balkans —
small states, as the German Emperor had once written to the
Tsar, were 'an awful nuisance ! Quantités négligeables !
The slightest encouragement from any quarter makes them
frantic' † — but Europe generally had grown to take squab-
bles as a chronic condition in that quarter, and the fear of
Russia championing some Slav state of kindred blood and
thus kindling a general conflagration had so often proved
to be a vain disquietude that it had lost its acuteness. Not

---

* Sir G. Arthur, *King George V*, pp. 293–296 ; Topham, *Chronicles of the
Prussian Court*, pp. 245–247 ; Bülow, *Memoirs*, 1909–1919, p. 198.
　† *Willy-Nicky Letters*, p. 245.

the wisest head in Europe could have conjectured that in the Balkans would now immediately be kindled the spark that set light to Europe. Europe was packed with far more obviously inflammable material. This spark, so to speak, was accidental ; any spark would make a catastrophic explosion when all Europe was a vast powder magazine of piled-up armaments by sea and land, and instead of a spark, in this spring of 1914, it was more likely that there should flare up some sudden sheet of flame between two of the Great Powers.

It was over five years ago that Austria had annexed the provinces of Bosnia and Herzegovina, and though the Powers had acquiesced in that act of brigandage for fear that war should follow, the small Slav states had never ceased to resent it. Chief among these was Servia, for Servia, in the crumbling of the Ottoman Empire, had dreamed of a Greater Servia, incorporating the two snatched provinces with a port on the Adriatic. She was riddled with secret anti-Austrian societies, and propagandist work of the Black Hand was busy in cafés in Belgrade, where excitable youths were kindled with tales of patriot heroes, from Obelic the Servian, who on June 28, 1389, had assassinated the Sultan Mourad, down to the Bosnian Bhogdan Zherajitch, who four years ago had unsuccessfully attempted to shoot the new Austrian Governor of Bosnia-Herzegovina and had then killed himself and was buried at Serajevo. In these cafés were sung songs in honour of such heroes and laments for enslaved Bosnia : 'O Bosnia, orphan before the gods, hast thou no patriots in thy land to-day ?' * Nor was this Black Hand movement confined to the lower classes ; officers in the Servian army organised it, officials in pseudo-Masonic associations worked for it and watched for an opportunity for revenge on the brigand Power. Early in 1914 it pre-

* Yeats-Brown, *Golden Horn*, p. 95.

sented itself. The Press announced that the heir to the
Austrian throne, Archduke Francis Ferdinand, would attend Austrian military manœuvres in Bosnia, and would
afterwards, with his morganatic wife, the Duchess of Hohen-
berg, pay an official visit to Serajevo, the capital of Bosnia.
The date was fixed for June 28, a day sacred to the memory
of the patriot Obelic. The Black Hand decreed that on
this commemorative day the Archduke should die.

Three youths, all under twenty, intoxicated with the dream
of becoming patriot heroes, were chosen for the insane outrage. They were furnished with bombs and pistols from
the State Arsenal at Belgrade by a major in the Servian
Army, they were smuggled across the frontier and reported
themselves to the agent of the Black Hand in Serajevo, who
gave them their instructions. On Sunday morning, June 28,
one of the boys, standing in the crowd, threw a bomb at the
Archduke's open motor as he drove to the Town Hall for
a civic reception given by the Mayor : it bounded from the
back hood of the car and exploded in the road. The Archduke drove on, and on his return from the Town Hall the
second of these youths, Gavrilo Princep, jumped on to the
footboard of his car and fired two pistol shots at point-blank
range. A quarter of an hour later both the Archduke and
his wife were dead.

That day the German Emperor was at Kiel, where a
regatta was going on. He had read service in the morning
on the *Hohenzollern,* there were yachting races for the afternoon, and his own yacht was competing. A motorboat
chunked out from Kiel harbour and came alongside the
Hohenzollern, and the officer in charge cried out that he had
a most urgent despatch for the All-Highest. No use : the
All-Highest was busy, and so he folded up his despatch in-
side his cigarette case and threw it on board : somebody
would pick it up, and its contents would be inspected. Ten

minutes later the Imperial flag was hauled down to half-mast, the Emperor was with difficulty persuaded to abandon the regatta, for he was most anxious that his yacht should win his own prize, and he returned to Berlin.*

Indeed he was sincerely to be pitied, for all the uncontrolled hounds of his own temperament, his panic fears, his impetuosity, his indecision, his bawling self-assertion, leapt out and savaged him. The murder of the heir to the Austrian throne was an anarchical outrage and exemplary vengeance must follow, for such crimes were aimed at the sacred principle of Monarchy, and who knew what the next target might be ? The Emperor was terrified for himself, and he scribbled on the margin of a despatch his imperial will : 'Servia must be wiped out, and at once !' Another hound bayed more remotely from the dangerous darkness. For if Austria carried out the capital sentence which he recommended, if she sent Servia some ultimatum which no country could accept without surrendering its independence, what would Russia do ? Often before now had Russia manifested her strong blood-sympathy with a Slav state, and she would never suffer Servia to be wiped out. That would mean war, and the Emperor erased his marginal note. Yet, on the other hand, the feeble, timorous Tsarlet would be the first to approve a condign punishment for regicide, since he himself lived in daily terror of it. In Russia the mere suspicion of an anarchist plot was enough to send to the scaffold any who could have the faintest connection with it, and Servia was riddled with anarchist societies. Perhaps it would be better to write to his venerable brother of Austria urging moderation, saying that he could not approve of too inexorable a punishment. In these first bewildering reactions he thought mainly in terms of Emperors.

The first loud bayings of panic died down and there as-

* Bülow, *Memoirs,* 1909–1919, p. 136.

serted itself the dread of Germany's being isolated unless she stood in with Austria. On July 5, a week after the outrage, the Emperor gave to the Austrian Ambassador in Berlin his personal assurance that Germany would support Austria whatever were the terms of the ultimatum to Servia, which he urged should be issued at once. He then left Berlin again, without convening his Crown Council, and rejoined the *Hohenzollern* for his usual northern cruise. Various conjectures have been made as to why, at such a time of crisis, he did not summon his Ministers and remain in Berlin. Possibly he thought that his absence on a pleasure cruise would produce a calming effect in Europe ; it would then be plain that he saw nothing alarming in the situation. Possibly the war party in Germany distrusted his habitual blusterings and withdrawals, and urged him, on the ostensible pretext of restoring confidence, to go away, while they could get on with their work. A more likely conjecture is that he recoiled from the responsibility to which his assurance to the Austrian Ambassador had already committed him. The most urgent need of that vacillating nature, which had so often screened its terrors under threats and sabre-rattlings, was that he should dissociate himself from the crisis which he had helped to precipitate. Despatches would follow him to those remote Norwegian fjords, but before he could read them, comment on them and return them events would have moved on. He was not yet seriously alarmed for any real danger of war, but if it came, it would not be he who could be blamed for it. Austria was to frame the ultimatum on the terms of which and on the consequent attitude of Russia so much depended. Then there was England : what would England have to say ?

While he was away President Poincaré paid a state visit to the Tsar. Very special honours were given to the guest : the Tsar himself had gone out on his yacht to meet the

French cruiser *La France* which conveyed the President to Cronstadt, and at the state banquet both laid stress on the solidarity of the Russo-French alliance as a guarantee for the peace of Europe : just so in Paris a few months before had the President and King George spoken of the Anglo-French *entente*. Apart from these assurances, Poincaré's mission was to bring Russia and England more closely together, and in a private conversation the Tsar bade him remit his personal message to the British Government that Russian policy in the East, where there had been friction over Persian questions, would now be framed in the friendliest spirit. One thing alone caused the President some uneasiness. More than three weeks had elapsed since the Serajevo murder, and as yet Austria had given no indication of the nature of the terms or guarantees she was to demand of Servia. He spoke to M. Szápáry, the Austrian Ambassador in St. Petersburg, about this, and gave him explicit warning against too great severity. 'With a little goodwill,' he said, 'this Servian affair is easy to settle. But it is easy also for it to become envenomed : Servia has very warm friends in the Russian people. And Russia has an ally. France. What complications are to be feared here !' * Szápáry had nothing reassuring to say : a judicial inquiry was being made, and a note to Servia was in preparation. After a three days' visit the President started on his return journey to France at midnight on July 23, the Tsar again coming on board to see him off.

A few hours before he sailed, the Austrian ultimatum had been delivered. It was extremely rigorous. It demanded that Servia should suppress all anti-Austrian propagandist societies and prohibit all such publications ; that Servia should dismiss from all public services officers and officials who had taken part in such a propaganda ; that Servia should

* S. B. Fay, *Origins of the World War,* ii. p. 281.

bring to trial all accessories to the plot that led to the murder of the Archduke ; and, finally, that Austrian officials should take part in the suppression of these propaganda and in these trials. The ultimatum would expire in forty-eight hours, *i.e.* on July 25. Servia accepted these demands with the exception of the clauses relating to the participation of Austrian officials in the inquiries, for no free state could suffer such interference with her internal affairs : it was a demand that could only be made of a conquered nation suing for peace. This reply was delivered to Baron Giesl, Austrian Minister in Belgrade, who at once informed M. Pasitch that diplomatic relations were severed. Within an hour the whole staff of the Austrian Legation had left for Vienna.

As yet the German Emperor, in his remote fjords, had no idea what the Austrian ultimatum would be. His terrors had been growing on him, and he heartened himself up by volleys of marginalia on the despatches sent him of contemptuous wrath against all those who presumed to question or advise. These fulminations were the more defiant because Chancellor Bethman-Hollweg kept assuring him that there was no fear of war : * he might therefore safely indulge himself. But the accounts of the Russo-French cordialities were disturbing : ever since Russia, an absolute monarchy, had allied herself with the French Socialistic Republic no dependence could be put on her. Even the Tsar might condone this regicide, and when Sazonov threatened that Russia might fight for her blood-brothers if Austria imposed impossible terms, he furiously scribbled on the despatch : 'Well, come on, then !' Then there was England : the German Ambassador in London, Prince Lichnovsky, had repeatedly warned Germany that England might intervene on the side of Russia and France, and a

* Bülow, *Memoirs,* 1909–1919, p. 161.

fresh abyss of peril yawned in front of him. So, dealing
with that in the usual manner, when Sir Edward Grey suggested that he might exercise a moderating influence, he
boiled over with fury. 'This is a piece of monstrous insolence on the part of England,' he wrote. 'The Servians are
a pack of criminals and should be treated as such. . . This
is the typical British attitude of condescending authority, and
I wish to put it on record that I entirely repudiate it.
William, I.R.' *

He dreaded his return home. He dreaded the Crown
Councils at which he would preside. It had been easy to
fulminate from afar, and let his Ministers deal with his
thunderbolts, but he must resume his responsibilties again,
among which was his assurance to Austria, made before he
went on his cruise, that he would support her. Not till the
morning after his return to Berlin (July 28) did he know
what reply Servia had made to the Austrian ultimatum, and
he read it with unspeakable relief. The nightmare of war
faded in this blessed awakening, and enthusiastically he
scribbled below it : 'A great moral success for Vienna ; but
with it every reason for war drops away and Giesl ought to
have remained quietly at Belgrade.' No longer did he repudiate as monstrous insolence Sir Edward Grey's suggestion that he should urge moderation on the Austrian Emperor. Only four days ago he had poured the full vials of
scorn on that counsel : 'I am not called upon to write to
His Majesty the Emperor [of Austria] prescriptions for the
preservation of his honour *à la* Grey.' Now he claimed
Grey's suggestion as his own and wrote to his Foreign Minister :

"I propose that we say to Austria : Servia has been forced
to retreat in a very humiliating manner, and we offer our
congratulations : naturally, as a result, *no more cause for*

* Ludwig, *Kaiser Wilhelm II,* pp. 388–390.

war exists, but a guarantee that the promises *will be carried out* is probably necessary, and that could probably be secured by a temporary military occupation of Servia. . . *On this basis* I am ready to mediate for peace with Austria.' *

Before Jagow could have received this letter, Austria had declared war on Servia : she announced also, secure of the German Emperor's backing, that she did not ask for nor would she accept any attempt at arbitration. Servia, anticipating this, was already mobilising, and negotiations instantly became more difficult, now that such definite steps had been taken. Far more serious was the consequence that Russia boiled up in sympathy with a Slav state suddenly threatened with annihilation in spite of her virtual acceptance of the ultimatum. The Tsar knelt before his ikons, praying that peace might yet be preserved, and inspired thereby he sent for his Foreign Secretary. Let Sazonov instantly telegraph to London and Paris and beg his friends to support his proposal that the whole dispute should be referred to the Hague Tribunal, which he had devised fifteen years ago to meet just such an emergency. Austria and Servia would surely then disarm, would they not ? Sazonov did not think very highly of this suggestion, and indeed he had first to recall to his mind what the Hague Tribunal *was.* Instead, as a more practical measure, he urged the Tsar to order a partial mobilisation on the Austrian frontier only. In face of such a demonstration, Austria would be likely to think twice before definitely committing an act of war. Then the Tsar bethought him of his old friend William. Their friendship had cooled off lately, but it was worth while telegraphing to him. He implored him to exert all his influence with Austria, for his Ministers were urging him to take 'these extreme measures which will lead to war.' Even while this telegram was being decoded in

* Fay, *Origins of the World War,* ii. p. 421.

Berlin, another from the Emperor was being decoded in St. Petersburg. In the name of their old friendship Willy implored Nicky not to take these 'extreme measures' or war must follow. Both of them hated and dreaded it : the wills of both, the one obstinate and weak, the other violent and timid, were set on peace. Though they still addressed each other as controlling the destinies of their realms, they were both powerless, for the day of Emperors was done. As for the third of them, he sat abjectly lamenting and tremulously signing all that his Prime Minister told him required his name.

The first act of war occurred on July 30, when the Austrian armies bombarded Belgrade. On the afternoon of the same day the Tsar signed the ukase for general mobilisation along the whole of his Western frontier. But this was not known in Berlin or Vienna till the next day, when already Austria had ordered general mobilisation and Germany had promised to support her unconditionally. This general mobilisation of the Central Empires therefore was ordered independently of the Russian mobilisation and was not consequent on it. But the news, when it arrived at Berlin, stunned the German Emperor. As he recovered himself, the whole past grew clear and illuminated, and he proclaimed the true and only begetter of the huge catastrophe. 'England, France and Russia,' he wrote, 'have conspired to fight together for our annihilation. That is, in a nutshell, the naked truth of the situation which was slowly and surely created by Edward VII. . . And so the notorious encirclement of Germany is at last an accomplished fact. England stands derisive, brilliantly successful in her long-meditated purely anti-German policy, stirring to admiration even him whom it will utterly destroy ! The dead Edward is stronger than the living I !' He believed what he wrote, and in this despairing cry he summed up all the spite and jealousy which had embittered his reign of twenty-six years. Now as he brought the sheaves of his harvesting with him there was nothing left in his soul but the desire for revenge, and again he wrote : 'Our Consuls in Turkey and India, our agents and all such must inflame the whole Mohammedan world to frantic rebellion against this detestable, treacherous, conscienceless nation of shopkeepers ; for if we are to bleed to death, England shall at all events lose India. W.' *

Two days later Germany declared war on Russia. France automatically ordered general mobilisation, but England still held her hand. President Poincaré was convinced that the issues lay with her, and that her declaration that she would stand in with France might still have averted the catastrophe. But the British Government, rightly or wrongly, believed that she could be a more efficient mediator as a neutral, and it was not till Sunday, August 2, that Sir Edward Grey promised M. Paul Cambon, French Ambassador in London, that if the German fleet came into the North Sea either for attack on the French ports in the Channel or, by sailing round the north of Scotland, on the Atlantic coast, the British fleet would render France all possible naval support. England thus conditionally abandoned neutrality before the violation of Belgian territory next day by the German armies. Up till then there had been a very strong feeling in the country against intervention in a dispute that originally concerned only Austria and Servia. But this violation of Belgian territory brought all parties together, and the ultimatum to Germany, expiring at midnight on Tuesday, August 4, was signed by the entire nation.

Next morning in Berlin, just before Sir Edward Goschen and the staff of the British Embassy left for England, the Emperor sent a message to the Ambassador by an aide-de-camp. He requested His Excellency to tell King George

* Ludwig, *Kaiser Wilhelm II*, p. 394.

that 'in consequence of what had occurred' he must resign
his posts as Field-Marshal in the British Army and Admiral
of the British Navy.*

Such was his final gesture, with which all his relations
with the country of his mother were closed.

* Wickham Steed, *Through Thirty Years*, ii. p. 30.

EPILOGUE

A DISCONCERTING telephone-call came for Count Godard Bentinck on the afternoon of Sunday, November 10, 1918. The Foreign Office at The Hague was ringing him up to know if he would entertain the Emperor William II of Germany and his suite of about thirty persons for a few days at his castle of Amerongen in the province of Utrecht, Holland. Count Godard replied that he could not manage it, and rang off. Three hours later The Hague rang up again urgently begging him to consent : the Emperor would stay for three days only. There were difficulties : there was a shortage of coal, petrol and food in Holland, but The Hague promised Count Godard to help him in the way of supplies, and he consented.[*]

Since early in the year the Emperor had made his General Headquarters at Spa, in the Belgian province of Liége, and from this centre a spider's web of telegraph and telephone wires to Berlin and other German towns and to the fighting fronts had been installed. A cordon of guards surrounded the town, and none of the inhabitants could leave it without a passport. The officers' mess was in the Hôtel Britannique, the English church was commandeered for the use of German troops, both Protestant and Catholic, and one Sunday morning the Emperor preached there. Most of the more commodious private villas were requisitioned for staff officers ; Hindenburg occupied the Villa Sousbois and the

---

[*] Lady Norah Bentinck, *The Ex-Kaiser in Exile*, pp. 1, 2, 15 and *passim*.

Emperor the Villa Neubois. Furniture had been sent from Berlin for the latter, and the suite which the Empress occupied when she visited her husband was upholstered in her favourite pale blue : a dug-out had been constructed below the terrace in case of an enemy air-raid. Across the road was a strip of woodland, and here the Emperor took his daily exercise, digging lines of miniature trenches and diverting the course of the streamlets that ran through it.*

He had spent the hours of Saturday, November 9, chiefly in consultation at the Hôtel Britannique. Before he left Berlin for the last time the thought of flight had occurred to him, for he had made inquiries of the Spanish Embassy whether Spain would receive him with due honour : perhaps he could land at San Sebastian from a German submarine.† But that was a rash, impetuous scheme soon abandoned, and now the end of the German resistance to the allied armies had come, and what was to happen to him ? Telegrams and telephone messages from Berlin had been treading on each other's heels. The fleet at Kiel was in mutiny ; revolution had broken out in the capital ; no troops there could be trusted, and it was impossible that he should return. He suggested that, after the armistice, he should lead back his troops now on the front. Quartermaster-General Gröner told him that the army would follow their own generals but that they would not follow him. He thought of committing suicide, but, so he tells us in his *Memoirs,* his Christian convictions forbade that : also he felt that he was bound to put himself at the service of his people in the evil days that were assuredly coming : what precisely that service should be he did not specify. Already his abdication had been proclaimed in Berlin by his Chancellor, Prince Max of Baden, as the sole chance of saving Germany from civil war, but to that he would not consent. He would abdicate as

* Private information.   † Bülow, *Memoirs,* 1909–1919, p. 280.

Emperor, but he must remain King of Prussia. Or how about entrenching himself with a small and loyal band in the villa he occupied and fighting till they were all killed ? That would have been consonant with his own ideal of himself in shining armour, as the legendary hero of one of Philip Eulenburg's romantic sagas. Here was an opportunity for such a visionary gesture, and he telegraphed to Berlin that 'the King of Prussia and German Emperor would resist to the last drop of his blood.' * But perhaps there was something more useful to be done than to commit so vain a self-sacrifice. 'Unspeakably arduous,' he tells us, were his soul-struggles, and at the end he came to the conclusion that he would secure better terms for Germany at the armistice if he left her to her fate : that was the way in which he could best serve her. Before dawn on November 10 he started from Spa in his motor, and drove away northwards to the Dutch frontier at Eysden. When the Crown Prince arrived a few hours later he was gone.†

His motor was stopped at the frontier, and the guard, demanding passports, learnt that this was the German Emperor, who asked to enter Dutch territory. The officer in charge rang up The Hague for instructions, and, after a long consultation between the Queen of Holland and her Ministers, it was decided to give him sanctuary in a neutral land. Hence the telephonic messages to Count Godard Bentinck that afternoon. The imperial train, all saxe-blue and gold and black eagles, with the rest of his suite on board, and with a newly fitted copper bath for the Emperor's ablutions, followed him to Eysden, and he lodged in it while preparations were being made at Amerongen to receive him : it was laden with large stores of provisions and many

---

* Bülow, *Memoirs*, 1909–1919, p. 287.
† William II, *My Memoirs*, pp. 280, 284 ; Ludwig, *Kaiser Wilhelm II*, pp. 435–445.

cases of champagne. He slept that Sunday night in the
stationary train, and next afternoon Count Godard Bentinck and the Governor of the province of Utrecht waited
in the rain for its arrival at Maarn, a wayside station near
Amerongen.

The train drew up : the Emperor stepped briskly out,
shook hands with his host, whom he had never seen before,
and got into the waiting motor-car. Perhaps he cast one
backward look at that shining train which had carried him
on so many imperial journeys to Rome, to Vienna, to Madrid
or to Flushing, where the *Hohenzollern,* with a sheaf of
despatches already on board, awaited him for his crossing
to England, and which in these last four years had so often
whirled him between Berlin and various headquarters behind the fighting fronts. Now his travelling days were
done, though once again the imperial train would halt at the
same station to carry back to the Mausoleum at Potsdam the
body of the faithful wife who would now soon follow him
into the exile to which he had sentenced himself.

'Cease Fire' had been bugled on the front that morning,
and as dusk fell Count Godard's car crossed the bridge over
the castle moat at Amerongen and the gates, strongly
guarded by Dutch soldiers, clashed behind it. At last the
War Lord felt safe : he rubbed his hands together and said :
'Now for a cup of real good English tea.' Life, as he had
hitherto known it, since the days when he first realised his
crippled arm, had been a campaign of defensive psychical
combat. Always he had been driven, by the Furies that
presided over his pitiful nativity, into concealing by smoke-
screens of bombast the ill-manned fortress of his soul, or by
Sinaitic clamour of thunder and trumpets proclaiming his
consecration as chosen instrument of the Lord of Hosts.
Now all was over ; he need compete no more, and above all
he need tremble no more at the machinations of the encir-

cling nations. He had lost his crown, he was an exile in a foreign land, his personal defeat amounted to annihilation, and now there was nothing to fear, for all his fears had been realised and with their fulfilment came the tranquillity that was attendant on unconditional surrender. Just one further ceremony, and that merely formal, lay between him and his emancipation from his imperial slavery. Before the end of the month he signed his abdication, and released all the officials of his vanished Empire from their oath of fealty to him. The large military staff which had come with him in the imperial train from Eysden went back to Germany, leaving him an elderly Hof-Marschal and a young aide-de-camp, Captain von Ilsemann. He was free.

Destiny had been cruel in ordaining that a man of his temper and temperament should be Emperor of a great nation. Throughout his reign he had never shown any grasp of the serious responsibilities of kingship, never once, for all his sincere patriotism, had he rendered any true service to his country, nor ever had he failed to use his great abilities in the cause of European disquiet. Save for those moments of hysterical exaltation when some impetuous and imprudent impromptu had satiated his craving for imperial gestures, he had been the prey of fear and jealousy and deep-seated self-mistrust. His happiest years were now to come, for the wicked ceased from troubling, and he, far from weary, could be at rest. If only Providence had consecrated him to be a squire of ample means and estate, just outside some county town in England, what a pleasant and useful existence might have been his ! His defects, ruinous in a monarch, would have been merely humorous and even endearing. He would have been a magistrate on the County Bench, and have motored into the town whenever it sat, hectoring in manner to his colleagues, but diligent in his duties. As a member of the Borough Council he would have proposed a hundred reforms on such subjects as drainage, overcrowding, slum clearance, postal deliveries and the lighting and paving of the streets. Every Sunday morning with his wife and family he would have walked into the town, to save Sunday labor, for Cathedral service, and the Bishop, the Dean and the Chapter would have been frequent guests at his hospitable table and eaten the good dinner provided by his economical and faithful wife. We can see him in the card-room of the County Club, laying down the law to his partner at bridge, and soon afterwards revoking amid general satisfaction. He would have been president of the local cricket and golf clubs, he would have contributed large pictures to the annual Art Exhibition, he would have got up penny-readings in his village, and recited the more famous passages in Shakespeare's plays. He would have had shooting parties in the autumn and told tall stories about his prowess ; he would have composed a hymn tune and been highly indignant when the organist had refused to use it at Cathedral service ; he would have written to *The Times* about hearing a cuckoo in March. No doubt he would have been a trying neighbour, apt to think himself the victim of imaginary plots and conspiracies, meddlesome, fond of making mischief, but nobody would have believed his malicious inventions. Morally he would have led a blameless life, and his boundless energy would have spent itself in harmless and often beneficent enterprise. But destiny denied him this humbler and happier sphere, and cruelly thrust into a crippled hand the sceptre that he was not strong enough to wield with steadiness and discretion.

The Empress joined him. The revolution and her husband's dethronement had shattered the very foundations on which her life was built. 'Nevertheless,' he recorded, 'she still tried to afford consolation to me.' * But indeed it was

---

* William II, *My Memoirs*, p. 330.

she who was in far more urgent need of consolation than he, and he was quite powerless to render it. He was bitter sometimes against his own people who, not knowing the sublimity of the motives which, he claimed, had prompted his flight, thought that he had forsaken them, but, otherwise, he was like a business man, not yet sixty years of age and hale and hearty, who had a sufficient fortune to enable him to enjoy, in retirement from the city and its disturbing fluctuations, a well-earned and vigorous leisure. The sheer relief at having got rid of the intolerable burden banished all regrets, and for a while there was never a savage word even against the English, whose machinations, he had long been convinced, had always been directed to procuring the ruin of his country.

His cheerfulness was natural and unaffected, and he settled down to a life of well-earned holiday. He went out for a brisk walk alone in the park at eight in the morning, he attended family prayers and chose the hymn to be sung, and after breakfast he interviewed his Hof-Marschal, and Captain von Ilsemann read the German papers to him. When that was done he went out again, clad in a blue serge suit with shirt open at the neck, and spent the morning with a saw cutting down negotiable saplings. These he chopped into faggots small enough to make firing for the narrow-mouthed Dutch stoves, and piled them in orderly stacks which grew sufficiently substantial to feed his host's stoves throughout the winter. After lunch he walked or motored in the park of Amerongen — brisk, sunny weather was 'regular Hohenzollern weather' ; if it was wet he took further exercise pacing up and down the long picture-gallery. He never shot ; such mild sport as this demesne could afford would be a childish pastime for one who had so often massacred the huddled, driven fauna of imperial forests ; he never rode or donned a uniform again, for he had had enough of horseback in a Field-Marshal's uniform, and, as exercise, there was always that difficulty with his powerless left arm.

He appreciated the excellent cooking, and at dinner he was the life and soul of the party, enjoying family jokes, and making those puns which Eulenburg had found so trying at breakfast on the *Hohenzollern*. He was not disturbed at the solemn promises made by Mr. Lloyd George at the Khaki Election that he should be brought to trial in London, nor even when he repeated them in the House of Commons, for they were too like his own flamboyant utterances to be taken seriously. Fear had departed, for there was nothing more to fear, and with it had gone that inward necessity of proclaiming his fearlessness. Such traces of the old habit of being Emperor which still remained were very harmless : there was that incessant monologue, when he was in the mood, which it was not etiquette to interrupt, and when he was pleased to walk about the smoking-room instead of sitting down, the necessity to stand was a little trying, but he was a much-travelled man of great observation and a picturesque talker, interesting to any audience. If he was pleased with the intelligence or humour of some guest, he would take a piece of wood of his own chopping from the fuel basket by the stove and, inscribing it with 'W,' present it to the low-curtseying beneficiary. He learned Dutch and soon spoke it fluently. He grew a beard, which had scarcely a streak of dark colour in it, he suffered the martial moustache to assume its natural hue and a civilian droop. He was an elderly, kindly man, with a sick wife, and a fund of striking experiences to discourse on. And he began to think over materials for his two books of autobiography.

Count Godard Bentinck had, with some reluctance, consented to offer his hospitality to the Emperor for three days. He and his wife with her lady-in-waiting, Countess Keller, and Hof-Marschal Lieutenant-General von Gontard, and aide-de-camp Captain von Ilsemann and a staff of servants remained at Amerongen for eighteen months. It suited him : he found the company of his host and his host's family exceedingly agreeable, and the search for a house of his own, anywhere in Holland, where he would be alone with his invalid wife, was not prosecuted with any great urgency. Eventually he purchased from Baroness van Hemstra the House of Doorn, outside the village of Doorn, about seven miles from Amerongen. In the Middle Ages it had been the summer residence of the Provost of the province of Utrecht, but the original house had been rebuilt later. It was surrounded by well-timbered grounds, and a notable feature was a Pinetum containing a fine collection of rare conifers. The house required extensive additions, and the Emperor built a large lodge by the principal entrance containing offices and quarters for his police-guard. When these alterations were finished, there were poured into the house magnificent furnishings of his own property from the New Palace at Berlin, and he settled into it during the summer of 1920. On leaving Amerongen he presented his host with a life-size marble bust of himself in helmet and military cloak wielding a sceptre, and portraits of himself and his wife. The Empress bestowed a gold snuff-box encrusted with diamonds, and for the Bentinck children there were innumerable signed photographs of them both.

Ever since November 1918 the Empress had been ageing rapidly and her bodily powers failing. Her husband's forced abdication had dealt her a mortal blow : unlike him, she trembled at the idea that he was in real danger of being extradited to England and made to stand his trial, and she was homesick for Germany and German ways. She had been married to him now for nearly forty years, a faithful, adoring and submissive *hausfrau,* to whom in the imperial days he had been a hero, and in his exile a martyr, and in both the Lord's Anointed. Her children and grandchildren visited her, but in comparison with his great light they were but flickering candles. She smiled brokenly at them and sighed and bent her eyes again on her eternal knitting, for she was always fashioning little garments for the ill-clothed, ill-nourished children of the Fatherland, and with every stitch she knitted into her wool her hatred for England. From the early days of her married life she had never made friends with her husband's English relations : the Crown Princess Frederick had at first been disposed to like her as 'gentle and good,' but, as William's relations with his mother grew worse, there came a definite break between the two, and soon the ex-Empress Frederick was writing to Queen Victoria of 'Dona's grand condescending airs,' of her ignorance and want of education.* The younger woman took note of this attitude ; she shared, too, and encouraged William's dislike and contempt for his uncle, and underneath her restrained silences, her discretion and her devoted domesticity, her antagonism to all things English had been long inveterate. Now it was England who had brought ruin and starvation on the beloved Fatherland, and above all it was England who had deprived William of his throne. Silent and unforgiving and deeply pathetic she nursed this quiet enmity, till love and hatred alike grew dim in the shadow of death. Before she had been at Doorn for a year she died, and once more the Emperor saw the imperial train, now draped in black, draw up at the wayside station of Maarn, bearing back to the Royal Mausoleum at Potsdam the remains of this devoted and broken woman.

The first relief at being free and unthreatened wore off, and as he got engrossed in his *Memoirs,* the past grew bitter and vivid to him again. Surely the whole world had ever

* Ponsonby, *Letters of Empress Frederick,* pp. 400, 401.

been in constant conspiracy to hamper and humiliate him ! He had with him a series of his father's diaries, a schoolboy diary of his own keeping, and letters he had written to his grandmother,* but his marvellous memory was in little need of documentary refreshment. He had no access to state papers, and indeed these would have been a handicap rather than a help for his purpose. For his object was to vindicate himself from the slanders of a malignant Europe, to declare the abiding rectitude and wisdom of the principles which had guided him in his reign of thirty years. No autobiographer ever undertook so agreeable a task, for he found that throughout that period he had never faltered in prudence, in moderation and in consistency, nor had he ever failed to foresee, when his Ministers preferred their foolishness to his wisdom, the sad consequences that invariably followed. Historically the book is of little value, for facts are distorted to fit the author's theories. He wished, for instance, to demonstrate that for years England had been making all possible preparations for the moment when she thought the time was ripe for forcing war on Germany and, on the instant, for sending to France an Expeditionary Force. He therefore tells us that his armies invading Belgium had found in various towns large stores of English military greatcoats, and that the inhabitants deposed that they had been sent there from England during the last three years. He had corroborative evidence of that : 'most of the English infantry men who were made prisoners by us in the summer of 1914 had no greatcoats : when asked why, they answered quite naïvely : "We are to find our greatcoats in the stores at Maubeuge, La Quesnoy, etc." ' † There we have romance grafted on to a stem of fact, for it is true that, in the broiling weather during the retreat from Mons, men were told to abandon their greatcoats, and these no doubt were found by

---

* William II, *My Early Life*, p. viii.   † William II, *My Memoirs*, p. 252.

the Germans in villages *en route*. But the British War Office had not for the last three years been providently piling up stores of greatcoats at Maubeuge and La Quesnoy to be distributed to the Expeditionary Force on arrival there.

And how little he himself had believed in the possibility of war ! German diplomacy was to blame for that : his ambassadors ought to have known and to have warned him. In the spring of 1914 he had been excavating for Greek antiquities in Corfu : was that like an Emperor who knew that war was imminent ? But the Tsar knew, for when he was asked what were his plans for that summer, he replied : 'Je resterai chez moi cette année, parce que nous aurons la guerre.' William had not learned that till months after the Imperial Family had been murdered at Ekaterinburg, but what a piece of treachery from the man who had sworn that he would never draw the sword against Germany ! And when, halfway through July 1914, he was peacefully yachting off the coasts of Norway, he was told and thought worthy of record that ships had been secretly detached from the English fleet in order to kidnap him. . . Such are a few specimens of these fantastic memories.*

But psychologically this book is of great interest : it is written in the calm, dispassionate style of an historian who, in justice to the victim of iniquitous plots and in refutation of cruel slanders against a prudent and far-seeing statesman, is only concerned that the whole truth and nothing but the truth should be known. Long ago Field-Marshal Waldersee had observed : 'The Emperor often lies to other people, but still more often to himself,' and the conclusion is forced on the reader that persistence in this habit had brought him to believe every word he wrote, and that, in this testament to his own changelessness 'without shadow of turning,' he con-

* William II, *My Memoirs*, pp. 242, 243.

sidered that he had proved before any impartial jury of sober minds and steady heads that, among the mischief-making monarchs and treacherous governments of Europe, whose impetuous policies, whose sabre-rattlings and pilings-up of armaments had brought about the great catastrophe, he alone had never uttered a provocative word nor made a threatening gesture. Instead of himself being tried, as Mr. Lloyd George had promised, he puts the world on trial, William *contra mundum,* and as prosecuting counsel exposes its criminal career, and as jury finds it guilty on every count. He was convinced of the truth of what he wrote, and was confident that he would convince his readers. He had climbed to the supreme pinnacle of egotism, and had come to believe anything that harmonised with his own conception of himself.

The consciousness of being Emperor remained with him still, himself undiminished ; and his House of Doorn, furnished with pictures and marbles and tapestries from the New Palace, with its hundred acres of land in place of his innumerable castles and illimitable estates, became his Empire. Every morning he received the domestic report of his Hof-Marschal instead of giving audience to his Imperial Chancellor or his War Minister, and his aide-de-camp read him news from the eight German papers which he took in. Captain von Ilsemann was married now to the daughter of Count Godard Bentinck, but he must be ready for his duties every day, so he slept alternately at Doorn and Amerongen, and after a night at Amerongen he bicycled seven miles so as to be at Doorn by nine in the morning. The wood-chopping went on, and the Emperor planted a rose garden, now one of the finest in Holland : gifts of rose-trees were made him by innumerable friends in Germany and labelled with royal and distinguished names. Sometimes he thought that Germany would turn to him again, but his flight now represented itself to him as being an abominable ingratitude on *her* part, and she must sue to him. 'If the Germans want me,' he said, 'they shall come and fetch me after the way they have treated me.' Countless letters and telegrams poured in every year on his birthday from Royalists in Germany, but as yet the remorseful nation made no sign. He married again : Princess Hermine of Reuss was herself a widow with children who came to stay with their mother at Doorn, and in this secure domesticity he kept all his interests alive, musing on his achievements in painting and in music — those great allegorical pictures which he had designed, his *Hymn to Aegir* — and, recalling his sunny marble palace at Corfu and his discovery of archaic sculptures, he wrote and delivered a lecture on their archaeological importance : they were the link, as he had pointed out twenty years before to Professor Dörpfeld, the long-sought link between Asiatic and European art.*

Among these memories the most vivid and imperishable was the treatment he had suffered at the hands of the nation he hated and loved. Indeed it was less a memory than an abiding consciousness, quiescent for the most part, but always liable to burst into volcanic eruption. Something one day recalled to him an Englishman, General Waters, with whom he had been on terms of very frank friendliness twenty-five years ago, and he wrote to him asking him to pay a visit to Doorn. But was there ever a stranger prologue to an invitation ? 'An ocean of abuse, vilification, infamy, slanders and lies has rolled over me coming from London, disclosing a spirit of debased, venomous hatred I never imagined in the British people, once so proud of their "fair play." ' Again he enumerated the benefits and sym-

* November 1935.

THE EX-KAISER AT DOORN

From left to right: The Chief of Police, the Court Doctor, Captain von Ilsemann (adjutant), the Ex-Kaiser and the Court Chamberlain

pathy he had showered on them : had he not mourned with them in their grief over the death of Queen Victoria and of King Edward ? They had acknowledged that by putting him to 'an ordeal of lies, slanders, misrepresentations, venomous hostility the like of which was never spent upon any ruler at the hands of Britain. . . And when she was on the verge of losing the unjust war she had for many years engineered against me and my country, she led America into the fight, and *bought* the subversive part of my people with money to rise against their ruler.' In postscript almost he said how glad he would be to see his English friend at Doorn, 'where I reside as an outcast by the vile intrigues of the British Statesmen.' *

He loved England still — there was the pathos of it — even as he had always loved her. Treacherous and black-hearted though he held her to have been, he had never succeeded in killing that love, and he could not have flamed into such white heat of hate unless it had been still alive, and unless in his tormented soul he felt that it had ever been repaid with scorn and mistrust. Hate without such furnace of underlying longing can never remain molten.

Sunday morning, and bright Hohenzollern weather : the church bells in Doorn were ringing with a mellow clarity. One of them had a deep and resonant tone, and it reminded him of some very solemn occasion when the voice of a bell like that vibrated through the still air. . . Yes : the tolling of the Sebastopol bell from the Round Tower of Windsor Castle at his grandmother's funeral. He stood listening by the open window, and soon he heard the bell no more but only the innumerable echoes which it awoke in his brain, as of footsteps in memorial chantries and of voices growing

* Waters, *Potsdam and Doorn,* pp. 95–97.

fainter as they receded down the corridor of past years. . .
Why, why had it all happened like this ?

The Hof-Marschal appeared and bowed : it was time for
His Majesty to read prayers for the Household and to preach
the sermon which the Court Chaplain had written for him.

INDEX

ADOWA, 123
Aehrenthal, Baron von, 236, 237, 238, 255
Afghanistan, 144, 202
Agadir incident, 261-2
Albany, Duke of, 143
Albert, Prince Consort, 6, 9, 90, 223 ; and marriage of the Princess Royal, 1-2, 3, 6-9, 10 ; aspiration for Anglo-German friendship, 2, 6, 14, 34 ; views of, on marriages between Royal families, 2 ; his German sympathies unpopular, 4, 8 ; imbues his daughter with idea of a mission, 6, 7, 14, 15, 20, 32 ; influence over the Queen, 7, 74 ; work for England, 8 ; liberal ideas, 9 ; and Schleswig-Holstein question, 17 ; views as to France, 20, 125 ; ideas on education, 23 ; versatility, 223 ; death, 15, 26
Prince William's recollections of, 26, 141, 242
otherwise mentioned, 12, 29, 225
Albert Victor of Wales, Prince (Duke of Clarence), 87
Aldershot review : Emperor William at, 104 ; President Loubet at, 187
Alexander II : Tsar of Russia, 53
Alexander III : Tsar of Russia : and Prince William, 38-41, 87, 88 ; rebuff to Bismarck, 40 ; reception of French fleet, 84-5 ; death, 106
Alexander of Battenberg, Prince : marriage question, 53-7, 61
Alexandra, Queen (Princess of Wales), 5, 17, 26, 41, 61, 106, 127, 189, 217, 221 ; and Prince William, 37, 249

Alexandra, Tsarina (née Princess Alix of Hesse-Darmstadt), 103, 104, 106, 124, 125, 126, 191, 196, 254 ; and Queen Victoria, 104
Alexis, Tsarevitch, 196, 254 ; Emperor William's present to, 196
Alfonso, King of Spain, 189, 207, 217, 221
Alfred, Prince (Duke of Edinburgh and Duke of Saxe-Coburg), 102, 142
Algeciras Conference, 209, 219
Alice, Princess (second daughter of Queen Victoria) : Princess Louis of Hesse, 57, 102
Alix, Princess of Hesse. See Alexandra, Tsarina
Alsace-Lorraine, 114, 211, 213, 251
Prince of Wales' question to Count Herbert Bismarck, 28, 62, 66-9
America, 136, 214, 221, 229 ; naval construction, 71 ; relations with Russia, 165, 171-2
American Pacific Fleet, 228
Angeli, von, 32, 71
Anglo-French relations, 27, 123, 139, 177, 180-1, 185-8 ; Siam, 93-4 ; Egypt, 109-10, 204 ; Morocco, 204 ; exchange of naval visits, 209-10 ; the *entente*, 186-7, 195, 202, 203, 209, 219, 233, 251, 270
Anglo-German relations, 20, 26-8, 63, 110, 120-1, 149, 162, 165, 172-6, 180, 195-6, 217, 227-9, 234, 250-1 ; Queen Victoria and, 69-70 ; King Edward and, 180, 194, 234
Anglo-Japanese treaty, 176, 180, 193, 229
Anglo-Russian relations, 103, 105-8,